MORAL SKETCHES

OF

PREVAILING

OPINIONS AND MANNERS,

FOREIGN AND DOMESTIC:

WITH

Reflections on Prayer.

By HANNAH MORE.

Let us make a stand on the ancient ways, and then look about us, and discover what is the straight and right way, and walk in it.   LORD BACON *on Innovation.*

I know not which is the greater wonder, either that prayer, which is a duty so easy and facile, so ready and apted to the powers and skill and opportunities of every man, should have so great effects and be productive of such mighty blessings; or that we should be so unwilling to use so easy an instrument of producing so much good.   BISHOP JEREMY TAYLOR.

LONDON:

PRINTED FOR T. CADELL AND W. DAVIES,

IN THE STRAND.

1819.

Printed by Strahan and Spottiswoode,
Printers-Street, London.

PREFACE.

It is with the sincerest satisfaction, and the most lively gratitude to God, that the writer of these pages is enabled to bear her feeble but heartfelt testimony, to the progress which religion has made, and is making, amongst us, especially in the higher, and even the highest, ranks of society.

At a period, therefore, abounding and advancing in almost every kind of religious improvement, she may be thought by those who would be looking for congratulation rather than caution, to have imposed on herself an invidious task, in choosing to dwell less on the triumphs of

Christianity, than on the dangers or the errors of some of its professors. Yet she is persuaded that they who have made the greatest proficiency in piety will be the most ready to forgive the intimations, of which they stand in the least need.

It may, however, justly be said, that the writer might have found more appropriate objects of censure amongst the worldly and the irreligious, than in the more respectable classes whom she has taken the liberty to make the subject of animadversion. But the truth is, the thoughtless and the profligate have been so successively and so perseveringly attacked by far more powerful pens; have been so long assailed by the monitory maxims of the moralist, pelted by the missile weapons of the satirist, and chastised by the grave rebuke of the divine, that, with due deference, she turns over the hitherto incorrigible to stronger and more efficient hands; while she ventures to address her observations to other quarters, where there will be more hope of forgiveness, and less despair of success.

She does not therefore appeal to those who "hear not Moses and the Prophets," but rather to those who, hearing, neglect them; and especially to those who, in some awful instances, misrepresent them. She presumes, with respect and diffidence, to expostulate with some, who, though exempt from palpable defects in practice, yet require to be reminded that speculative errors cannot be indulged without danger; and to intimate to others, that the practice may be faulty where there are no material errors in the creed. Doubtless indifference to religion will hereafter be more severely judged, than mistakes in it, especially if the latter be found to proceed from the head, as the other more apparently does from the heart.

The remarks in the early part of this volume, on the excess of continental intercourse, will probably be accused of blamable scrupulosity, and the writer be charged with unnecessary rigour. Yet what enlightened conscience will deny that some of the habits to which allusion is made, militate as much against the self-denying spirit of our religion as more ostensible faults. They would not, however, have been noticed, had they been confined to trifling and common characters; but the least error that grows into a habit, and that habit sanctioned by the countenance of the worthy and respectable, becomes more important than even the vices of ordinary men or frivolous women. In lamenting the probably injurious consequences to a large proportion of the myriads who are still, with unabated eagerness, crowding to a foreign shore, the author is fully persuaded that many amongst them carry out principles too deeply rooted, to be shaken by unprofitable intercourse, and morals too correct to be infected by the fascinations of pleasure. But who will deny that the countenance of those who escape the injury gives an authority to those who receive it? In this view, the wisest and most correct of our emigrants, may, by lending themselves to the practice, furnish in the result, an apology for things which they themselves disapprove, and thus their example may be pleaded, as favouring what they would be amongst the last to tolerate.

That long and frequent absences from our home, and especially from our country, are not favourable to the mind, is but too visible in that spirit of restlessness induced, by so many who have *repeatedly* made the experiment. For it is observable that the desire once indulged, instead of being cooled, is inflamed; inclination becomes voracity. Appetite has grown with indulgence. And is it not to be feared that the sober scenes of domestic, and especially of rural life, will continue to appear more and more insipid in proportion to the frequency with which they are deserted? Will not successive and protracted carnivals convert the quiet scenes of home enjoyment into what the poet calls "a lenten entertainment?"

Home is at once the scene of repose and of activity. A country-gentleman of rank and fortune is the sun of a little system, the movements of which his influence controls. It is at home that he feels his real importance, his usefulness, and his dignity. Each diminishes in proportion to the distance he wanders from his proper orbit. The old English gentry kept up the reverence and secured the attachment of their dependants by living among them. Personal affection was maintained by the presence of the benefactor. Subordination had a visible head. Whereas obedience to a master they do not see savours too much of allegiance to a foreign power.

We know that the Roman hero who transgressed the boundaries of his own province by *once* crossing the Rubicon, changed the whole condition, circumstances, constitution, and character of his country. May not the reiterated passage of the Straits of Dover eventually produce moral changes not less important?

The mischiefs effected by these incessant migrations may, indeed, be slow, but they are progressive. Principles which would revolt at the idea of any sudden change, are melted down by the gradual relaxation of continued contact. Complacency in the soothing enjoyment creeps on by almost imperceptible advances. The revolution is not the less certain, because it is not acknowledged. The conscience, too, is quieted by the geographical anodyne — " I would not do in England what I think it no harm to do in Paris."

Might not a fair practical appeal be made to the different state of the feelings of many of our travellers, on witnessing the open violation of the sanctity of the *first* Sunday, and the *twentieth* repetition of the same abuse? Who can affirm, that familiarity has not gradually diminished the alarm, and in a good measure suppressed the indignation? Who will assert, that this succession of desecrated sabbaths has produced no alteration in the state of their feelings, except that of reconciling them to the practice. They, indeed, who had made such a proficiency in religion as to maintain an unabated sense of the evil, would be the least likely unnecessarily to expose their principles to such a risk.*

For the bold remarks on this dangerous and delicate subject, the culprit throws herself on the mercy, and the anglicism of her readers; on the courtesy of those, whose kindness she hopes will not be forfeited, by her having shewn herself too exclusively an Englishwoman. Anxious, perhaps to a fault, for the welfare, the

* Some friends of the writer, men of the first respectability, who during the late war commanded volunteer corps, have acknowledged to her, that when first called out to drill on Sundays, their religious feelings were most painfully wounded, but by long habit, it gradually became a matter of indifference to them.

honour, the prosperity, the character of this Queen of Islands, she yet believes that there are to be found worse prejudices than those national attachments, which in her are irreclaimable.*

It is not, however, to be conceded, that the term *prejudice*, so frequently applied to these attachments, is, by this application, legitimately used. If prejudice, in its true definition, signifies prepossession, judgment formed beforehand, fondness adopted previously to knowledge, notions cherished without inquiry, opinions taken up, and acted upon without examination, —if these be its real significations, and what lexicographer will deny that they are? then how can this term be applied to the more enlightened Britons? How can it be applied to men who, independently of the natural fondness

---

* These prefatory apologies for the offences of a subsequent chapter, will, it is to be feared, remind the reader of the prudent sinner mentioned by Luther, who in going to purchase indulgences for the faults he had *already* committed, purchased another or a fault he *intended* to commit.

for the soil, and all the objects which endear it; who, in addition to this instinctive attachment, feel, acknowledge, and enjoy, in their native country, all the substantial blessings which make life worth living for; a constitution, the best that mortal man has ever yet devised; a religion, above the powers of man indeed to conceive, but reformed and carried to perfection by his agency, taught by the wisdom of God, led by the guidance of his word, and the direction of his Spirit. A system of civil and religious liberty, which, while certain miscreants at home are labouring to destroy under the pretence of improving, some foreign countries are imitating, and all are envying. Institutions, which promise to convey the chief of these blessings to the remotest lands;—if all these assertions are true, let it be again asked, whether, if an intimate knowledge, and a long enjoyment of these blessings, should have produced a filial fondness for such a country, that attachment can be denominated *prejudice*, a word which, let it be repeated, was only meant to express blind zeal, neglected examination, and contented ignorance?

May not this growing attachment for foreign manners, by wearing out domestic attachments, create a powerful preponderance in the opposite scale? The English partialities being cured, may not those who shall have conquered them, become more satisfied with their acquired, than their former tastes; may they not fancy, that they are grown more candid, when, perhaps, they are only become less conscientious? When the mind is softened down by pleasurable sensations, pleased with every thing about it, it becomes pleased with itself; begins to look back on its former scrupulous character with present triumph, rejoices in its enlargement from its previous narrowness; congratulates itself on its acquired liberality, calls what was firmness, bigotry; and thus to the altered character, the strictness it carried abroad, appears rigour on its return home?

That the attraction may be inviting, and the temptation considerable, is readily allowed; but if once the rightness of an action should come to be determined by its pleasantness, an entirely new system of morals must be introduced amongst Christians; the question then would be no longer, what *ought* we to do, but what should we *like* to do? That the temptation is not irresistible, appears in the self-denial of those who continue to withstand it: many who have felt the desire have prudently deferred its gratification to a safer season; while others continue to doubt its *general* expediency.

That many among our innumerable travellers, have gone abroad on the reasonable ground of health, as well as for the necessary purposes of business, is not to be doubted. And who will deny that some men of great ability and high principle, have gone with the meritorious desire, of doing moral and religious good, in various directions; and that they have, in no inconsiderable degree, effected it, or at least have opened a door for further improvement? On the other hand the disgraceful truth must not be concealed, that others have carried out more evil from home, than they found abroad.

It would be uncharitable and unchristian, to desire to maintain a spirit of hostility between near neighbours; but when neighbours have been so frequently on the alert to find pretences for disagreement, and national safety has sometimes been endangered by the quarrels of individuals, will not good neighbourhood be more probably promoted by friendly dispositions and mutual good offices on the respective shores, than by obtrusive visits, which, if they were thoroughly liked, would doubtless be more frequently returned?

For is it not worthy of remark, that we only refuse to imitate our continental neighbours, in the very point in which they are really respectable? *They stay at home.* Even if they do so with the same proud self-preference, which made ancient Rome call all the other nations of the world barbarians, it is at least an honest and a patriotic partiality. Would not the natives of our happy land who have less to gain, and more to lose, do well to follow their example in this honourable instance? *They* prudently augment the resources of their country in two ways, by spending their own money in their own land, with the additional profit of holding out to us those allurements, which cause ours to be spent there also.

> O England! model to thy inward greatness,
> Like little body with a mighty heart!
> What might'st thou do that honour bids thee do,
> Were all thy children kind and natural!
> But see, thy fault France hath in thee found out.
>   SHAKESPEARE.

While the pen is in the hand of the writer, fresh intelligence is brought of conspiracies forming in different parts of the kingdom for its destruction. Can she, therefore, forbear repeating, that if her degenerate sons betray her, and her honourable sons desert her, her perils are indeed imminent?

At her advanced age the writer has little to hope from praise, or little to fear from censure, except as her views may have been in a right or a wrong direction. She has felt that a renewed attention to growing errors is a duty on those who have the good of mankind at heart. The more nearly her time approaches for her leaving the world, there is a sense in which she feels herself more strongly interested in it; she means in an increasing anxiety for its improvement; for its advance in all that is right in principle, and virtuous in action. And as the events and experience of every day convince her, that there is no true virtue which is not founded in religion, and no true religion which is not maintained by PRAYER, she hopes to be forgiven if with declining years and faculties, yet with increasing earnestness, from increasing conviction of its value, she once more ventures to impress this last, important topic, on their attention.

If then she has enlarged even to diffuseness on the subject of prayer, it is because she is fervently desirous to suggest it, as the surest counteractive of those many aberrations of heart and practice but too visible amongst us. In some former publications, however, she had expatiated so largely on this inexhaustible topic, that, in order to avoid repetition, she has chiefly limited her present observations on prayer to the errors which may prevent its efficacy, together with allusions to certain classes of character in whom these errors most abound.

In taking her final leave of her readers, may she be allowed to express her gratitude for their long and unwearied indulgence; for a patience which the too frequent demands made on it could not exhaust; for their candour in forgiving her bold remonstrances; for their kindness in bearing with her faults in consideration of her desire to be useful; and for extending to one who had nothing to offer but right intentions, that favour to which merit might have put in a fairer claim.

Barley Wood,
July 24th, 1819.

CONTENTS.

FOREIGN SKETCHES.

	Page
Foreign Associations	3
French Opinion of English Society	24
English Opinion of French Society	43
England's best Hope	81

DOMESTIC SKETCHES.

On Soundness in Judgment, and Consistency in Conduct	117
Novel Opinions in Religion	131
Ill Effects of the late Secession	169
Exertions of pious Ladies	192
High Profession and negligent Practice	215
Auricular Confession	232
Unprofitable Reading	238
The Borderers	250

REFLECTIONS ON PRAYER.

	Page
On the Corruption of Human Nature	277
False Notions of the Dignity of Man, shewn from his Helplessness and Dependence	295
The Obligation of Prayer universal.—Regular Seasons to be observed.—The Sceptic and the Sensualist reject Prayer	306
Errors in Prayer, which may hinder its being answered.—The proud Man's Prayer.—The patient Christian.—False Excuses under the Pretence of Inability	322
God our Father.—Our Unwillingness to please Him.—Forms of Prayer.—Great and Little Sins.—All Sin an Offence against God.—Benefit of habitual Prayer	348
The Doctrine of imputed Sanctification, newly adopted.—The old one of progressive Sanctification newly rejected.—Both Doctrines injurious to Prayer.—St. Paul's Character	361

Character of those who expect Salvation for their good Works.—Of those who depend on a careless nominal Faith.—Both these Characters unfavourable to

Prayer.—Christianity a Religion of Love which disposes to Prayer, exhibited in a third Character - 377

Prayer.—The Condition of its attendant Blessings.—Useless Contention about Terms - - - - 394

Vain Excuses for the Neglect of Prayer.—The Man of Business.—Case of Nehemiah.—Prayer against the Fear of Death.—Characters to whom this Prayer is recommended - - 404

The Consolations of Prayer.—Its perpetual Obligation - - - 423

On intercessory Prayer - - - 441

The Praying Christian in the World.—The Promise of Rest to the Christian 451

The Lord's Prayer, a Model both for our Devotion and our Practice.—It teaches the Duty of promoting Schemes to advance the Glory of God - - 471

Conclusion - - - - 496

SKETCHES

OF

FOREIGN MANNERS.

FOREIGN ASSOCIATIONS.

We had fervently hoped, during a war unparalleled in duration and severity, that if ever the blessing of peace should be restored, all would be well again: we had hoped, that at least we should be brought back to our previous situation with that improvement in humility and gratitude, which the remembrance of past sufferings, and recent deliverance from those sufferings, would seem naturally to produce. If our pleasant feelings in such a prospective event were shaded at all, it was simply by the irreparable and individual loss of a father, son, or brother, which almost every family, of every rank, had sustained. Peace was at length providentially granted to our arms and to our prayers; but all the blessings we had anticipated did not return in her train:

> Ease still recants
> Vows made in pain as violent and void.

Were it not almost doubtful whether in some respects the change may have proved a benefit, if it should be found to be the choice between the two evils, the waste of human lives, or the decay of moral principles? Some scrupulous persons may even think it requires no very correct arithmetic to determine on the comparative value of perishable lives and immortal souls.

What then was the first use we made of a benefit so earnestly implored,—a blessing which we fondly flattered ourselves would be converted to so many salutary purposes? This peace, for which so many prayers were offered, so many fasts appointed;—this peace, whose return was celebrated by thanksgivings in every church, and, as we hope, in every house, and in every heart, to what purpose was its restoration devoted?

This peace was seized on, not as a means to repair, in some measure, the ravages which were made on the commerce, the property, the comforts, as well as the population of our country; but must it not, in many instances, be said truly, though most painfully said, to vary their nature, and enhance their malignity? Instead of sedulously employing it to raise us to our former situation, by a prudent restriction in our indulgences, an increased residence in our respective districts, and an endeavour to lighten the difficulties of government, by the continued contribution of its rightful supplies;—instead of using it to mitigate the distresses, and to restrain the crimes of the lower orders, by living in the midst of them, each at his natural and appropriate station, and thus neutralising a spirit of disaffection, which took advantage only of their absence to break out;—instead of improving its opportunities, or providing against the impending scarcity, which the desertion of the rich increased almost to famine, in giving employment to the industrious, relief to the sick, and bread to the famished;—instead of each centinel remaining at his providentially appointed watch,—at this critical moment, a very large proportion of our nobles and gentry, an indefinite number of our laity, and not a few of our clergy, that important part of the community, of which the situation is peculiarly local,—all these, as if simultaneously seized by that mania which, in fabulous history, is said to have sent *one* unfortunate object of divine persecution wandering through the world,—all these important portions of our country at once abandoned it. The only use they made of peace was to fly, with most unrighteous speed, to the authors of our calamities, and of such calamities as it might be thought could not at once have been forgotten, to visit a country which had filled our own with widows and orphans, which had made the rest of Europe a scene of desolation.

Not only hundreds of thousands of our country, men, and women, and children, but millions of our money, so severely wanted at home, were transported from every port to visit this lately execrated country. To *visit*, did I say? that had been little;—a short excursion to feed the eye, and gratify the taste with pictures and statues, might have been pleaded as a natural temptation.

Here we conceive the grave Christian moralist will censure the writer, as much as she censures the emigrants. He will say, "the desire is too natural to be right." If we plead in mitigation of damages, that it was innocent curiosity, we shall be told, that it was a curiosity, which one of our first parents believed innocent, but which lost them both Paradise. If it was a desire of knowledge, it might be a knowledge better unknown;

if to cure those prejudices, "for which our country is a name so dear," such prejudices may better be retained than cured.

But be this as it may, the truth is, that to multitudes, France was not made a place of visit, but a home. For when these wonderful productions of art were restored to the places from whence they had been feloniously taken, did that allay the hunger of emigration? France became the settled residence of multitudes. France was made a scene for the education of English, of Christian, of Protestant children! Sons and daughters, even in the middle ranks of life, were transported thither with an eagerness, as if the land of blood had been the land of promise. And as all fashions descend, not a few of our once simple, plain-hearted English yeomen were drawn in to follow the example of *their betters*, as they are not very correctly called. The infection became general, nor has time as yet stayed the plague.

A late French wit*, who always preferred a calumny to a fact, and was more fond of giving a neat turn to a sentence, than of speaking truth, after visiting this country about the middle of the last century, characterised its natives by saying, the English people resembled their own beer, the top was all froth, the bottom all dregs, but the middle was excellent. If this were at that time true, the middle class has now merged its distinctive character in the other two; it is abandoning the honourable station in the cup which it then held, is adopting its worst ingredients from above and below; and by its mixture with the froth and the feculence, has considerably lessened its claim to its once distinct commendation.†

But the evil, great as it is, does not end here; numbers of a higher strain

---

* Voltaire.

† It is almost too ludicrous to assert, that the wife of a reputable farmer, being asked lately what she had done with her daughter, replied, "I have *Frenched* her and *musicked* her, and shall now carry her to France."

remain domiciliated in France, and too many who are returned, are more than ever assimilated with French manners. It is to be feared, that with French habits, French principles may be imported. French alliances are contracted, as almost every newspaper records. We are losing our national character. The deterioration is by many thought already visible. In a few years, if things proceed in their present course, or rather with increasing velocity—which is always the case with downward tendencies—the strong and discriminating features of the English heart and mind will be obliterated, and we shall be lost in the undistinguished mass.

In the mean time let us take warning from the consideration, that the first stage of decline is the beginning of dissolution. Whatever has begun already to decay, is not far from perishing. This contagious intercourse has been too probably the cause of the recent multiplication of those great Sunday entertainments, in the diminution of which we had begun to rejoice; a multiplication which is as likely to contribute to the decline of religion in the domestic arrangements of the great, as any more obvious and ostensible evil.

What would the veteran moralist, who, in his beautiful and vigorous satire, indignantly exclaimed,

I cannot bear a French metropolis;

What would Johnson have said had he been spared till now?

How would he laugh at Britain's modern tribe,
Dart the keen taunt, and edge the piercing gibe!

How would he have poured out his ready wrath, his cutting sarcasm, his powerful reasoning, his robust morality, on a country which is in danger of deserting its own character, impairing its own virtue, and discrediting its own religion?

We set a just value on the French language as the introduction to much elegant literature; to much indeed that is valuable, but to more that is pernicious.

But even this agreeable language, for the higher acquisition of which so many important sacrifices are made, so much domestic duty is relinquished, so much religious principle is hazarded, may be bought too dear. Even if this supreme excellence, the perfection of the Parisian accent, *should* obtain for an English lady the coveted distinction of being taken for a Frenchwoman; does she not run some risk, even in her own country and her own home, from the habit of domesticating in our families persons of whom all she may know is, that their accent is good; of whose morals she knows little; and of whose religion she knows nothing, except that, if they happen by great chance to have any, it is of a character hostile to her own. The only hope is, that the foreign teacher may care so little about the matter, as never to introduce religion at all: but this is not a very consoling consideration in the instructors of our children.

There is another grievance connected

with this mania for whatever is foreign, — a grievance not the less serious because it is overlooked, and because it affects only a subordinate class in society;—we allude to the injury sustained by our domestic manufactures from the abundant importation of French articles of dress and decoration. We forbear to enter on the subject in all its painful extent; we forbear to advert to the looms that are standing still, to the gloominess of our trading streets, to the warehouses that are left solitary, to the shops which are nearly deserted; and shall confine our humble remonstrance to pleading more particularly the distress of those unfortunate females who used to procure a decent support by their own industry, and of whom thousands are now plunging into misery. We would fervently but respectfully advocate the cause of this meritorious and most pitiable class.

If British patriotism be not a plea sufficiently powerful to restrain a temptation, which can only be indulged by the violation of laws, which perhaps the husbands and fathers of the fair offenders have established, we would appeal to the sensibilities of a well-regulated heart, to the tenderness of an enlightened conscience, and to the dictates of justice and of charity, whether it be pardonable to yield to every slight temptation, merely to gratify vanity, or, to speak more tenderly, to indulge a capricious taste.

When tempted to make the alluring purchase by the superior beauty, real or imaginary, of the article, might we not presume to recommend to every lady to put some such questions as the following to herself:— " By this gratification, illicitly obtained, I not only offend against human laws, but against humanity itself; by this purchase I am perhaps starving some unfortunate young creature of my own sex, who gained her daily bread by weaving her lace or braiding her straw. I am driving her to that extremity of want, which may make her yield to the next temptation to vice, which may drive her to the first sinful means that may offer of procuring a scanty, precarious, and miserable support. It is in vain that I may have perhaps subscribed for her being taught better principles at school, that I have perhaps assisted in paying for her acquisition of her little trade, if by crushing that trade I now drive her to despair, if I throw her on a temptation which may overcome those better principles she acquired through my means. Shall I not then make this paltry — this no sacrifice? Shall I not obtain a victory over this petty allurement, whose consequences when I first gave way to it I did not perceive?"

The distress here described is not a picture drawn by the imagination, a touch of sentimentalism, to exhibit feeling, and to excite it. It is a plain and simple representation of the state of multitudes of young women, who, having been bred to no other means of gaining their support, will probably, if these fail, throw themselves into the very jaws of destruction. Think, then, with tenderness, on these thousands of young persons of your own sex, whom a little self-denial on your part might restore to comfort—might snatch from ruin. Many ladies, who make these unlawful purchases, do not want feeling, they only want consideration. Consider, then, we once more beseech you, consider, that it is not merely their bread, but their virtue, of which you may be unintentionally depriving them; and you will find, that your error is by no means so inconsiderable as it may hitherto have appeared to you.

If the superiority of the foreign purchase you are about to make be not great, you have gained little or nothing by your fault; if it is, and you forego it, you have gained a victory over your own inclination,—the victory of an honest principle over a misleading fancy.

Spare yourself, then, the pain of feeling that, if you hear of any of these unfortunate beings having, previously to their entering on other sinful courses, been tempted by famine to commit a robbery — spare yourself the pain of reflecting, that you, perhaps, by a thoughtless gratification of your taste, first robbed her of that subsistence, the failure of which has driven her to a crime she abhorred. The evil which appeared little, considered by itself, considered in its possible consequences, is of no small magnitude.

But to return. — It was from the land of polished arts that ancient Rome imported the poison of her sturdy morals, the annihilation of her masculine character. England has a palladium for her protection, which Ilium, which Rome never possessed. Yet on that guardian genius depended, as the people thought, the safety of the former; of the latter, it was considered as the destiny. Our palladium is the CHRISTIAN, the PROTESTANT RELIGION. It cannot be taken by storm; but, like that of Ilium, it may be taken by stratagem. The French are to us as much more formidable than the Greeks were to Rome, as we have more to lose. While our guardian genius remains inclosed within our walls, we shall be safe, in spite of wars and revolutions; if we neglect it, like the besieged city of antiquity, we fall: losing our religion, we lose all with it. Religion is our compass, the only instrument for directing and determining our course; and though it will not save the trouble of working the vessel, nor diminish the vigilance of guarding against rocks and shoals; yet it constantly points to that star which, by ascertaining our course, insures our safety.

In making our country an island, Divine Providence seems to have made a provision for our happiness as well as for our security. As that circumstance has protected us from the sword, it should also protect us from the manners of our continental neighbours. The more she labours to resemble them, the more she will lose of her independent character. *Le goût du teroir* is often mentioned as the distinctive mark of the country which produces certain wines. The British character, we hope, will always retain its indigenous flavour.

But if Britain, blest by Heaven above all the nations, ancient or modern, recorded in the annals of history, sacred or prophane, has not made the most of all the advantages bestowed on her; if she has not yet made the best use of that elevation on which Divine Providence has placed her; if she has not yet applied to the best possible ends, the rich gifts with which he has endowed her; nor turned the provision made for her happiness to the best account: if, standing on the loftiest summit of naval, military, and literary glory; if, favoured with the best civil and religious constitution the wit of man has yet devised;—if, with all these advantages, she has yet some steps to ascend before she reach the height to which the Almighty seems to have destined her, let her remember, she has resources within herself, by which, with the blessing of Him who conferred them, she may still set an example to all the kingdoms of the earth. We will not say she may acquire a superiority over other nations — of that she has long been in possession — No; we must not try her by her comparative, but her positive merit: not by placing her in juxta-position with other countries, but with the possibilities of her own excellence.

Britain, we repeat, has abundant resources. If it be true that she has lately, in any respect, gone back, rather than advanced; if, when her public character has reached its zenith, her private character is in any thing deteriorated, she has still within herself all the materials of moral renovation; ample means, not only of recovering what has been lost, but of rising to heights yet unattained. It is only to be wished that she may use these resources, and consider them as raw materials, that will not produce their effect without being industriously worked up.

If the familiar and protracted intercourse with a neighbouring nation; if, during this intercourse, the long witnessed contempt of religion, morbid insensibility to morals, desecrated Sabbaths, and abandonment to amusements the most frivolous, to pleasures knit in one eternal dance; if all this should happily have left unimpaired, or have only tinctured, too slightly to make a lasting impression, the noble simplicity, the ancient rectitude, the sound sense, and the native modesty which have long been the characteristics of the British people; if the growth at home, and within our own doors, of an intolerant and superstitious church, be not too fondly fostered — be not promoted instead of tolerated; if the paramount fondness, in the more delicate sex, for unbounded dissipation, for prophane and immoral writers, should decline; if the middle classes among us should return to their ancient sobriety and domestic habits, should cease to vie with the great in expensive dress, and the decorations of high life, and to give their daughters the same useless accomplishments, which are carried too far even in the highest station, and in theirs are preposterous; if the instruction we are at length giving to the poor be as conscientiously conducted as it is generally adopted, and the art of reading be made the vehicle of true religion; if a judicious correction of our criminal code, and a prudent rectification of the demands of pauperism, be successfully followed up; if the African slave-trade should be effectually abolished—not in promises, and on paper, but in very deed and act; if our prisons be made places of reform, instead of increased corruption; if the young offenders be so instructed, that they come not out as bad as the old, and the old come not out worse than they went in; if our venerable universities should fulfil the promise they give of becoming as distinguished for moral discipline and strict religion, as they have ever been, and still are, unrivalled for learning and ability of every kind; if churches be as readily attended, as they will be cheerfully provided; if there be the same honourable attention paid to filling the pulpits, as to raising the buildings; if the Bible be as generally read by the giver, as it is liberally bestowed on the receiver; if the good old practice of family prayer should be revived, and public worship more carefully attended by those who give the law to fashion; if those who are " the makers of manners" will adopt none but such as deserve to be imitated:—if all these improvements should take place, and which of them, let me ask, is impossible—then, though we laugh to scorn the preposterous notion of human perfectibility, we shall yet have a right to expect that England, so far from being satisfied to excel other nations, will not only excel her present self, but be continually advancing in the scale of Christian perfection.

FRENCH OPINION OF ENGLISH SOCIETY.

The French nation have lately had many opportunities for forming their opinion of the English. It may be worth our while to consider what opinion they *have* formed; since by ascertaining their present judgment of the English character, we may form some instructive conclusions as to the change their tuition is likely to effect in it.

Foreigners are of opinion that we want polish. If this were all, we should rather blame their discernment, or their deficiency in fair deduction. For grant us that we are solid, and we have high authority for saying that solid bodies take the brightest polish. And if in point of fact the English character, like the English oak, be susceptible of no inconsiderable polish, it is owing in both to the inherent soundness and firmness of its substance. Soft bodies admit of little polish: in them, therefore, recourse is had to varnish, which hides all flaws; and the thicker it is applied, the more surely it conceals the meanness of the materials beneath its surface.

A late brilliant female writer*, whose genius it would be a reflection on our own taste not to admire, and on our own candour not to extol; has, towards the end of her admirable posthumous work, done, in general, noble justice to the English character. She had talents to appreciate, and opportunities to examine it, in its highest condition and most advantageous forms. It must be observed, that we here presume to touch on no part of her able delineation of English habits and manners, but only so far as private society and conversation are concerned. On these points we are to look for her ex-

---

* Madame de Staël.

ceptions: though on the society of the gentlemen she animadverts with the most flattering consideration; and even to that of the ladies she makes a frequent and generous, but not very successful, effort to be civil.

However, with all the politeness and good nature of this fine writer, two qualities which she seems to have possessed in no ordinary degree, it frequently escapes her, that she found the English ladies deplorably deficient in those shining talents and airy graces which embellish society. Had her visit to London been three or four years later, she might possibly have found, in some quarters, stronger marks of improvement in this talent so near her heart; at least if any expectation might be formed from their subsequent intercourse with the society of Paris, the charms of which she never fails to exhibit in those glowing colours which she so well knows how to lay on, even on the worst ground.

But this eloquent panegyrist of animated conversation seems to be a little mistaken in some of the causes to which she ascribes the heaviness of London parties. She laments with deeper concern than the occasion, even had it been real, seems to require, that the great English gentlemen regularly retire, and spend nine months in the year on their estates in the country. We wish she had happened to mention in what quarter of the kingdom this annual retreat is made, where this voluntary exile *to* the native home is to be found.

We say voluntary, for British gentlemen are not *rélegués* from our capital, as ex-ministers and discarded favourites used to be from Paris. Neither the fate, nor the credit, nor the liberty, nor the choice of habitation of a man of rank in this country, depends on the favour of an arbitrary king; nor does his happiness, his general acceptance, nor his respectability, hang on the smiles of a despotic and capricious master. And if her concern be excessive for the annual voluntary banishment of our men of taste from the centre of social delights, which she would wish to see converted into a circle "never ending, still beginning;" had this lady never further heard of such places as Bath, or Tunbridge, or Brighton, or any other of those numberless felicitous resources, those supplemental relaxations, those by-reliefs of the *ennui* of retreat, which always stand ready to intercept the speed of the fashionable exile, and to break the fall between the London and the country home?

But if even the fact were as desperate as she intimates, the self-imposed relegation would not be likely to produce the effect she deprecates. This lady, born herself to excel in polished society, regrets this injurious retreat, chiefly because it interrupts the brilliant intercourse of the metropolis, and causes conversation to suffer so tedious and melancholy a suspension. Now we should almost as soon have expected that a philosopher would have imagined a supernumerary eclipse of the sun for the same period, and then have brought it to account for the late dreariness of the natural world and the inclemency of the seasons.

She laments that the manner in which these absentees from the source and centre of intellectual enjoyment spend their time in the country, not a little disqualifies them for the charms of society. With all due deference to this able reasoner, from whom it is hazardous to differ, we should have really thought, that the long leisure for reading, to which this supposed solitude must be at least as favourable to some, as that indolence, sleeping, and drinking which she too indiscriminately ascribes to most, would have been generally seized on for the former purpose by men, who are all scholars by education, and frequently studious from taste. Thus, instead of starving the intellect, would not this leisure rather serve to nourish it; and, instead of lowering the mind, furnish it with fresh images, enrich it with new ideas, and aided by the "short retirement urging sweet return," dispose it to repair with a full mind, additional spirit, replenished resources, and increased energy, to that more splendid society which she deems the life of life; that feast of intellect, of which the writer of these pages is fully disposed to acknowledge the pleasure and the profit? Those to whom she alludes, who only hunt, and loll, and drink, and sleep at their country seats, are not, we presume, of that race of active intellect who would swell the flow of soul by their contributions, were they even tied as closely and constantly to the metropolis as the tavern waiter who draws their corks, or the more respectable purveyor who supplies the market with their luxuries.

As we presume that there is at this time at least as much genius, and taste, and literature, at home, as in any capital abroad, consequently there can be no deficiency of the finest materials for enriching and embellishing society, were their possessors a little more disposed to imitate a neighbouring nation in one talent, in which they must be allowed to excel all others — the talent *se faire valoir*.

There is more sterling weight than show in the genuine English character; and Mr. Addison was not the only one of his countrymen who, with respect to intellectual wealth, could draw for a thousand pounds, though he may not always have a guinea in his pocket. But if they are not incessantly producing all they are worth to every comer; when called out in public situations, in the senate, the pulpit, or at the bar, we see all the energies of genius in all its opulence and variety. We see the most powerful reasoning, adorned by the most persuasive eloquence. With these ample materials for conversation, they are not perhaps driven, like some of their more volatile neighbours, to talk for the sake of talking. Talking is not with Englishmen so completely a *besoin*, so entirely a natural necessity. They are more disposed to consider conversation as the refreshment than the pabulum of life. Added to this, their professional and laborious duties abroad, may make some of them frequently consider society as a scene in which rather to repose their minds, than to keep them in full exercise.

Learning, in this country, is not confined to academicians, authors, and professional men. There is scarcely a man of fortune in the kingdom who, if he be not actually learned, has not, however, been bred to learning. The effect of that high institution, brought from the halls and bowers of our distinguished seats of learning, is generally diffused; it serves to fill and adorn the stations of dignity, honour, and utility of public, as well as to grace the shade and raise the tone of private life. So that an illiterate gentleman is more rarely to be met with in this country, than in any other in the world. When a learned dignitary of our church enquired of one of the French emigrant clergy, who took refuge in England, if he understood Greek, he coolly replied, "*Monsieur, nous avons un professeur!*"

But to return to the other sex.—Our only fear on this subject is, lest they should not always remain what the writer in question represents them as being at present. If, indeed, we were only sent into this world to be entertaining; if we had nothing to do but to talk, nothing to aim at but to shine, nothing to covet but admiration; we should more readily coincide in opinion with this sprightly lady.

A great ancient has pronounced silence to be no unimportant art in society, and points, in a particular instance, at one man, as the wisest in an enlightened assembly, because he knew how to hold his tongue. If there had not been many discreet imitators of this taciturn orator in the London parties, what a diminution would it have been in the number of this lady's delighted auditors, and what a lessening of their own gratification in enjoying the exhibition of her superlative talents!

There are, indeed, very frequently sounder causes for being silent than deficiency of talent, or lack of information; and how happily would the multitude of idle talkers be diminished, if they never opened their mouths, but when they had something to say. The writer in question ascribes to causes, which appear quite new, the reserve and insipidity of the English ladies, when she says, that the true motive is the fear of ridicule; and that as they are not called upon to enliven conversation, they are more struck with the danger of talking, than with the inconvenience of silence. She then, somewhat unaccountably, goes on to attribute the frigidity of their society to the dread of newspapers; and conjectures, that because they do not delight in political warfare, they keep themselves back as much as possible in the presence of others. We did not know that English ladies were either so political or so discreet, or that vivacity and the graces were such heavy losers from these unsuspected causes. Perhaps this lady did not know that the English educate, or rather *did once educate*, women of fashion for *home*. A man of sense will desire to find in his domestic associate good taste, general information, and a correct judgment. In the course of their literary pursuits and conversation together, he will take pleasure in refining and improving her mind; but he would not delight in a wife who will be always introducing subjects for debate, who will be always disputing the palm of victory. Competition and emulation do not contain the elements of domestic happiness. He married for a companion, not for a competitor. Rivalry is no great promoter of affection; nor does superiority in wit always confer superiority in happiness. A professed female wit, like a professed devotee to music, will be soon weary of wasting her talent on her husband; and even he, though he might like such an occasional display in a visit to the house of his friend, will find other talents wanting in a constant home-companion; talents which will not only embellish, but improve society; qualities which will eclipse wit, and outlive beauty.

We do not find that those brilliant French women, who had spoiled this sprightly writer for English society, reserved their wit for the entertainment of their husbands, or their learning for the instruction of their families. Their most graceful ethic and courtly poet, who had the best opportunities of ascertaining the real value of professed wits in society, has given his estimate in a single line:

Diseurs de bons mots, fades caractères !

Among other deductions from brilliant society in England, this lively writer laments an evil, which, if things proceed as they have now begun, we fear may not always remain a subject of lamentation, as coquetry is, in her recipe book, the flavour which gives to society its poignancy: and this zest she complains is not to be found in England, except in the unmarried! If, however, the growing imitation of French manners should hereafter add this new savour to the real accomplishments of English ladies, their fathers and husbands may not think it the most desirable finishing. She accounts for the fondness of our ladies for foreign travel in a manner not the most flattering to their purity, by supposing it to arise as much from the desire of escaping from the restraint on their manners, as from the influence of the fogs on their constitutions.

She is at no loss to know the true cause of a fact, which we are entirely indebted to her sagacity for discovering at all, namely, why *the disgust of life* seizes on those women who are confined to these inanimate societies. Certainly this explanation admits the following preliminary question, — Are the movers in these lifeless circles disgusted with their existence? By the way, we do not quite understand whether by *le degout de la vie* she means a dislike to company, or a taste for suicide.

But let us do justice to her who has in most respects done ample justice to our country. If she is a little sickened with the moody taciturnity, and unassuming manners of our ladies, she graciously redeems their characters by making them a full allowance of the more solid virtues; she acknowledges that sincerity and truth form the basis of their conversation, even where all the graces are wanting. It is somewhat doubtful, however, whether she would not willingly have relinquished the actual, in exchange for the absent qualities.

While we continue to preserve, or rather to improve in, this only true foundation of Christian intercourse, we will less regret the want of its embellishments; and while reserve is protection, and delicacy security, we will console ourselves under these minor evils, which are considered as so cruelly detracting from the fascinations of polished society.

Lord Chesterfield, who adorned conversation by his wit as much as he impaired it by his principles, has defined " politeness to be the art of pleasing." Saint Paul, one of the few writers with whom this accomplished peer was not acquainted, recommends, with as much warmth as his lordship, the duty of pleasing our neighbour. But here the two moralists part. The noble writer would have us please others to benefit ourselves. All his precepts originate, proceed, and terminate in that one object—self. The christian writer directs us to " please others for their good," their highest good, their moral " edification." The essence of the worldly code of ethics is selfishness; that of the Christian is disinterestedness.

There is a generosity in christian intercourse, the very reverse of that little and narrowing spirit ascribed to it by those who do not know, or do not love it.

It cannot be otherwise; for are not those who cultivate it ever the followers of Him, whose sublime characteristic it was — "that he pleased not himself?"

In the society of Christians, every man does not so much look on his own things as on the things of others. Christians do not make conversation a theatre for dispute or display. They consider it as a reciprocation of benignity; a desire to draw out the talents of those who with more merit have less pretension. An interchange of sentiment between intellectual and highly principled persons confers both pleasure and benefit. To make it at once pleasant and profitable, there must be an accordance of principle, if not of opinion. The conversation will frequently have a tincture of religion, even when the topic under discussion is not religious. Topics purely secular are susceptible of this spirit; and in pious and discreet hands, they will be treated in a way to promote religion without professing it.

True religion keeps the whole man in order, whether he be engaged in business or in company. It sheds its benign influence far beyond its own sphere, and by a reflex light casts a ray on actions or speculations to which it has no immediate reference. The Christian does not go out of his way in search of wit, or embellishment, though he does not refuse them when they naturally present themselves, when they grow out of the subject, and the story is not invented for their forced introduction, nor any sacrifice made of something better than themselves. The Christian uses his talents temperately, seeks not to eclipse the less brilliant; and had much rather not shine at all, than shine at the expense of another. The religious man in society finds means for the exercise of many christian virtues without descanting on them,—candour, charitable construction, patience with the less enlightened, and temper with the less forbearing, a scrupulous veracity, an inviolable sincerity, a watchful guard against every vain thought and every light expression. He is careful to preserve wit unsullied, gaiety pure, and vivacity correct. He is constantly on the watch to introduce subjects of a higher strain; when the occasion offers, he gladly embraces it, but with a due regard to time, place, and circumstance. Let it be observed we are not here speaking of select society, associating for religious improvement, but of the duty of keeping ordinary conversation within the bounds and under the discipline of correct principle.

ENGLISH OPINION OF FRENCH SOCIETY.

It may at first sight be censured as a departure from the general design of these slight pages, to introduce any allusion to the manners of foreign countries, as exhibited in their own journals, memoirs, and letters. But when it is considered how deeply our own manners are now becoming assimilated with theirs, it may not be thought quite irrelevant to the subjects under consideration, to take a cursory view of the habits of society in a neighbouring metropolis, so far as they may be likely to affect and influence those of our own country, avoiding every thing public or political, or general, and confining the few cursory remarks to be made, to the fashionable circles of private society.

Paris has long been looked up to by many with admiration, as the centre of all that is brilliant in wit, or fascinating in conversation. In a capital, which before the Revolution was said to contain twenty thousand men of letters, high society was not likely to want eulogists. The extravagant encomiums bestowed on these societies by their own people, and echoed back by ours, may prevent its being thought inexpedient to give a superficial sketch of a few of the leading characters which seem to have set the superiority of the circles over which they presided above all competition. It is, we repeat, the apprehension that this boasted superiority may kindle undue admiration, and even excite envy, in the ardent and ingenuous mind of young persons of taste, who feel themselves precluded from the enjoyment, which must apologise for the freedom, whilst it explains the motive, of these observations.

It is indeed wounding to delicacy to speak explicitly on things which should not be so much as named. Yet though it is painful to touch on such topics, how shall we be so likely to prevent evils, as by exposing them? Perhaps it may check the desire of imitation, lightly to touch on a few of the *bad characters* who presided over these *good societies.*

That many have escaped their pollution, is a thing more to inspire wonder than to excite imitation. All do not die of the plague where the plague rages; but the preservation of the few is no proof of the salubrity of the air, where so many have been infected.

In certain societies, the difficulty of being witty is materially diminished by the readiness of the speaker to make any sacrifice, both of piety and modesty, to the good thing he is about to utter. While the feeling of that very sacrifice may perhaps give a keener relish to the pleasure of the profane hearer, the Christian, not inferior in talent, rejects with horror the reputation for wit to be obtained by any such sacrifice himself, and disdains to sanction or applaud it as the hearer of others.

Though the late sanguinary revolution in France overturned law, order, government, and religion; and had given a more emphatical character to crime of every description; yet if we take a cursory view of the period immediately preceding it, we shall see that this tremendous convulsion rather aggravated than introduced many of its moral corruptions. To be convinced of this, we need not travel so far back as that period which the natives consider as the *acmé* of human glory, — the age of *Louis Quatorze*, of Richelieu, and the Academy, the immortal Forty, as this academy had the modesty to call itself.

More sober thinkers are, however, of opinion, that what characterised that splendid reign, was unbounded extravagance, elegant profligacy, and tolerated debauchery. Surely these, which were its notorious distinctions, are practices which contribute little to the real grandeur of a country; unless, indeed, it can be proved that, according to the fearfully unguarded expression of the otherwise moral Burke, that the exhibition of vice in a better taste, by taking from it all its apparent grossness, takes away half of its real turpitude.

What arts of refinement could neutralise the evil, when all the bounds of moral restraint were so far broken through, as that the royal wife and the royal mistress were every-where received with the same appearance of respect, when they were even met together in the same societies?

Louis has lately obtained in certain quarters, a kind of resuscitation of his buried fame, by the only method perhaps by which it could have been raised,—a comparison with the prisoner of St. Helena. But surely to have committed fewer crimes than the man who has committed more than any other man, is not to have attained a very high degree in the scale of moral excellence. Are splendor in decoration and magnificence in expense a mantle broad enough to cover that injustice and those exactions on a plundered people by which they were purchased? The piety of the king's latter days is frequently thrown into the scale against the disorders of his earlier life. But surely the transition from profligacy to persecution is no great improvement in the human character. Were not his false virtues even more destructive than his avowed vices? Did matters take a better turn, when the monarch, by exchanging gross immoralities for the exercise of a superstitious and intolerant religion, indulged himself and his directress in a long and bitter persecution of his own subjects? a persecution accompanied with every act of the most unrelenting cruelty. Exile, proscription, torture, death, were the rewards of four millions of his faithful protestant subjects! To these rigorous exercises of arbitrary power, he was encouraged and impelled by a woman who had herself been educated in the faith she now endeavoured to exterminate. We pass over the intermediate government of " the godless Regent trembling at a star," in whose character, in addition to the most disgraceful vices, we see a shocking, but not uncommon union of the wildest superstition with the most avowed infidelity.

During the reign of the next equally corrupt successor, we have endless records of the state of society among persons in the higher walks of life. These notices are to be found in a multitude of the letters and memoirs of the individuals who were themselves actors and interlocutors in these scenes of familiar life. These fashionable societies are all that come within our present design. Many of these works have preserved the history of characters, principles, and sentiments, which, had they been consigned to eternal oblivion, religion would have had less to mourn, and virtue less to regret.

Many of these writings, for life would be too short, and time ill-spent to peruse them all, are adorned with elegancies of composition, and graces of style, which, had they been devoted to the purposes for which they were given, might have benefited the world as much as they have injured it. Out of all these mischievous but lighter writings, we shall only mention one or two; nor would they have been noticed in a little work of this nature, but for the popularity they have obtained among us, and our dread of that natural progress, the tendency of admiration to produce imitation.

In the Life of Marmontel, written by himself, we have an extraordinary specimen of decorous vice and accredited infamy — of abandoned manners, to which reference is frequently made, at least to the characters which exhibited them, without the slightest feeling of their turpitude. Vices abound, and are revealed without the least apparent suspicion of their guilt. The intimations, indeed, are not repeated in the way of boasting, but look as if the writer did not think that concealment of the vice would raise the character he was eulogising. If there are no offensive descriptions of vicious manners, it seems to be because they were not understood to be vicious; and if gaiety of spirit seems to conceal from the writer the complexion of his own morals, gaiety of style seems almost to make the reader lose sight of the character of the company in which he is passing his time. In fact, the delineation of these characters consists rather in a morbid insensibility to sin, than in an ambitious display of it. The slight veil thrown over corrupt manners by decency of expression, seems the effect of some remains, not of principle, but of good taste. It is the cool-bloodedness of a heart stagnated by long habits of impurity; for while the passions are inflamed by criminal indulgences, the sensibilities of the soul are chilled. The mind insensibly loses that delicacy of perception which nicely distinguishes not only the shades of evil, but the very existence of the distinction between vice and virtue. This deadness of principle, and liveliness of language, it is which makes this writer, and others we could name, so peculiarly dangerous.

Women of fashion, of the very worst description, to whose parties the writer referred to was familiarly admitted, are named with unbounded admiration, not merely of their talents, but their virtues. The charms of their conversation, and the amiableness of their characters, are the theme of his unmixed panegyric. Incidentally, however, as a thing by the by, as a trifle not requiring to be named expressly, as a thing not invalidating any of their perfections, it comes out, that these women, so faultless and so panegyrised, are living in an illicit commerce with different men — men, whose wives are, with the same uncensured guilt, carrying on similar connections with the husbands of other women! Sobriety, chastity, the conjugal and maternal virtues, are not thought necessary to be called in to complete their round of perfection. Impurity of heart and life, dereliction of all the domestic duties, are never brought forward as any deduction from the all-atoning merit of graces of manner and vivacity of conversation.

Divine Providence seems to have intended advanced age as a season of repose, reflection, and preparation for death; and to have sent its infirmities, sufferings, and debility, as gracious intimations of our approaching change, and with a merciful view of our attaining by those remembrances, to the end of our faith, even the salvation of our souls.

But one of the unhallowed projects on which these accomplished societies seem to have congratulated themselves, was in defeating this providential procedure. It was their boasted aim to cheat old age of itself—of its present inconveniences, its decays, and its prospective views, by a more amusing method. They contrived to divert the stage of infirmity into a scene of superinduced gaiety and increased levity. Instead of desiring to invest it with the peaceful attributes of calmness and resignation, they invented the means of making old age lose itself, as it were, in youthful images, not only by indulging in light reading, but loose composition. One of them was so successfully boiled in Medea's kettle, that his eulogist triumphantly tells us he translated Ariosto, and published tales exhibiting pictures of voluptuousness without indecency; and these boasted exploits are adduced as adding fresh laurels to a being on the very verge of eternity!

Hear a celebrated academician immortalise one of the deceased confraternity in his public oration! In illustrating the character of his friend, who died in extreme old age, he describes this period as "a season when ingenious trifling is peculiarly graceful; a period in which men might give themselves up to levity with the least scruple and the most success. It is in old age, says the orator, that *the mind is disabused on all subjects, and that a man has a right to jest upon every thing!* It is then that long experience has taught him the wit of concealing reason under a veil which may embellish it!" *

Whoever has cast an eye on the lately published letters of Madame du Deffand, — a most unnecessary and unprofitable addition to the late load of similar literary mischiefs, — will have beheld such a picture of the manners even of private and select society, among persons of high rank, science, taste, and literature, as must make him look on these distinctions without envy, when beheld disconnected with those principles which alone render talents estimable.

* Speech of Condorcet to the Academy on the death of Monsieur De Tressan.

In the history of this distinguished lady, we find these striking circumstances: they present a melancholy instance how completely, in Paris, at that time, a disregard of all the obligations of duty, all sense of religion, all the charities of domestic virtue, all the purposes of social usefulness, was, on *her* part, perfectly compatible with her being received in the first society. On the part of her associates, all the objections, insurmountable, we trust, in any other place, were there sacrificed to the reigning idol — the fondness for display in conversation, the vanity of eclipsing those who eclipsed others.

We see also how little splendid talents contribute to the felicities of the life, or to the virtues of the possessor. We even see that, when not under the control of sound principle, they awfully increase the present capacity for evil, and the responsibility of a future reckoning. Instead of promoting improvement, they carry contamination. In morals, as well as in politics,

"Great power is an achievement of great ill."

Some of these brilliant societies fostered in their bosoms the serpents that were so soon to sting, not only their own country, but all Europe. Here were cherished those academical philosophers, wits, and political economists, who first sounded the alarm for the simultaneous extinction of thrones and altars; who first exhibited the portentous remedies for curing despotism by anarchy, and superstition by atheism; who sowed the first prolific seeds of those revolutionary horrors which so rapidly sprung up into the poisonous tree of liberty, and who hurled their arrows at the God of heaven, and erected on the meditated ruins of his kingdom, the temple of the goddess of reason.

Previously to some of Madame du Deffand's numerous intrigues, she had been separated from her husband, on the ground which, it is presumed, the laws of

England would not recognise as a lawful impediment — *that " he was a weak and tiresome companion!"* She was extraordinarily acute, but her acuteness, though it was frequently just, was always malicious. It is difficult to say whether she was more completely deficient in sensibility or principle. She possessed all the qualities which attract, but wanted all those which attach; or rather, she wanted no talent but that of turning those she possessed to a better account. Not possessing the female virtues, she either did not believe in their existence, or despised them. If she wanted any vice, it was that of hypocrisy; for she takes little pains to hide qualities which were not fit to be seen. If she possessed any virtue, it was frankness, which yet was often disfigured by coarseness, and not seldom counteracted by falsehood. She wanted all the good feelings of kindness, affection, and tenderness; and possessed in perfection all the bad ones of ill-nature, jealousy, and envy; but her ruling passion was a selfishness the most deeply rooted, and an egotism the most completely unconquerable.

The dark and hollow character which she takes little pains to conceal, is rendered more broadly conspicuous by the warmth of her colouring, the strength of her language, and the power of her wit, all frequently exercised in proclaiming her own impieties.

It is a striking proof of the unrelenting rancour of her heart, that a friend, of the same class of character *, whom she had formerly loved as much as she could love any woman; one who had been her select companion in her own house fifteen years, but who had quitted her in disgust, and set up a *talking house* for herself, which drew away some of " the best feathers in her wing;"— on hearing the death of this rival lady, she only exclaimed, " I wish she had died many years ago, and then I should not have lost D'Alembert!"

* Mademoiselle de l'Espinasse.

We learn from her letters, that her splendid society was composed not merely of wits, philosophers, and academicians, but of women of rank, of nobles, and of statesmen, with one of whom she was connected. From those, it must be confessed, admirably written epistles, we profitably learn much of the hollowness of worldly friendships, much of the insincerity of mere wits and mere men of letters — of persons who associate together, partly for the credit of having it known that they are so associated — who mix acrimony and adulation, venturing to indemnify themselves for their reciprocal flattery when together, by their cutting sarcasms when separated. Happily, the more we see of these communications, the more we are convinced that nothing but sound principle, "godly sincerity," a conquest over vanity, a triumph over egotism, an habitual struggle against selfishness — can establish an honourable, virtuous, and durable friendship, or shed a benign lustre on the most polished society.

We repeat, that these reports are not industriously gleaned from rival parties, ill-informed journalists, nor even from virtuous writers, eager to expose the vices they detested; but from the principal performers in the scene — from a woman whose uncontrollable openness prevents her concealing her own vices.

We see, not without pain, her exposure of the faults of some of the associates whom she so sedulously courts, and so constantly abuses; we see the malignity which forces itself through all her endeavours to appear amiable in the eyes of the distinguished person to whom she writes; we see the corroding envy, the gnawing jealousy, and sometimes the obvious aversion to the individuals of a society, without which she cannot exist; which society probably entertained a reciprocal hatred of their flattering hostess, and yet could not exist without *her*. All this exhibits a scene, from which an unsophisticated English heart turns away, sickening with disgust.

This unhappy woman, old, deaf, blind, repining, and impious, yet drew this accomplished society about her by their mutual fondness for conversation. They met without affection, they parted without regret; yet meet they must—they were necessary to each other, not for comfort, for they knew neither the name nor the thing; but society being an article of the first necessity for the support of existence, it must be had with companions hating, and hated by, each other. Under such circumstances, the fondness for society seems not so much a taste, as a raging appetite.

It is, however, a cheerless, heartless society, where persons of talents and breeding meet, not so much to enjoy each other, as to get rid of themselves. Intimacy without confidence, and intercourse without esteem, add little to the genuine delights of social life. Competition, while it inflames vanity, is no improver of kindness.

In a city like Paris, where men were

wits and authors by profession, and ladies judges and critics by courtesy, nothing was considered as an exclusion from these societies but want of talents to amuse, or taste to decide. The poet produced his work, not, however, so much to be corrected as applauded; not so much to be counselled as flattered; he, in return, paying usuriously, in the same counterfeit coin, the honour conferred on him, and the benefit done him, by their proclamation of the beauty of his work; his fame, perhaps, suspended on the avowed patronage of a woman whom we, in our plain language, should call infamous. He is grateful to receive his imprimatur and his crown of laurel from fair and fashionable, but impure hands; and Paris resounds, next morning, with the immortality assigned him by the decision of this coterie.

All this might be very well, or at least would not be so very bad, if there were no future reckoning; but to see old age without consolation, dreading solitude as only less terrible than death,—to contemplate loss of sight as only augmenting spiritual blindness, yet to see the afflicted sufferer clinging to this miserable existence, and closing a life of sin with a death without penitence and without hope,—to consider talents capable of great things, abused and misapplied,—a God not merely forsaken, but denied;—all these are images from which the sober mind turns away with horror softened by compassion. May every daughter of Britain say, with the patriarch of old, " Come not into their secret, O my soul; to their assembly let not thine honour be united!"

Some ladies of unimpeached morality were found in these coteries. True; yet we hope to be forgiven for saying, that they could have retained but little of that delicacy which should preserve the purity of society, when they made no scruple of mixing intimately with women whose practices they would not by any means adopt. In such society virtue withers, delicacy is impaired, and principle finally extinguished.

In this view it is impossible not to make a short digression, to observe with gratitude on the obligations of English society to our late venerated queen. Not to insist on the admirable example she set in her exact performance of all the domestic duties; her public conduct, in one important instance, will ever reflect honour on her memory — we mean her solicitude to prevent the impure mixtures to which we are now alluding. She raised, as it were, a rampart between vice and virtue; and her strictness in excluding from the royal presence all who had forfeited their claim to be introduced to it, had a general moral effect, by excluding them also from the virtuous society of others of their own rank. Discriminations of this nature are of incalculable value in preserving the distinctions between correctness and impurity, when no offender, though of the highest rank, can preserve the public dignity of the station she has dishonoured.

> " 'Twas hard, perhaps, on here and there a waif,
> Desirous to return, and not received;
> But was an wholesome rigour in the main,
> And taught th' unblemish'd to preserve with care
> That purity, whose loss was loss of all."
> COWPER.

London also has had its select assemblies for conversation. They were neither trifling, dull, nor pedantic. If there were less display of wit, less pains to be easy, less study to be natural, less affectation of being unaffected, less effort to be unconstrained, there was more sincerity, integrity, and kindness. If there was a less perpetual aim at being ingenious, ingenuity was never wanting. If there were less persiflage and sarcasm, there was more affection, truth, and nature. Religion, though not discussed, was always venerated, and no degree of rank or talent would have procured an introduction where there was any taint on the reputation.

The tone of social intercourse is at present, perhaps, likely to be raised by the recent adoption of more direct religious improvement in the private parties of some persons of rank and talents. But to return to Paris.

One instance more of the substitution of talent for virtue, and of the little regard paid to the absence of the one where the other abounded; one instance more, and we will relieve our Readers, and carry them to breathe a purer atmosphere in better company. The celebrated Madame d'Epinay is described by one of her admirers [*], who came in the order of succession next after Rousseau, not only as the most attractive, but most *discreet* of women! This discretion, which is his rather than hers, appears in his making her indulgence in forbidden gratifications, consistent with her constant regard for public opinion, and the desire of reputation. He records, intentionally

---

[*] Le Baron de Grimm.

to her honour, that being above all prejudices herself, (that is, above the weaknesses of Christianity,) yet no one knew better what was due to the prejudices of others. She conformed, he observes, as scrupulously to old usages, as to new opinions, and kept up the outward observances of the church as much as a woman of an ordinary mind could have done; that is, she was at once an infidel and a hypocrite. He proclaims to her glory, that, "without believing in any catechism but that of good sense, she never failed to receive the sacraments, painful as the stupid ceremony was, with the best grace imaginable, as often as decency, or the scruples of her friends, made it becoming." "Perhaps," adds her prophane panegyrist, "there was as much greatness in receiving them with *her* notion of them, as there would have been in refusing them." Is it any wonder that, with such a conformity of principles, she obtained the prize of the academy, as well as the homage of the academician?

We are amused to think with what a contemptuous smile of pity these ladies, with all their allowed taste and learning, must, if they were consistent, have beheld the pictures of those obsolete wives, Andromache and Penelope, as delineated by the Grecian bard — pictures of female excellence and domestic virtue, which have drawn the tear of admiring sympathy from many a British eye. The poet has omitted to mention whether their valiant lords loved them the less for having spent the hours of *their* absence in scenes of bloody warfare or perilous adventure, in mournful solitude, cheating the time in simple occupations, yet such as served to keep up the memory of their beloved heroes; in one, by contriving decorations for a living lord, or, in the other, honouring the memory of the dead one, by preparing funeral honours for his father, ingeniously deferring the detested second nuptials by nightly unravelling the daily labour, and thus keeping her promise of consent when the work should be finished, and preserving her fidelity to her lord by never finishing it.

What manly English heart would not prefer the fond anxiety of the Trojan wife, which led her in secret to the watch-tower to mark the battle, and tenderly seek to explore her husband so soon to bleed,—to all the Aspasias of Greece, to all the Du Deffands, the De l'Espinasses, the D'Epinays, to all the beau ideal of the fancy, and all the practical pollutions of the life, of the "*bonnes societes*" of the metropolis of France?

But, happily, we need not go back to ransack antiquity for *examples* in the finely-imagined females of Troy or Ithaca, nor for *warnings* to the polished, but profligate courtezans of Athens, nor to the criminal countesses of Paris;—we may find instances of the one, and a complete contrast to the other, nearer home. We need go no further for the highest examples of female dignity, talent, and worth, than are to be found in the private biography of our own country.

We could produce no inconsiderable number in the highest rank of women, who, if their names are not blazoned in the book of fame, will be recorded in more lasting characters in the book of life — who, if their memoirs are not spangled with their *bons mots*, have yet had their good actions and holy principles embalmed in the writings of their faithful Christian friends. But we shall confine ourselves to a very few.

The Lady Mary Armyne, descended from the ancient Earls of Shrewsbury, was eminently skilled in human, but especially in divine learning. But the remembrance of her talents, which appear to have been of the first order, is lost in that of her Christian virtues. Among numerous other instances of her pious exertions, she contributed largely to the support of a society for converting the Indians in New England, long before missions were thought of by her lady countrymen. On hearing of the fatal massacre of St. Bartholomew, she instantly devoted a large sum to those exiled and destitute clergymen who had fled hither for protection. Her piety was as exemplary as that extensive benevolence of which it was the source.

In Birch's Life of the Hon. Robert Boyle, there is a most interesting account of Mary, Countess of Warwick, of whom it is saying every thing to say that she was entirely worthy of being sister to that illustrious Christian philosopher. Of the eminently pious Lady Frances Hobart, the ornament of the court of James the First, Dr. Collings has preserved an interesting memorial. A long and unwearied attention, for many years, to the bodily sufferings of her lord, could only be surpassed by her anxiety for his spiritual interests. Through the blessing of God she became the honoured instrument of a total change in his character, who never named her by any other appellation but that of his "dear saint." This term had not then fallen into reproach.

Of Susanna, Countess of Suffolk, it is impossible to say too much. For brevity's sake, however, we must restrict ourselves to one or two particulars in speaking of a life which was a constant series of secret piety and active benevolence. When near her end, which happened in her twenty-second year, she implored of her lord, that whatever provision might be made for the fortunes or acquirements of her children, that they might be educated in the strictest principles of Christianity, in comparison of which she esteemed all worldly accomplishments as nothing. To her dying father, who had been inattentive to Christian duties, she administered such spiritual supports, that in rapture he praised God that he should live to receive his best religious consolations from his own child!!

To the memory of the Lady Cutts, the incomparable wife of the gallant Lord Cutts, so distinguished at the siege of Namur, noble justice has been done in an admirable funeral sermon of Bishop Atterbury, which we would recommend to every reader who has a taste for exalted piety or fine writing.

The Lady Elizabeth Hastings was not less distinguished for superior talents than for eminence in every Christian attainment. She has been celebrated for both in the Tatler, under the very inappropriate appellation of Aspasia. No two characters could form a more perfect contrast.

But the time would fail to enumerate all the English ladies who have conferred honour on their country. Of those already mentioned, all possessed considerable talents. Some were eminent for their skill in the dead languages; others for their knowledge of philosophy and the admiration due for their high religious attainments. All were practical Christians, who adorned their profession by the strictest attention to the domestic, the relative, and the social duties.

But what shall we say to Rachel Lady Russell? *Many daughters have done virtuously, but thou excellest them all!* She has unintentionally bequeathed us her character in her letters. Though there is little elegance in her style, there is all the dignity of wisdom and truth in her sentiments. Many specimens of epistolary writing might be produced, which excel these in the graces of composition, but few which surpass them in that strong sense, solid judgment, and those discriminating powers which were the characteristics of her intellectual attainments, as heroic fortitude, Christian humility, unshaken trust in God, and

* For a full account of these, and many other equally eminent ladies, see " Memoirs of Pious Women."

submission to his dispensations, were of her religious character. Such a combination of tenderness the most exquisite, magnanimity the most unaffected, and Christian piety the most practical, have not often met in the same mind.

An acute, but sceptical French writer, calls "Magnanimity the good sense of pride, and the noblest way of obtaining praise." How well has the prince of pagan philosophers, by anticipation, corrected this tinsel phrase! "If thou art not good, thy magnanimity is ridiculous, and worthy of no honour." How did our sublime Christian sufferer practically improve upon both! "Seek not the honour which cometh from men, but that which cometh from God."

Whether we view this illustrious daughter of the virtuous Southampton taking notes on the public trial of her noble consort, concealing the tender anguish of the wife under the assumed composure of the secretary; whether we behold her, after his condemnation, prostrate at the feet of the unfeeling monarch, imploring a short reprieve for her adored husband, while the iron-hearted king heard the petition without emotion, and refused it without regret; whether we behold her sublime composure at their final separation, which drew from her dying lord the confession, "the bitterness of death is past;" whether we behold her heroic resolution rather to see him die, than to persuade him to any dishonourable means to preserve his life; whether we see her superiority to resentment afterwards towards the promoters of his execution,— no expression of an unforgiving spirit; no hard sentence escaping her, even against the savage Jeffries, who pronounced his condemnation, adding insult to cruelty; no triumph when that infamous judge was afterwards disgraced and imprisoned; if we view her in that more than temperate letter to the King a few days after her dear lord's execution, declaring that, if she were capable of consolation, it would only be that her lord's fame might be preserved in the King's more favourable opinion:—had long habits of voluptuousness left any sense of pity in this corrupt king; or, rather, if a heart had not been forgotten in his anatomy, it must have been touched at her humble intreaty that "he would grant his pardon to a woman amazed with grief, to the daughter of a man who had served his father in his greatest extremities, and his Majesty in his greatest perils:"— if we view this extraordinary sufferer under all these trials, while we admire the woman, we must adore the divine grace which alone could sustain her under them.

After this imperfect sketch, may we not say, that, for an example of conjugal tenderness, we need not go out of our own country for a perfect model? Portia swallowing fire because she would not survive her Brutus, the *Pæte non dolet* of the faithful Arria, as she stabbed herself, and then presented the sword to her husband, to set him an example of dying bravely; these heroic instances of conjugal affection, which have been the admiration of ages, are surpassed by the conduct of Lady Russel: *they* died a voluntary death rather than outlive their husbands; Christianity imposed on *her* the severer duty of surviving hers,—of living to suffer calamities scarcely less trying, and to perform duties scarcely less heroic. After weeping herself blind, after the loss of her only son the Duke of Bedford, let us view her called to witness the death of her daughter, the Duchess of Rutland. After seeing her dead corpse, let us behold her going to the chamber of her other daughter, the Duchess of Devonshire, then confined in child-bed, of which the other had just died. When her only surviving daughter enquired after her sister, the mother cheerfully replied, " I have just seen her out of bed!"—It was in her coffin.

In whatever attitude, then, we consider the portrait of this illustrious lady, it is with fresh admiration. Each lineament derives additional beauty from its harmony with the rest, the symmetry of the features corresponding with the just proportions of the whole figure.

ENGLAND'S BEST HOPE.

We have dwelt on the present and the past, as well with reference to our neighbours as ourselves. If we have shown that we have little regret in any still remaining difference between the inhabitants of the opposite shores, and much to fear from a growing resemblance between them;—if we have successfully hinted at the grounds of our own real superiority, and the possibility of maintaining, and even increasing our greatness, to any extent consistent with human imperfection;—if we have, in the two preceding chapters, anticipated what might be our ultimate degradation, whilst in the first we had pointed at the heights to which we may reasonably aspire;—let us not think it unworthy our attention to inquire how we can alone answer our high destination, revive what we have lost, attain what more is within our reach, or having attained it, how we may perpetuate the inestimable blessing.

We have at length, though with a slow and reluctant movement, begun to provide a national education for the children of the poor. Prejudice held out against it with its accustomed pertinacity,—knowledge would only make them idle, ignorance would preserve subordination, the knowledge of their duty would impede the performance of it. This last we did not perhaps say in so many words, but was it not the principle of our conduct? We put off the instruction of the poor till the growth of crime made the rich tremble. We refused to make them better till they grew so much worse as to augment the difficulty, as to lessen the probability of their reform.

The alarm came home to the opulent. They were afraid for their property, for their lives; they were driven to do what it had long been their duty not to have left undone. But they did it not, till "the overflowings of ungodliness made them afraid." They discovered, at length, that ignorance had not made better subjects, better servants, better men. This lesson they might have condescended to learn sooner from the Irish rebels, from the French revolutionists. We have at length done well, though we have done it reluctantly. We have begun to instruct the poor in the knowledge of religion.

But there is another class, a class surely of no minor importance, from whom too many still withhold the same blessing. If, as is the public opinion, it is the force of temptation which has produced so much crime among the poor, are not the rich, and especially the children of the rich, exposed to at least as strong temptations, not indeed to steal, but to violate other commandments of equal authority? Laws, without manners, will not do all we expect from them: manners, without religion, will be but imperfectly reformed. And who will say that religious reformation will be complete, whilst it is confined to a single class, or deemed at least a work of supererogation by some among the higher ranks? There are, however, many honourable exceptions, the number of which is, we trust, increasing.

Why should the poor monopolize our benevolence? Why should the rich, in this one instance, be so disinterested? Why should not the same charity be extended to the children of the opulent and the great? Why should the son of the nobleman not share the advantage now bestowed on the children of his servant, of his workman, of the poorest of his neighbours? Why should not Christian instruction be made a prominent article in the education of those who are to govern and to legislate, as well as of those who are to work and to serve? Why are these most important beings, the very beings in this enlightened country whose immortal interests are the most neglected?

The Apostle tells us, that "he who provides not for his own house has denied the faith, and is worse than an infidel." If this be true of temporal, what shall be said of him who neglects to make "for his own" a spiritual provision? Does not he far more emphatically deny "that faith" which is violated even in the other inferior case?

If we have begun to instruct the poor with a view to check the spirit of insubordination, that spirit requires little less suppression in our own families. In all ranks it is the prevailing evil of the present day. The diminished obedience of children to parents, of servants to masters, of subjects to sovereigns, all spring from one common root — an abatement of reverence to the authority of God. Fathers should therefore keep up in their offspring, as long as possible, a dependence on themselves, without which they will gradually shake off their dependence on their Maker. Independence of every kind, as it is the prevailing wish, so it is the most alarming danger. With filial obedience, obedience to Divine authority will become connected; but the muzzle of domestic restraint shaken off, there will be no controul of any kind left. Might not a more exact Christian institution help to arrest the same spirit which has, within a few years, so frequently broken out in our, in many respects, excellent public schools? We mean not altogether to censure these honourable seminaries. Do not the youth carry thither, rather than acquire there, this want of subordination? Is it not too often previously fostered at home by the habits of luxury, the taste for expense, the unrestrained indulgences, the unsubdued tempers, which so ill prepare them to submit to moral discipline? Laxity of manners and of principles act reciprocally: they are alternately cause and effect.

Tender parents are, indeed, grieved at the indications of evil dispositions in their children; but even worthy people do not always study the human character: they are too much disposed to believe this budding vice but accidental defect—a failing which time will cure. Time cures nothing; time only inveterates, only exasperates, where religion is not called in as a corrective. It is in vain to hope to tame the headstrong violence of the passions by a few moral sentences;—the curb is too weak for the natural ferocity of the animal. If the most religious education does not always answer the end, what end is an education, in which religion does not predominate, likely to produce? How is the Christian character likely to be formed without the strict inculcation of religious principles, without the powerful discipline of religious and moral habits?

Parents are naturally and honourably

anxious about advancing the interests of their sons; but they do not always extend this anxiety to their best interests. They prepare them for the world, but neglect to prepare them for eternity. We recal our words; they do not even make the best preparation for the world. Their affection is warm, but it is short-sighted; for surely that principle which is the root of all virtuous action, of all the great qualities of the heart, of integrity, of sober-mindedness, of patience, of self-denial, of veracity, of fortitude, of perseverance in a right pursuit, is likely to produce a character not unqualified for the best services to society — for advancement in life, for fitness for the most useful employments, for adorning the most honourable situations: for we do not recommend such a religion as would make Ascetics, as would abstract men from the business or the duties of life, or from the true enjoyments of society. There seems, indeed, little necessity for guarding against evils of which we see no great danger.

Gentlemen should be scholars; liberal learning need not interfere with religious acquirements, unless it be so conducted as to leave no time for its cultivation, unless it cause them to consider religion as an object of inferior regard. But no human learning ought to keep religious instruction in the back ground, so as to render it an incidental, a subordinate part in the education of a Christian gentleman.

Some apology might be made for the natives of a neighbouring kingdom for their contempt of religion, from the load of absurd and superstitious observances which degrade it. Though even *they* might have discovered, under these disadvantages, much that is good; for they have had writers who yield to none in elevation of sentiment, in loftiness of genius, and sublimity of devotion.* Yet the

* What has been said here and elsewhere of France, and of the religion of France, has been said " more in sorrow than in anger," and with the single view of caution to our own country. However we deprecate the past, we still cherish the hope,

labours of these excellent men have left the character of their religion unaltered.

But we have no such excuse to plead for the contempt or neglect of religion. Here, Christianity presents herself to us neither dishonoured, degraded, nor disfigured. Here she is set before us in all her original purity; we see her in her whole consistent character, in all her fair and just proportions, as she came from the hands of her Divine Author. We see her as she has been completely rescued from that encumbering load under which she had so long groaned; delivered from her long bondage, by the labours of our blessed reformers, and handed down to us unmutilated and undefaced.

that having witnessed the horrors of a political, we may one day hail the dawn of a moral revolution. A virtuous King, and an improving government, leave us not without hope that this fair part of the globe may yet rise in those essentials without which a country can never be *truly* great. May they eventually improve, in " that righteousness which alone exalteth a nation!"

If every English gentleman did but seriously reflect, how much the future moral prosperity of his country depended on the education he may at this moment be giving to his son, even if his paternal feelings did not stimulate his zealous endeavours, his patriotic, would.

May the unworthy writer, who loves her country with an ardour which the superior worth of that country justifies; who, during a long life, has anxiously watched its alternations of prosperous and adverse fortune; and who, on the very verge of eternity, is proportionally anxious for its moral prosperity, as she approaches nearer to that state, in view of which all temporal considerations diminish in their value;—may she hope that her egotism will be forgiven, and her pardon be obtained for the liberty she is taking? May she venture to suppose that she is now conversing with some individual father of a family in the higher ranks of life, and, presuming that he would permit the freedom, address him, and through him, every man of rank and fortune in the kingdom, in plain and bold language, with something like the following suggestions?

Let it be your principal concern to train up your son in the fear of God. Make this fear, which is not only " the beginning of wisdom" in point of excellence, the same also in priority of time. Let the beginning of wisdom be made the beginning of education. Imbue the youthful mind betimes with correct tastes, sound principles, good affections, and right habits. Consider that the tastes, principles, affections, and habits he now forms, are to be the elements of his future character; the fountain of honourable actions, the germ of whatever may hereafter be pure, virtuous, lovely, and of good report.

In his education never lose sight of this great truth, that irreligion is the death of all that is graceful, and amiable, in the human mind; the destruction of all moral beauty. Its foundations are in the dust, and it is a vain attempt to hope to raise a noble superstructure on so mean and despicable a basis. Tell him, that the irreligious man never looks out of self. He is his own centre; all his views are low; he has no conception of any thing that is lofty in virtue, or sublime in feeling. How should he? He does not look to God as the model of perfection. He will act nothing that is holy, for he does not honour *his* commands; he will conceive nothing that is great, for he does not look to the Archetype of greatness; there is no image of true grandeur in his soul. His mind will be reduced to the narrowness of the things to which it is familiarized, and stoop to the littleness of the objects about which it is conversant. His views will not be noble, because they are not excursive; they are confined, imprisoned, limed, entangled in earth and its concerns; they never expatiate in the boundless regions of immortality. He has no connecting link between himself and things

"Beyond this visible diurnal sphere."

His soul is cramped in the exercise of all its noblest faculties; his heart paralyzed in its best attempts after a fugitive, low-minded virtue.

There is no true elevation of soul but what the youth must acquire by the knowledge of God as revealed in his word; no perfect example but that exhibited to him in the character of his Divine Son; nothing but the Gospel, through the grace of God, will check his corruptions, give him a sense of his accountableness, and raise his nature above the degraded state to which sin has reduced it.

It is material to reflect that nothing really preparative to his well-being in this life, and conducive to his qualification as an ornament to his country, will otherwise than forward him in his progress for another country, " even a heavenly." Adopt the measures which even nature and reason suggest for making him a distinguished member of human society, and it will not lessen your satisfaction, nor lower your gratitude, when you see that you have not only trained him to be a useful and virtuous citizen, but also a candidate for heaven.

Let your child be made familiarly acquainted with God's word, his providence, his controlling power, his superintending eye. Let him be taught not barely to read, but to understand, to love, to venerate his Bible. Implant at a proper season, in his mind, the evidences of Christianity, in the clearest, simplest, and most explicit manner. Furnish him with arguments to defend it, for he will not fail to hear it attacked. Teach him to despise ridicule, that last resort of the bad defender of a bad cause; for he will find that those who cannot argue can sneer, and he may feel it harder to withstand the one than the other.

Inform him that in France it was the ignorance of religion which produced the contempt of it; and that both together overturned the state, by inculcating principles hostile to all virtue, fostering passions destructive of all order, and an impatience of control subversive of all government; all springing from one common source, all meeting in one common centre, a combination to throw off the government of God himself. Impress upon his young mind that important truth, that there can be no security for a state in which religion is not warmly yet wisely taught by its ministers, cherished by its government, and believed and reverenced by the people.

There are certain traditional sayings which claim a sort of prescriptive right to be received, which pass unexamined, and are credited as oracular. Guard him against these false and sordid, but popular maxims, which, though the phrases may be used chiefly by the lower orders, the things themselves are practically adopted, pretty equally, by "the great vulgar, and the small." Some vindicate speculatively loose principles, by the assertion that "thoughts are free." Tell your son this is not true. A Christian must endeavour to bring his thoughts to the same correct standard with his actions, and from the same awful motive, "Thou God seest!"

There is another popular but unfounded axiom respecting the use of wealth, namely, that "A man may do what he will with his own." Christianity denies this assertion also. Every man has indeed a legal right to the disposal of his own property, but religion interdicts his right to spend it in vanity or vice; or if he be exempt from these grosser temptations, she still abridges his right to monopolise it. Christianity expects that the deserving and the distressed shall come in for such a proportion of his wealth as an enlightened conscience shall dictate. The divine person who refused, in a legal sense, to be " a divider, or a judge," over a contested property, did not fail to graft on the question he avoided answering, the imperative caution, "Take heed and beware of covetousness."

There is another fatal lesson which he will learn in the world, and which the natural pride of his own heart will second; namely, that to resent an injury is a mark of spirit, while to forgive it shows a base mind. The prince of darkness, in his long catalogue of expedients, never invented a maxim which has brought more generous, but ill-disciplined souls to destruction.

The uncurbed desires, the unrestrained passions, to which we have before adverted, the contempt of submission, the supposed meanness of forbearance, the hot resentments not controlled betimes in the boy, may have been preparing the man for an act which may hereafter fill his whole life with cureless remorse.

Boys well born, and accustomed to well-bred society, have a sort of instinctive notion of *honour*, which is strengthened by the conversation to which they are sometimes exposed. Seize upon this spirit, whether instinctive or contracted, but seize it with a view to convert it to higher purposes. This popular notion of honour may seem to give dignity to the tone of his conversation, while it is inflating his heart with arrogance. It may indeed set him above doing an act which some fashionable men may agree to call base, but it will not preserve him from a duel, which these same men agree to call honourable. But whatever acquittal a jury of the world's men of honour may pronounce on such a transaction, it will, by that awful decision from which there lies no appeal, by the definitive sentence of the great Judge of quick and dead, be pronounced murder;—murder of one of them in the act, of both in the intention; murder as criminal as that which brings its vulgar perpetrator on the highway to his ignominious catastrophe.

Lay hold then on this high-minded feeling, and endeavour to direct it into a purer channel. Lead his aspiring mind to higher objects. Let the hope of the favour, and the dread of the displeasure of God, expel from his heart a too eager desire to court the applause, or escape the censure of irreligious men, by acts which, while they would offend his Maker, would destroy his own soul. Let him learn to distinguish between the swellings of human arrogance, and the consciousness of Christian dignity. Worldly maxims of honour are tumid, but they are not great.

There is no sure preservation from these mischiefs, but in an education formed on the religion of Jesus Christ. The principles drawn from the spirit of the Gospel, conscientiously adopted, and acted upon, would subvert all the hollow and destructive maxims of the worldly code. How many boiling passions might have been cooled, how many disappointed hearts and mourning spirits healed, how many duels, how many suicides (both now so dreadfully prevalent) might have been prevented, by the early and unremitted application of this one grand specific.

Cultivate in your son whatever is valuable in science, or elegant in literature. Independently of its own intrinsic worth, it will, by filling up his time and engaging his thoughts, assist in setting his mind above low and sordid tastes, and leave him little leisure or relish for the base and grovelling pursuits of sensuality. A love of learning judiciously instilled, is amongst the most probable *human* preservatives from vulgar vice; though since it is human, it can go but certain lengths as to moral benefit; and we have witnessed many deplorable instances of its failure, in minds of the highest literary attainments, for want of being under the direction of a superior principle. It is, however, a most valuable auxiliary, not only in improving the intellect and refining the taste, but, as we have already observed, in rescuing so much leisure from inferior pursuits.

But learning, be it repeated, though it invigorates the mind, will not reform it. It is a shining ornament, but not of the nature of a corrective. Moral evil is not cured, is not regulated,—nay, it might even be inflamed by it, where intellectual science is made its own end, and not considered subservient to a higher. Learning will strongly teach him to despise what is worthless in composition, but will feebly lift him above what is unworthy in practice. It will correct his taste, but will not enable him to resist temptation: it will improve his judgment of the world, but will not secure him from its pollutions. Human learning will only teach him the knowledge of others, the Bible that of himself.

Let him therefore enter into the battle of the world armed with weapons from the divine armoury; stoutly furnished with motives and arguments drawn from religion, of potency to fortify his resolutions, convince his understanding, and affect his heart. Let him see in your own example, that religion is neither unmanly nor ungentlemanly. Accustom him not to hear the three dominant spiritual, and intellectual sins, PRIDE, SELFISHNESS, and EGOTISM, treated with an indulgence not shown to such as are more disreputable, gross, and scandalous. Against both classes the whole artillery of the Gospel is impartially levelled. Of the first, peculiar condemnation is intimated in Scripture. Of pride it is observed, that " God resisteth the proud," and that it is hard to be found " fighting against God." Against selfishness it is specifically proclaimed, that " no man" with any pretensions to a Christian character " liveth to himself;" that we are not to " seek our own things," and that we must " bear one another's burdens." Against egotism a host of precepts present themselves in battle array, — " to esteem others better than ourselves, to avoid vain glory, to look on the things of others; to be slow to speak, ready to hear."

Though these interior and mental sins are as much cherished by impiety as those which are coarser and more notorious, yet as the latter can produce no plausible pretence for their indulgence; as they cannot be qualified by any sophistry, nor covered by any artifice, they are less likely to hold out to the end. Morality is disgusted by vulgar vice, by the practical sins of the sensual man; but mere morality can never extirpate the vices of the heart and mind: it is not always her aim, nor if it were, could she accomplish it.

In your conversation with the young person, do not be satisfied to *generalise* religion. Religion is an indefinite term, a vague word, which may be made to involve a variety of meanings, and to amalgamate a number of discrepancies. It may release a man from all the prescribed institutions of Christianity; it may set him loose from all its peculiar doctrines and restraints; turn him adrift, and dismiss him to his choice between the " Jehovah, Jove, or Lord," of the sceptical poet. Since life and immortality have been brought to light by the Gospel, a *general* religion is no religion at all. His must be the religion of the New Testament. Be not ashamed to teach your son the Gospel of Jesus Christ. If you believe that there is no other name under heaven by which yourself can be saved, you must be assured that there is no other salvation for your son. Defer not then too long to communicate to him the distinctive peculiarities of our faith. Other notions will occupy the space which you leave vacant. O! stamp the right impressions on his heart while it is soft, tender, and ductile; and he will hereafter mix these early imbibed feelings, and sentiments, and principles, with his other sweet associations, his other pleasing recollections of the vernal season of life; cherished images!

which the matured mind is fond of retracing, and which commonly remain vivid when most others have faded, or are obliterated.

Fancy not that these acquisitions and pursuits will blight the opening buds of youthful gaiety; that they will check his vivacity, or obstruct his amiable cheerfulness. The ingenuous unvitiated mind is never so happy as when in a state of virtuous exertion, as when engaged about some object to which it must look up; something which, kindling its energies, raises its views; something which excites the ambition of lifting it above itself.

Much less fear that the pursuits here recommended will depress his genius; it will exalt it; his mind will find wider room in which to expand; his horizon will be more extensive; his intellectual eye will take in a wider range; the whole man will have an ampler region in which to expatiate. To know that he is formed for immortality, is not likely to contract his ideas, or to shorten his views. It is irreligion which shrinks and shrivels up the faculties, by debasing the spirit, and degrading the soul.

And if to know that he is an immortal being will exalt his ideas, to know that he is an accountable being will correct his habits. If to know that "God is," will raise his thoughts and desires to all that is perfect, fair, and good,—to know that "God is the rewarder of all them that seek Him," will stimulate him in the race of Christian duty;—to know that there is a day in which God will judge the world, will quicken his preparation for that day.

As he advances in age and knowledge, impress upon his mind, that in that day of awful inquisition he must stand unconnected, single, naked! It is not the best attachments he may have formed, the most valuable societies to which he may have belonged, that will then stand him in any stead. He must therefore join them now with a pure and simple intention; he must not seek them as something on which to lean, as something with which to share his responsibility—this is his own single, individual concern. It is vain to hope that by belonging to any society, however good, to any party, however honourable, he can shrink from his own personal, individual accountableness. The union of the labourers gives no claim to the division of the responsibility. In this world we may be most useful among bodies of men; in the great judgment we must stand alone. We assist them here, but they cannot answer for us hereafter.

From his Bible, and from his Bible only, let him draw his sense of those principles, of that standard by which he will hereafter be judged; and be careful ever to distinguish in his mind between the worldly morality which he may learn from the multitude, and that Christian holiness which is the dictate of the scriptures, and of the scriptures alone. Teach him to discover there,

he cannot discover it too soon; that it is
not a set of proverbial moral maxims,
a few random good actions, a code of
polite inoffensive manners, the effect
naturally of fashion, of career,
of regard to health, of desire of reputation, that will achieve any valuable
character. This is not to be acquired
by certain popular virtues, or rather
fractions of virtues, for there is no
integral virtue where there is no religion. Pleasing manners will attract
popular regard, and worldly motives
will produce popular actions; but genuine virtue proceeds only from Christian principles. The one is efflores-
cence, the other is fruit.

After all, though you cannot by your
best exertions, seconded by the most
fervent prayer, without which exertion
will neither be rightly directed nor successfully prosecuted, command success,
yet what a support will it be under the
possible defeat of your fairest hopes,
that you strove to avert it! Even if,

through the prevalence of temptation, the perverseness of his own nature, and the malignity of his corruptions, the barbarous son *should* disappoint the best founded hopes of the careful parent, what a heart-felt consolation would it afford you, under this heaviest of all trials, that the misconduct of the child is not imputable to the neglect of the father! The severest evil—and this perhaps is the most severe,—is supportable, when not aggravated by the consciousness that we have contributed to bring it upon ourselves. Though it will not pluck the sting from his guilt, it will render the poignancy of your own anguish more tolerable.

But let us indulge higher hopes and brighter prospects for our country. We refer to those hopes with which the first chapter of this little work concluded, namely, the rich provision which God has put into our hands for accomplishing his great designs in our favour. The hope therein expressed, and the means humbly suggested for accomplishing it, was the reformation of the British character. We have here, feebly indeed, but honestly, shown what obviously appears to be the best security, the most effectual barrier, against the vices and contamination of our prolonged continental intercourse. Religious education, with God's blessing upon it, which every truly Christian father will not fail to invoke, is all in all towards the restoration, the elevation of our national character. And let it never be forgotten, that it is the education of the rich which must finally determine the fate, at once, of rich and poor; and by consequence, which must determine the destiny of our country.

Here then is Britain's last, best hope; and when we consider the unparalleled advantages we possess in a learned and orthodox clergy, who instruct us in the sanctuary, and who preside over our public and private seminaries, why need we despair? Why need we doubt, that the Christian religion, grafted on the substantial stock of the genuine British character, and watered by the dews of heaven, may bring forth the noblest productions of which this lower world is capable; though neither the security nor the triumph will be complete till these " Trees of Righteousness" are transplanted into the paradise of God.

Reader, if you are indeed a Christian father, anticipate in idea that triumphant moment, when, having cast your crown at the foot of the eternal throne, you shall be called upon to give an account of your own conduct, and, as far as had depended on you, of that of your offspring. Think of the multiplied felicities of meeting, in the presence of God, those whom your example and instruction have, through his grace, contributed to bring thither! Think what it will be, to be able, amidst all the hosts of heaven, amidst the innumerable com-

we despair? Why need we doubt, that pany of angels, and the spirits of just men made perfect—think of being able to say to the Universal Father, "Behold, I and the children thou hast given me!"

ON

DOMESTIC ERRORS

IN OPINION,

AND

IN CERTAIN PRACTICAL HABITS.

ON SOUNDNESS IN JUDGMENT, AND CONSISTENCY IN CONDUCT.

As a preliminary to the following pages, the writer begs leave to observe, that it consists rather of miscellaneous observations on a variety of topics, than in an attempt at a systematic view of religion or morals. It does not pretend to present an exhibition of Christian doctrine, or to prescribe the duties of a Christian life. It is presumed that the generality of readers who shall honour these pages with their attention, are already, in a greater or less degree, religious characters; consequently, standing in little need of such information as her humble talents could have imparted. But as religion is become a subject of increasing and more general interest, it may not be unseasonable, as we proceed, to point out some of the dangers to which the less advanced Christian may be liable, as well as some of the evils which may subsist with a high outward profession. To those who are beginning to see the importance of religion—and of such persons, adored be Almighty goodness! the number is rapidly augmenting—to those interesting characters, may the writer venture to address a few words of affectionate and respectful counsel? Carefully encourage the first dawning dispositions of piety in your heart, cherish every indication of a change in your views and an improvement in your sentiments. Let not the world, nor the things of the world, stifle the new-born principle, nor make you ashamed modestly to avow it.

But while you cultivate this principle by every possible means, avoid the danger of fancying that your religion is confirmed when it is scarcely begun. Do not conclude that a complete change has been effected in your heart because there is a revolution in your opinions, and a favourable alteration in your feelings. The formation of a Christian character is not the work of a day; not only are the views to be changed, but the habits to be new-moulded; not only is the heart to be convinced of sin, but its propensities are to be bent into a contrary direction. Be not impatient, therefore, to make a public disclosure of your sentiments. Religion is an interior concern. Try yourselves, prove yourselves, examine yourselves, distrust yourselves. Seek counsel of wise, established, sober Christians. Pray earnestly for more light and knowledge, and especially for perseverance. Pray that you may be able to go on with the same zeal with which you set out. Of how many may it be said, "Ye did run well — what hindered you?" You ran too fast; your speed exhausted your strength; — you had not counted the cost.

Carefully distinguish between the feverish heat of animal fervour, and the vital warmth of Christian feeling. Mere youthful energy, operating upon a newly-awakened remorse for a thoughtless life, will carry the mind certain lengths; but if unaccompanied with humility, repentance, and a continual application for a better strength than your own, this slight resource will soon fail. It is not that principle which will encourage progress; it is not that Divine support which will carry you on to the end. The Christian race is not to be run at a heat: religion is a steady, progressive course; it gains strength by going, and eventually it gains speed also: progress quickens the pace; for the nearer the approach to the goal, the more ardent is the desire to reach it. And though, in your further advance, you may imagine yourself not so near as you did when you first set out, this is not really the case;—you have a lower opinion of your state, because you have obtained

AND CONSISTENCY IN CONDUCT. 121

heighten views of the spirituality of the law of God, and a close building upon your own experience. Had the first Christian prophet to whom we have been referring, indeed conceived of himself as having had so bright a view of the glory of the Divine vision, he exclaimed, "Mine eyes have seen the King, the Lord of Hosts!"

The persons who address you as of a promising character, sadly disappoint the hopes their early stages in religion had excited. By taking too high a tone at first, they not only lost all the ground they had gained, but sunk into indifference themselves, accompanied with a prejudice against serious piety in others. They not only became deserters, but went over to the enemy's camp. Amid their errors, The world is too much disposed to impute rashness, presumption, and enthusiasm to the purest and most correct religious characters. In no instance let them not be furnished with any ground for this censure

G

by your deserving it. If you advance, you glorify God, and promote your own salvation; if you recede, you injure the cause you now intend to serve, and bring upon yourselves a fearful condemnation. Self-abasement, self-examination, and prayer, are the best preservatives for all who have entered on a religious life, and are especially becoming incipient Christians.

There is one thing we would more particularly press on the important class we are now taking the liberty to address; —*it is the cultivation of a sound judgment.* Of all persons, religious persons are most bound to cultivate this precious faculty. We see how highly the great Apostle of the Gentiles valued it. In directing the spiritual labours of his beloved young friend, in stirring him up to every good word and work, he does not forget this exhortation:—" *The Lord give thee a right understanding in all things!*" Again, he prays for his beloved Philippians, " that their love may abound more and more in *knowledge* and in all *judgment.*" And in his Epistle to the youthful Bishop of Crete, he repeats the admonition to young persons of both sexes to be *sober-minded.* These admonitions acquire great additional force when it is considered, that he who gave them was a man of exceeding ardency of temper, and of zeal without a parallel. This experienced saint must have frequently seen the danger of imprudent piety, of self-confidence, of a zeal not regulated by knowledge; and therefore presses the great importance of a *sound judgment.*

Judgment is to the faculties of the mind, what charity is to the virtues of the heart; as without charity the latter are of little worth, so without judgment talents are of little comparative use.

Judgment, with the aid of God's spirit, and the instructions of his word, is the balance in which qualities are weighed, by which the proportions of our duties, and the harmony of our virtues, are preserved; for it keeps not only the talents in just subordination, but the principles in due equipoise. When exercised in subservience to the Divine rule, the faculty becomes a virtue, and a virtue of a higher order. It restrains irregularity, it subdues vanity, it corrects impetuosity, it checks enthusiasm, and it checks it without diminishing zeal.

One of the most powerful defenders, not only of our church polity, but of our church doctrines, has had the renown of all his great qualities so absorbed in the quality we are recommending; or, rather, this was so much the faculty which maintained his great talents and qualities in their due order, that we never read the name of Hooker without the previous application of this weighty epithet — THE JUDICIOUS.

Judgment is so far from being a cooler of zeal, as some suppose, that it increases its effect by directing its movements; and a warm heart will always produce more extensive, because more lasting good, when conducted by a cool head.

We speak of this attribute the more positively, because it is one which, more than many others, depends on ourselves. A sound judgment, indeed, is equally bestowed with other blessings by Him from whom cometh every good gift; yet it is not, like the other faculties of the mind, so much born with us, as improved by us. By teaching us to discern the faults of others, it warns us to avoid them; by detecting our own, it leads to their cure. The deepest humility is generally connected with the soundest judgment. The judicious Christian is watchful against speculative errors, as well as against errors in conduct. He never adopts any opinion because it is new, nor any practice because it is fashionable; neither does he, if it be innocent, reject the latter merely for that reason. Judgment is, in short, that quality of the mind which requires to be kept in ever wakeful activity; and the advantages it procures us, and the evils from which it preserves us, will be more apparent, the more it is kept in exercise.

Religious charity more especially demands the full exercise of the judgment. A judicious Christian will double the good done, by his selection of the object, and his manner of relieving it. All things that are good are not equally good. A sound judgment discriminates between the value of the claimants which present themselves, and bestows on them more or less attention, according to their respective claims.

Above all, an enlightened judgment will enable you to attain and to preserve CONSISTENCY, that infallible criterion of a highly-finished Christian character, the want of which makes some really religious persons not a little vulnerable. It was this want in some of his people, which led an eminent divine, at once a man of deep piety and lively wit, to say, that " there were some good persons, with whom it would be time enough to be acquainted in heaven." So much to be regretted is it that goodness of intention is not always attended by propriety in the execution.

In another class, the want of consistency makes not a few appear over scrupulous as to some minor points, and lax in others of more importance. These incongruities not only bring the individual into discredit, but religion into disgrace. When the world sees persons, whose views are far from high, act more consistently with *their* avowed views, and frequently more above them, than some whose religion professes to be of a loftier standard, they will prefer the lower, as exhibiting fewer discrepancies, and less obvious contradictions.

Consistency presents Christianity in her fairest attitude, in all her lovely proportion of figure, and correct symmetry of feature. Consistency is the beautiful result of all the qualities and graces of a truly religious mind united and brought into action, each individually right, all relatively associated. Where the character is consistent, prejudice cannot ridicule, nor infidelity sneer. It may, indeed, be censured, as holding up a standard above the attainment of the careless. The world may dislike, but it cannot despise it.

In the more advanced Christian, religion may seem to be less prominent in parts of the character, because it is infused into the whole. Like the life-blood, its vital power pervades the entire system: not an action of the life that is not governed by it; not a quality of the mind which does not partake of its spirit. It is diffused through the whole conduct, and sheds its benign influence, not only on the things done, but on the temper of the doer in performing them. The affections now have other objects, the time other duties, the thoughts other employments. There will be more exertion, but with less display; less show, because the principle is become more interior; it will be less obtrusive, because it is more rooted and grounded. There will be more humility, because the heart will have found out its own corruptions.

By the continual exercise of the judgment, and an habitual aim at consistency, the Christian, though animated, will be orderly. He will be less subject to the ebullitions of zeal, as well as to the languors of its decay. Thus, through the joint operation of judgment in the intellect, and principle in the heart, the religion is become equable, regular, consistent.

There never was but one visible exhibition of infallible judgment and complete consistency. In that Divine person who vouchsafed to pitch His tent among us, and to dwell with men on earth, that He might give us a perfect example in His life, before He obtained salvation for us by His death — in HIM alone was judgment without any shadow of error, consistency without any speck of imperfection. His Divine perfections none can approach; but all may humbly imitate those which come within the compass of His humanity.

ON NOVEL OPINIONS IN RELIGION.

Among the numerous innovations of this innovating age, it is deeply to be lamented, that religion should come in for so large a portion. Of this we have a melancholy instance in the system of the new secession. Many are distorting the sacred doctrines, and slighting the practical ethics of the New Testament. The religion of the Gospel is employed to furnish arms against itself. The truth, as it is in Jesus, is fearlessly controverted: its sanctity is no security; its Divine authority is no protection.

In the new system — strange to say! the hardihood of the sceptic is adopted for the professed purpose of purifying

Christianity. The dogmatism of the unbeliever is employed for improving our faith in the religion which the unbeliever denies!

This heterogeneous system, composed of different elements, made up of conflicting principles, unhappily is not brought forward by the avowed opposers, but by the professed and zealous friends of Christianity;—by religionists placing themselves much above the standard of their former pious associates, with whom they once went to the house of God as friends; by Christians so critically scrupulous, that they can no longer go to that house at all.

Novelties in the sciences and in the arts may be, and generally are, beneficial. Every invention may be an improvement; but in religion they are delusions. Genuine Christianity is not, as one class of men seem to suppose, a modern invention; serious piety is no fresh innovation. " That which was from the beginning declare we unto you," are the words of inspiration; the new and living way, therefore, now so much depreciated, is only a continuation in the good old way so long ago recommended by the Prophet.

Nor is Christianity, as the recent party seem to suppose, a superannuated thing, which wants repairing; nor is it an incomplete thing, which wants filling up; nor is it a redundant thing, whose excrescences want lopping; nor a defective thing, whose deficiencies must be supplied; nor an erroneous thing, whose errors must be expunged.

But to do these malecontents justice, they do not resemble those reformers who are contented to expose the defects of an existing system, without providing a remedy. This restoration, this purifying, this repairing, this expunging, this lopping, this grafting, this perfecting, they have actually and gratuitously taken into their own hands, with a view either to improve the old religion, or, as their progress rather threatens, to produce a new one; while the champions of the antiquated system all agree that " the old is better."

Some Christians of the primitive ages were not then, perhaps many of the present age are not now, aware, that he who overleaps the truth, errs as widely as he who falls short of it; nay, the danger is even greater, as it is more difficult to recede than to advance. It was the vain desire of overturning established truths, of being wiser than the wisdom of God, of being more perfect than the perfection of the Gospel, of giving new glosses to old opinions, and rejecting all opinions which did not hit their own distempered fancies; together with the temptation of being considered as the founders of a new school, — which gave rise to the Ebionites, the Cerinthians, the Marcionites, and various other sects; and which has continued, to this day, to introduce successive heresies into the church of Christ.

Of the two classes above mentioned,

—those who think true religion a novelty, and those who are endeavouring to introduce a novel religion, though they are the very antipodes of each other, yet it is difficult to determine which has wandered most widely from the truth. Scylla has its wrecks as well as Charybdis. Though each thinks that the only way to safety is to recede as far as possible from the other, yet, by this increasing desire of mutual recession, they are in more danger of gradually approaching to each other, if not of finally meeting, than either intended or believed at first setting out.

In one quarter we hear the most consoling of all doctrines — the doctrine on which the great hinge of Christianity turns, — rejected as false, and its defenders derided, as if they were adopting it to be a substitute for virtuous practice. We hear one community spoken of by its professors as triumphantly bearing away from all others the proud distinction of *rationality*. It is a monopoly not to be allowed. If by rational religion is meant a religion singularly adapted to rational beings, no church on earth has a fairer claim to the appellation than the Church of England. It is rational to exercise our reason in examining and weighing the evidences of Christianity; and, having clearly proved the authority on which they are grounded, it is then rational to submit our reason to its doctrines. It is rational to believe that we are apostates from our original brightness; not only because we perceive it to be a scriptural doctrine, but because we see it in all around us, and feel it in all within us.

It is rational for a being conscious of its weakness, to desire to lean upon something that is strong; we therefore lean upon a rock, and that rock is Christ. Our church is a rational church; for it is sober without coldness, and animated without enthusiasm. Its service unites the affections of the heart with the faculties of the mind; it teaches to pray with the spirit, and with the understanding also. Though it lays hold with a firmly grasping hand on the blessed doctrine of the atonement, yet it is so far from using this doctrine as a pretence for neglecting virtuous practice, that it draws from thence new motives, new sanctions, new encouragements. It teaches that without shedding of blood there is no remission for sin, while it declares that without repentance, and without holiness, there is no salvation for sinners.

The sound members of this church acknowledge that there are mysteries in our religion; but the same reason which employed its best energies in proving the Divine authority of Scripture, has convinced them that the secret things which belong to God must be adored now, and will be fully understood hereafter. The legitimate members of the church, for she has, it is to be feared, some spurious ones, are not surprised, that in a revelation from heaven there should be mysteries; but they believe that these sacred mysteries are meant as exercises of faith to the probationers for Heaven; are meant to promote humility; which *they* consider, whatever others do, as a grand fundamental in religion. They do not pretend to know in what manner the Holy Spirit operates on the human heart, but they know that it does operate, because it produces that change of heart which they are not ashamed to call the renewing by the Holy Ghost, and which distinguishes the vital from the nominal Christian. They leave to those who have sufficient natural resources in their own minds, if such there be, to reject assistance which *they* fervently implore; assistance without which they, who think they stand, may finally fall.

These humble dependants on Divine grace come at length to attain, in addition to the external evidences of Christianity, an internal evidence in their own bosom, which, so far from giving them any elation of heart, any eccentricity of doctrine, any irregularity of conduct, preserves them from each, while it affords them " all joy and peace in believing."

But while we put in the fair claim of our church to rational religion, we do not make an exclusive pretension to this, or any other excellence. Every human institution bears on it some marks, greater or less, that it is human, of course imperfect; and it is sufficient to guard *us* against the folly of such a pompous assumption to know, that an erroneous church not only assumes the appellation of *infallible* itself, but gives it also to its infirm, mutable, human head, to a being certain of death, and liable to sin.

But if we do not claim soundness as well as rationality, for our exclusive possession, we are more likely to perpetuate both, than the best societies of separatists. All that is good in our church is likely to be secured to it by the fence of an establishment. An enclosure is not so likely to be broken in upon from without, as a society planted in the waste. We are likely, I say, to be secured from the introduction of new dogmas, as well as to be preserved in our long adopted principles. The pale which encircles our church, and the formularies which belong to it, do not leave it open to the experiments of new projectors, to the incursions of fresh innovators. Above all it is enriched by a great mass of the Divine treasures of Scripture; the spirit of which is also expanded in our collects and prayers, so that, as we have observed in another place, if the pulpit should in any instance unhappily degenerate in doctrine, the desk will still furnish a perpetual antidote. It may indeed deserve the name of the *establishment* not only as being the national religion, but as being built on the foundation of the everlasting Gospel, on the doctrines taught by prophets and evangelists, Jesus Christ himself being the chief corner stone.

In another of the quarters alluded to, the more novel system, we hear much of opinions but little of practice; much of doctrines, but little of holiness; much of faith — a disproportioned and unproductive faith — but little of repentance. These grand ingredients, which, when severally coupled together, make up the sum and substance of Christianity, — these joint essentials, which St. Paul preached invariably, and which by never separating, he preached effectually, are now considered as separate interests, and severed from each other as having no necessary connexion.

We are very far from the injustice of accusing those who propagate doctrines which are evidently unscriptural, of being themselves unholy. In some of the leading characters we fully believe the contrary to be the case; but the obvious effect of such doctrines on those who hear them, is not only to lessen their value for practical preaching, but to lead them to consider personal holiness as making no part of the things which accompany salvation.

Those who are at all acquainted with ecclesiastical history, must know that in the most flourishing ages of the church, even when Christianity was best understood and most successfully practised, errors of opinion most readily started up, the ephemeral fungus of a luxuriant soil; they were frequently the suggestion of fanciful and mistaken, rather than of immoral men. Our great spiritual adversary, who successfully employs the *vicious* as the corruptors of morals, knows it to be a stale and fruitless device to make them his agents for misleading the judgment and bewildering the imagination; and therefore, by a refinement of ingenuity, prompts the more virtuous to the accomplishment of spiritual mischiefs. Moral men are his selected instruments for broaching novel, enticing, and dangerous opinions. These moral but wayward persons seem to have overlooked the fine supplication of the Apostle, that

God would " stablish, strengthen, settle them." These terms, which indeed are not synonymes, but shades; — these terms, a noble climax, implying not equality, but gradation, are now inverted. Every move in the new machine seems to shake, weaken, unsettle. One pin in the old system is pulled out after another, till the whole magnificent fabric, if its security depended upon them, would fall to the ground. The patriarch Jacob has shown us, in the character of his vacillating son Reuben, how destructive instability is of excellence.

We are assured that the changes in these ever varying theories are so frequent, that to confute them would be as difficult as unnecessary; for that which by some of the party is insisted on in one week, gives way in the next to some wider deviation; so that he who might wish to animadvert on some existing evil must be as rapid as its inventor, he must

" Catch ere it fall the Cynthia of the minute."

If in religious contemplation or discussion, we once give the reins to fancy, if we cherish every seducing thought, merely because it is new, if we set up for complete independence of opinion, if we assume individual release from all the ties that hold Christian society together, if we permit ourselves to plunge into the unfathomable ocean of discovery, without compass or rudder, there is no saying where we may land; it may be on the shore we now dread. Many of these leaders differ in opinion, but each seems to lay as exclusive a claim to truth as the Pope himself; but as the latter was equally infallible when there was one Pope at Avignon and another at Rome, so the infallibility here seems to be lodged by each in himself, only with this variation, that these last begin by differing from each other, till in their more advanced progress they come to differ from themselves.

Is not the recent secession founded on a kind of spiritual democracy, an overturning system; an aversion to whatever is established; a contempt of authority; an impatience of subordination, a thirst for dictatorship; with this difference, that these religious dissidents loose the reins of their self-government, instead of those of their country.

We know to what a degree the love of novelty, the longing to see any thing they have not seen before, though the object be ever so disgusting, is carried by our countrymen. The poet who best knew human nature, who best painted the characters of Englishmen, said, " in England any monster will *make* (be the making of) a man." This is so true, that a dwarf, a giant, an unnatural birth in an animal, will afford delight; the greater the distortion the higher the pleasure. We have seen to what excess this passion for what is novel and monstrous may be carried, in the instance of a late preposterous prophetess, a creature born and bred among the dregs of the people, with nothing to recommend her

H

but ignorance, presumption, extravagance and blasphemy; yet did this woman not only make numberless proselytes among her vulgar equals, but obtained advocates among those from whom better things might have been expected. But it is the very absurdity which is the attraction. Such preposterous pretences being obviously out of the power of human means to accomplish, the extravagance is believed to be supernatural. It is the impossibility which makes the assumed certainty. The epilepsy of Mahomet confirmed his claims to inspiration.

Extravagance in religion is a kind of spiritual empiricism, which is sure for a time to lay hold on the vulgar. The ignorant patient in both cases, who frequently pays little attention to the established physician, is sure to be attracted by any new nostrum from the laboratory of the irregular prescriber: he is resorted to with more confidence in proportion to the reputed violence of his catholicon;

and he who despised the sober practitioner, swallows without scruple the most pernicious drug of the advertising professor.

Without the slightest desire to detract from the personal character of our new empirics in divinity, we may be allowed to suspect that their education, and early habits of life, had not altogether qualified them for the arduous undertaking of new modelling a church. It is true, that " the erudition of a (common) Christian man" is not required to be very profound, but surely that of a Christian reformer should be something more than moderate.

The lapse of three centuries has added little clearness to the lucid exposition of Christian truth as exhibited in the writings of those reformers by whom the doctrines of the Church of England were modelled. Whatever defects might have escaped the notice of those eagle-eyed sifters and examiners of Christian truth, when they rescued it from the rubbish under which it lay almost buried, would not these defects have been detected, pointed out, rectified, by the penetrating mind of Bishop Jewel in his renowned challenge at Paul's Cross, or in his celebrated Apology for the Church of England? Would they not have been expunged or purified by the judicious Hooker, that bulwark of the establishment, in his immortal writings on *ecclesiastical polity*, and on *justification?* Would they have eluded the observation and correction of Archbishop Usher, that prodigy of erudition?

We need not be again told the well-known fact, that there may be abundant learning where there is little enlightened piety; but in these glorious champions of the faith of Christ, and of the Protestant church, learning was only a secondary excellence. Various and profound as were their acquirements, they were conscientiously devoted to the purpose of advancing and confirming the scarcely established church. Can we believe that Ridley, Hooper, Cranmer, and a long list of such distinguished men, would have made the sacrifices they actually made, without scrupulously examining into the momentous truths they professed to believe; that they would have suffered the most cruel tortures, rather than renounce the doctrines of a church to which they were first ornaments and then martyrs?— "There were giants in those days:" but to say no more of them, nor of the succession of profound divines and eminent scholars who succeeded them, "men of stature also"—would it not be casting a severe reflection on these bright luminaries of our country and church, to believe that the great truths of the gospel which were hid from these skilful and acute indagators, were reserved to be brought to light by half a dozen persons in the nineteenth century; that to men, most of them bred to secular pursuits, and living antecedently in secular habits, should be reserved the honour of detecting, not trifling faults, not imperfections, from which perhaps no human institution is exempt, but radical errors, but fundamental mischiefs, affecting the very vitals of our religion? If these evils really exist, if they indeed escaped the penetration, eluded the vigilance, and mocked the wisdom of those mighty champions, then to say those holy men were blameable, is saying little: they were indeed ideots, voluntarily to suffer a violent death, rather than renounce a church too erroneous for the new reformers, not only in which to preach, but in which to remain.

The penetrating genius of Luther seems not only to have exposed all existing, but to have anticipated all future heresies, especially when he inveighs against that which declared that "*The Ten Commandments ought to be taken out of the Church!*"

This Coryphœus of the doctrine of faith, in contradiction to the new system, says: "Faith is by no means an ineffective quality, but possesses so great excellency, that it utterly confounds and destroys all the foolish dreams and imaginations of sophisters; but if works only are taught, faith is lost." "But if nothing but faith is inculcated, carnal men begin to dream that there is no need of good works." Again: "If, indeed, faith saves us without works, let us have no anxiety about good actions; let us only take care and believe, and we may do what we please. It is true," adds he, "that Paul tells you, that faith without works justifies; however he also tells you, that a true faith after it has justified, does not permit a man to slumber in ignorance, but that it worketh by love." Again: "You now see, that though it is faith alone which justifies, yet that faith alone is not sufficient."

There is not a single doctrine of the New Testament which does not involve practical consequences. The necessity of holiness, now unhappily not insisted

ion] is more exalted by the death of Christ than by all other means that ever were devised. God's hatred of sin is more forcibly expressed by the sacrifice of his Son, than it could have been by any other method, although we do not presume to set limits to infinite power. Yet this most glorious doctrine, this cleanser from all sin, may be converted by the manner in which it is administered into an open door to that licentiousness which it is its special design, its obvious tendency, and when truly received on scripture grounds, its natural consequence, to cure.

But if men come to the perusal of the Bible with certain prepossessions of their own, instead of a simple and sincere desire after Divine truth; if, instead of getting their obliquities rectified by trying them by this straight line, they venture to bend the straight line till it fits their own crooked opinions; if they are determined to *make* between them a conformity which they do not *find*, they are not far from concluding that they *have* found it. By such means, a very little knowledge, and a great deal of presumption, has been the groundwork of many a novel and pernicious system.

Systems, indeed, there will be as many as they are novel and pernicious; for though men are as tenacious of error, for a time, as if their convictions were as strong as they could be if it were truth, yet the persuasion of error is not likely to be so lasting. As no error can be so irresistible as a known truth, it cannot long carry the same weight with it. He who adopted it, at length finding it not to go, as we say, on all fours, is more likely to plunge into a succession of errors, each deeper than the other, than to return to the truth which he has abandoned. Whether the pride of not going back, or the hope that in his wider wanderings, he may extricate himself, it is hard to say; for error is as endless as truth is powerful. Some minds are so constituted, that it is easier to them to produce objections to truth, than to embrace it; they therefore resist truth, when they might resist the obstacles which prevent their receiving it. Our adoption of error as naturally proceeds from our abuse of reason, as our adoption of truth from the right use of it. The question, to a plain Christian, seems to be settled by this declaration of our Lord: "He that doeth His will shall know of the doctrine, whether it be of God."

As, in many of those to whom we have been alluding, their aberrations seem to have been occasioned rather by the vagrancy of the imagination, than the corruption of the heart, we are not without hope that they may yet retrace their steps; that the way they have lost may be recovered; that their involution in this labyrinth may not be past extrication; that Divine grace may furnish a clue to lead them back to the plain, obvious, intelligible meaning of the unsophisticated word of God. That this may be the case, is the cordial wish and prayer of many who loved and respected them before they were unhappily led astray, by erratic fancies, into these seducing theories.

There is no method which the subtle adversary of mankind has not devised to injure religion. When the church is at a low ebb, when she is sunk in forms and outward observances; when zeal is asleep, and all seems safe because all is still, he sometimes rouses her, but it is to wrong purposes: it is not to advance the interests of Christianity, but to bend his force against some symptoms of its returning spirit, which begin to break out: these symptoms of incipient zeal he calls enthusiasm, though an evil which perhaps in that stage of the church, does not exist; he, however, strives to prevent the existence not of enthusiasm but of zeal, that the frigid may enjoy their doze, and not be reproached by the threatened exertions in the quarter which is beginning to open its eyes.

At another period when the church is beginning to be triumphant, he sends out his favourite engine persecution, with his faggot and his axe, burning where he could not refute, and subduing by force what he could not silence by argument.

He is now pursuing a different course. The same malignant spirit which once laboured to drive men from Christianity by martyrdom, now draws them from it by sophistry. He now deteriorates truth instead of persecuting it; and as the process is less revolting, it succeeds better. Men are no longer terrified into error, but coaxed into it. They are not frightened, but wheedled out of their belief. Their understandings become so bewildered, that they are persuaded that every new advance in heresy is a fresh step towards truth. Advantage is made even of their prejudices, which become more deeply rooted by the very change which they are made to believe is to extirpate them. New converts, who once valued themselves on their incredulity, have become credulous to excess; and those who were previously indifferent to sober religion, are led to swallow the wildest perversions of Christianity, to adopt opinions which she as heartily rejects as she did their former unbelief.

Some subjects are placed out of the reach of the human mind. Presumptuous spirits lose themselves by attempting to pierce through forbidden bounds; by endeavouring to explain things beyond the limits of created comprehension, they subvert the truth they pretend to serve, they involve themselves in the very difficulties they undertake to clear. The humble Christian, like the seraphim, "covers his face" before the infinite Majesty of Heaven, and exclaims, "O the depths of the riches both of the wisdom and knowledge of God!"—

"Verily Thou art a God that hidest Thyself."

We are not called upon to unravel intricacies, but to hold fast the form of sound words. While to the ill-informed these new teachers appear profound because they are unintelligible, they remind those of better judgment of certain animals, who, burrowing in shallow ground, just beneath the surface of the earth, fancy they are deep only because they are dark.

Many a metaphysical reformer, by the manner of conducting his system, so exposes and defeats his own cause, as to resemble in fate, though we say not with any similarity of intention, the Neapolitan atheist Vanini, who, with eleven others of the same class (we presume the number to be a match for the twelve apostles) endeavoured to establish a regular college of infidelity. The object was nearly the same with that of the late atheistical school in France; and by having the priority of two centuries, they robbed that recent rabble of the meritorious claim to original wickedness.

Vanini's object was to exterminate the very idea of a God, and for this, he adopted a most singular method. He undertook to prove there was no God by stating the general idea of God. He strangely fancied that to define the idea was to destroy it; and that to pretend to say what God is, was the surest way to disprove his existence! His definition is so artfully made out, and part of it is so ingeniously written, that while he thought he was drawing only the creature of his imagination, it appears as if he were enthroning rather than deposing his Creator. A marvellous delusion, to argue against the being of God from the very magnitude of his perfections! Let the delirious metaphysics of modern times alone, and we had almost said they will also argue themselves into the abyss of forgetfulness.*

* For a fuller account of this metaphysical atheist, see Mr Saurin's sermon on "The deep things of God."

We want more simplicity in the exercise of our religion; we want to be reformed by it, and not to reform it; we have need to be sent back to our first rudiments. We should imitate the plainness and uncomplicated method of the New Testament, where the doctrines are few, but of importance inestimable, infinite, eternal! We should examine the grounds of our faith by this unerring guide, and not by the pullulations of our own visionary fancies. We want to be sent back to elementary principles. We need not even think it beneath our wisdom to be directed by that familiar summary, the Apostles Creed. It were well if we fixed our own faith by the articles comprised in, and enclosed by, that safe compendium, instead of turning it over to our children as if we were got above its beggarly elements. Even the way-faring man cannot stray, while he is contented to keep close within this hedge.

Many do not virtually adopt its first simple declaration, "I believe in God;" for to believe in God on the Christian scheme, is not merely to believe in a first cause, is not merely to believe in His existence, we must also believe in His attributes, His promises, His threatenings, His Son, His word, His Spirit; to believe in those attributes especially which harmoniously meet in the glorious union of truth and mercy, the blessed combination of righteousness and peace in the person of his Divine Son; those promises which are eternal life to as many as keep his commandments; those threatenings which say to the ungodly, "Depart from me I never knew you;" that holiness without which no man shall ever see his face.

A bad principle is of much more extensive mischief than a bad example; the latter it is true, like a conflagration, has a tendency to destroy whatever comes within its reach; but a pernicious principle, like the variolous matter, may be conveyed to any distance, and infect the patient, though he had never come in contact with him from whose eruption it was taken. "It is time for thee, Lord, to lay to thine hand, for they have destroyed thy law!"

But it is not the entertaining a dangerous opinion, it is this rage for proselyting to new opinions, which constitutes the most malignant part of the mischief; an erroneous doctrine not propagated, hurts none but him who holds it; but by propagating it to unsettle the minds of multitudes, to deteriorate the Gospel, and to disturb the peace and unity of the church, is surely no light evil, especially in a country like ours, proverbial for its credulity and love of novelty; and in a church like ours, which has been reformed, sifted, and purified, beyond the example of any other in the Christian world.

The everlasting edifice of the Gospel is founded on a rock, whose stability neither storms can shake, nor waves undermine. Nor can any contrivances of man improve the beauty of its superstructure. Its depths cannot be fathomed by our short line, nor its height fully apprehended by our short sight! Christianity then is no appropriate field for the perplexities of metaphysics, nor the industry of new discoverers. This brief title of the Bible — THE WORD OF GOD — excludes the censure of all cavillers, annihilates the emendations of all critics!

It is with unfeigned sorrow the writer has witnessed the rise and progress of the new community. If she knows any thing of her own heart, the preceding remarks have not been dictated by a censorious spirit. But it may be said, she was not called upon for any such impertinent animadversions. The probability of such a reproof makes her feel herself obliged to account for the liberty she has taken.

Those who have condescended to look into her former writings, need not be reminded, that she has through life, in a considerable degree, though not exclusively, devoted her humble talents to the service of her own sex; and has conscientiously, though feebly, laboured to be useful to their best interests in every way she could devise. She has endeavoured to strengthen them in the pursuit of what was right, and they have had the goodness to bear with her when she has reminded them of any aberrations from that pursuit.

Though the deep interest she has taken in their credit and their welfare has by no means invested her with a right of interference on the present painful occasion, yet it would not have been consistent with her antecedent practice, to overlook a circumstance in which they are so deeply involved.

It has excited the most lively feelings of regret in many minds, to hear, in a recent instance, of the departure of some ladies of consideration, from that reserve and delicacy so peculiarly the characteristics of their sex, and so naturally appendant to their own respectable characters and situation in life. They appear not only to have entered very warmly into all the tenets of the seceding school, but to labour very assiduously for their propagation. They are, it seems, not only followers, but joint leaders in the several departments of the government of the seceding party.

Tenderness of heart, warmth of feeling, and liveliness of imagination, form a most interesting part in the composition of an amiable woman; but the qualities which adorn, are also the qualities which mislead. The very attractions which cause them to please, may become snares. If not carefully directed, they give a wrong bias to the character, and a dangerous tendency to the conduct. They lead their possessor more widely astray than is commonly the case with those who are destitute of these pleasing powers.

That providential economy which has clearly determined that women were born to share with men the duties of private life, has as clearly demonstrated, that they were not born to divide with them in its public administration. If, then, they were not intended to command armies in war, nor to direct cabinets in peace, to legislate in the senate, or debate at the bar, — doubtless they were not intended to be public teachers of religion, to be makers of canons for a new church, nor to invent dogmas to controvert an old one; nor to be professors of proselytism, nor wrangling polemics, nor conductors of controversy, nor settlers of disputes — disputes which will continue to be agitated as long as men have hot heads and proud hearts; as long as they possess vanity or curiosity, impatience of restraint, or a love of opposition; a weariness of sober truths, and a thirst after the fame to be acquired by their subversion.

Why will women of sense, then, defeat their providential destination? why desert their proper sphere, in which they were intended to benefit, to please, even to shine, at least as stars of the *second* magnitude? Why fly from their prescribed orbit? Why roam in useless and eccentric wandering,

"And, comet-like, rush lawless through the void,"

and then, having for a season astonished with their false and momentary blaze, fall disregarded and forgotten?

These well-meaning ladies would be among the last to use their allotted measure of grace and accomplishment, to any purpose which they believed to be improper; yet they require to be told, that neither should their talents be exerted to the purposes of spiritual seduction; that they should not be employed to disturb the faith, to shake by dispute, or weaken by persuasion, the steadiness of persons who, without their endowments, are perhaps in a safer state.

But, though the writer cannot hope that these observations will produce any effect on those who are already embarked on this sea, without a shore, and without a bottom — happy would she be, if they might become the means of preserving one inexperienced female from the perils to which novelty, curiosity, and pressing invitation, too easily allure. The sure preservatives from this danger are to cultivate deep humility and self-distrust, to keep clear of the very threshold of innovation, to avoid the first step; for all the subsequent ones are easy. Let her bear in mind, that, once seduced, she may find, that "when she would inherit the blessing, she may be rejected, and find no place of repentance, though she may seek it carefully with tears."

ILL EFFECTS OF THE LATE SECESSION.

Among the evils to which the late secession has contributed, those we are about to mention are of no light nature. It has been the means of exciting a sort of spiritual vanity, of awakening a desire of departing from received opinions, in certain young persons, who may be designated by the name of premature instructors. It has increased the alienation of the lower orders from the church; it has afforded to some who are not favourable to serious piety, a pretence for indiscriminately classing together men of different views, characters, and principles. Among the more respectable, it has stirred up a spirit of debate and controversy, by no means friendly to the cause of genuine Christianity. We shall mention these effects in their order.

There is scarcely a greater mistake in morals, than is committed by those who habitually speak of vanity as a trifling fault, as a small pass not worth guarding. There is perhaps scarcely an error which is so generally adopted, and so carelessly overlooked. It finds its way into characters of every species, and almost into every individual of the species. There is not only the vanity of beauty, of rank, of riches, of learning, of talents, but, as we have already observed, the vanity of religion.

A bold familiarity with Scripture, an unhallowed touching of the sacred ark, not as formerly by sceptics and scoffers only, but by persons professing, and we believe intending to be religious, are, it is to be feared, becoming too common. This, like many other of our offences, has its foundation in vanity. It is obvious that an unwillingness to be taught, and an impatience to teach, marks the character of the present day.

There is a scion from this presumptuous stock, which perhaps has not had sufficient time to grow, in order to become generally known, but which is beginning to sprout up in certain provincial towns and villages. There is a growing disposition in a few arrogant young men to read the Bible with their own glosses and interpretations, and to aim at proselyting, and " taking captive" not only " silly women" but silly girls. Several of these persons, as soon as they began to open their eyes on the importance of religion, or rather before they were broad awake to its truths, have undertaken this gratuitous tuition. Instead of taking time to promote their own advancement, instead of learning wisdom by an increasing discovery of their own ignorance; instead of improving in Christian knowledge by the only legitimate methods, diligent study of the

Bible with the aid of the soundest commentators, both accompanied with fervent prayer for that light they profess to seek,—without consulting able ministers — without taking this straight and obvious road, — on their own very slender stock they set up for teachers themselves. Instead of looking to the experienced and the wise, they collect a little groupe to look up to them, thus inverting the Apostle's observation — for *they* " when for the time they seek to be teachers, have need to be taught themselves, which be the first principles of the oracles of God." If this spiritual vanity should flourish we shall soon have none left to learn; all will be teachers.

Thus the raw and rash Christian, confidently jumps over all the intermediate steps between the enquirer and the instructor, and despising the old gradual approach to the sacred temple, despising the study of books, of men, and of himself, starts up at once a full-grown divine;—the novice seizes the professor's chair, erects himself into a scholar without literature, and a theologian without theology. On the strength of a few texts, ill understood, and worse applied, he undertakes to give his young neighbours new views of the Bible, and without eyes himself, sets up for a guide of the blind.

These young persons in reading the Scriptures seem to be setting out on a voyage of discovery of something new, rather than on a course of observation on what their precursors have done for them. They search, not with devout enquiry, but fearless curiosity; they look out for passages written in a different connection, and applied to different purposes, and then try to prove that they produce not consecutive reasoning, that they do not establish the generally received doctrines. How should they? They were never intended to produce the one, or to establish the other. They bring together propositions which have no relation, and which require different proofs, and then triumph in the supposed opposition of what was never intended to agree.

"Thus fools rush in where angels fear to tread."

Suffer a few friendly hints. Though Holy Scripture was given to be searched, it was not given to be criticised. It was "written for our learning," not for our cavilling: it was given not to be pertly scrutinized, but to be " inwardly digested;" not to make us wise in our own conceits, but " to make us wise unto salvation." It is not to be endured to hear questions, on which hang all our hopes and our fears, speculated upon as if they were a question of physics or history, and explained till they become contradictions.

Men taught of God, and possessing those depths of erudition which qualified them to teach others, depend upon it, have left nothing for your discovery except the discovery of your own insufficiency. If there are obscurities, they will not be cleared by such shallow expositors. The sun of righteousness will not be made to shine brighter by the light of your farthing candle.

Boldness in religion, we repeat, is one of the great evils of the present day. The more we cavil the less we shall obey. We may explain truths till we come to deny them. We may be so involved in intricacies of our own weaving, that we may end by opposing the doctrine we undertook to clear. Oh! there is no security like a humble mind; a mind always distrusting its own wisdom, and always confiding in the wisdom of God.

Why, then, will not the premature instructor wait till he is himself instructed? Why not look up for information on difficult and disputed points to wiser and older heads? Why not in their little parties turn their attention to practical points, rather than to speculative niceties? Why not cultivate that self-inspection and heart-humbling prayer which would cure those conceits that lead to a critical, and often end in a sceptical spirit; such habits would best preserve them from that inflation of heart which arises from the vanity of some supposed new discovery, in a religion which was given us by the Spirit of God.

The Scripture no where teaches us to indulge this audacious curiosity; it stirs up no eagerness for pushing speculation beyond its legitimate bounds. It furnishes no invitation for ranging beyond the limited sphere allotted to our imperfect human condition. Its incitements are not irritations but encouragements. The Bible wisely represses all that spiritual vanity which would dive into unprofitable, because impenetrable mysteries. It teaches us all that is necessary for us to learn, and there it stops. It teaches what is of prime importance for us to know,—that we are fallen creatures. It shows what we ought to *believe* in order to our being rescued from this state of apostacy. It instructs us in all that is necessary for us to *do* to be restored to the favour of God, which by sin we had forfeited. It is enough that it lays open the disease, presents the remedy, and offers God's Holy Spirit to render it effectual. In short, it reveals all that as probationary beings we should desire to know, and of all we know it expects us to make a practical use.

The present is, especially among the lower ranks, an age of rebuke and blasphemy; and what is so likely to augment the popular hostility to Christianity, and neglect of the established church, which is founded upon it, as when they see some of its ministers reprobating at one time, the church which they warmly defended at another?—when they see them actually renouncing it as unchristian, and setting up a new system in opposition to it? Where, then, is truth to be found; may not even the more sober amongst the people say, if it is not found in that church, in defence of which so many of her divines, so many of her bishops, were led to the scaffold and the stake? Will not the loose and careless be likely to be confirmed in impiety, when they see these men, who were fostered in her bosom, who had subscribed to their belief in her articles, who had been warm beyond their fellows in the admiration of her liturgy, her doctrines, and her discipline, —when they see these men not only desert her altars, but take up arms against her; when they behold a perpetual conflict between Christian ministers?—for a church that is attacked must be defended—will they not think that an establishment which is so frequently assailed, which requires such continual vindication, from which there are so many recent deserters, must needs be an erroneous and unsound church, and even the Scriptures on which it is founded, uncertain, if not false?

What is so likely as this defection to give confidence, without the least intention of doing so, to that spirit of infidelity which used to skulk in corners, and stab from behind a mask, but now avows itself boldly, bares its unblushing front to public gaze, spurns at law as well as decency, openly defies government, whom it used to fear, as well as God, whom it never feared?

Was it not enough that these low, designing demagogues — men who think one religion as good as another, and no religion best of all, — was it not enough that these open violators of order, truth, and justice, should, as the most probable means to accomplish their political mischiefs, endeavour to overturn the church, by bringing her creeds, and her other holy services, into contempt; insulting, by their profane parodies, all that is grave, and rendering ridiculous all that is good? Yet, from such men, such attempts excite our regret and astonishment less than those we have been contemplating. How grievous is it, when persons of a totally different description are, perhaps undesignedly, contributing to help on the work which, we are persuaded, they abhor!—when decorous and religious men, though by other devices, and with other weapons, may be contributing to accomplish the work of these vulgar politicians, and assisting, in no inconsiderable degree, to discredit the church which the others are labouring to subvert!

Nay; in one respect the better men are doing the worse deed; for the factious assailants of the church injure those alone who were injured before; for, by the grossness of their attacks, they shock all who are not totally given up to impiety; while, in the present instance, those more decent characters are more likely to be led astray, who have shown some disposition to be serious; and are, therefore, in more danger of being misled by the specious subtleties, and the assumed tone of confident security, of these religious dogmatists.

The inexperienced and the wavering —those who are unconfirmed in their principles, together with others who have their religion to seek, and who like to have one pointed out to them which will not disturb their repose by the severity of its practical injunctions, nor the self-denying spirit of its tendencies,—are likely to be led astray by these false lights; while the sober and self-distrusting Christian will only be driven, by these alarming novelties, to adhere more closely to the humbling and consistent doctrines of the New Testament,—will, with deeper prostration of heart, implore the aid of the Holy Spirit, not only to lead him into all truth, but to *keep* him in it. Such a one will find that it does not require profound knowledge, or deep learning, to perceive the awful dangers of the presumptuous innovations which lead to these perilous subtleties—which terminate in these bold conclusions. He will see that common sense, an humble mind, and a competent acquaintance with Scripture, are all that is wanting to discover that the Bible, and the novelties of the seceding community, cannot both be right.

But the evil does not end here; for some of the adversaries of serious piety are, it is to be feared, disposed to take a most unfair advantage of this secession; and the very circumstance of that separation which ought to have rescued men who firmly adhere to the church, and to the principles on which it is founded, from suspicion, increases it, and causes them to be involved in one common charge of extravagance and error, with men whose opinions they abhor: whereas, when the vessel is assailed by an unexpected storm, instead of throwing themselves out to sea in quest of imaginary safety, the tempest only makes the experienced Christian mariner cling the closer to his hold. Men of more than ordinary zeal and activity, then, should not be suspected of disaffection, unless they afford other, and more substantial reasons, for doubting their want of orthodoxy. Does it not look as if there were no soundness but in apathy, no security but in inertness?

One of the great evils of the times is rash judgment, indiscriminate attack, and a zeal for censure without examination; a not separating men who are materially dissimilar, but lumping them into one common reprobated mass; or, at best, speaking as if the difference were so little, that it was not worth the pains to separate them.

Perhaps there are no church communities in the world, that do not hold some doctrines in common. We are identified in some important points with the Church of Rome; but that does not blind us to its errors, nor does it prevent our keeping clear of them. There are both rational and orthodox communities in our own country; but our holding some opinions in common with them, neither makes us adopt those opinions which we disapprove, nor condemn those who profess them, as if they held none that were right. Why, then, should not the case be the same in our own church?

This lumping system is not a little hard on the steady and orderly divine. It weakens the hands of the faithful pastor, when his auditors, who have just been hearing him speak the words of truth and soberness, find him, perhaps, in the next controversial pamphlet they take up, coupled with the half insane, and the wholly absurd. It is hard that the zealous Christian, who is at the same time a pattern of propriety and correct demeanor, should be dragged in to make common cause with those at whose principles he shudders. Yet these men of opposite characters, principles, and pursuits, are forced into contact, are together plunged into the crucible of undistinguishing prejudice, and melted down together; all distinctions so lost in the fusion — the sober Christian so mixed with the fanatic, the temperate with the fiery, the regular with the eccentric, that they come out of the furnace blended into one common mass, and are reproduced as if formed of one common material.

Ours is also pre-eminently an age of controversy. Is not charity sometimes recommended with uncharitableness, and religion vindicated irreligiously? But are there not a thousand other subjects better calculated for its legitimate exercise? "Let the potsherds strive with the potsherds of the earth," on all other topics; but here, though one dash the other in pieces, he does not always escape unhurt himself. But shall the word of "the High and Holy One, the word of Him who sitteth on the circle of the earth," be made an arena for the combats of its puny inhabitants, whom the prophet represents by the most contemptible insect?

But although, as we have already observed, if truth be attacked, it must be defended, the Christian controvertist never engages in offensive war. He does not fight for victory, but truth. And the surest way for him to ascertain this, is, to examine the temper with which he defends it. Rivalry is not his motive, nor is railing his weapon.

If, as it is said, warfare is the natural state of man, let its hostility among Christians be directed to a foreign enemy; let them not engage in civil war. You have already " provoked each other to good works," which is part of the law; go on, and provoke each other to "love, which is the fulfilling of the law." Let both sides rejoice in the good done, without caring which does it. " There are diversities of operations, but it is the same God which worketh all in all." If there is so much done separately, what a mighty mass of good would be produced by cordial co-operation! Let me not be accused of levity in applying the words of the poet,

The Douglas and the Percy *both together*,
Were confident against a world in arms.

We know that, in the sight of God, he is not the most successful champion who may have given most falls to his adversary; but he who has obtained the most victories over his own spirit. And *he* will be found, in the great and tremendous day of reckoning, to have been the most valiant soldier of Jesus Christ, not who has been the fiercest combatant in the field of controversy, but who shall have brought most glory to God, and most souls to heaven.

If we made, as surely we ought to make, the Holy Scripture our standard of judging, as well as of believing, of charity as well as of faith, of brotherly kindness as well as of orthodoxy;—if we brought the Bible to be the constant arbiter of our debates, as well as the professed rule of our lives, we should attack nothing with warmth but what that Bible condemns. All differences of opinion in which God has not set to His seal that it is false, should be treated with candour; men should not then make their own "purged eyes" the universal medium of clear vision, they should not vilify others for seeing the same object with other optics. Want of charity is probably no less a fault than the one we may be reviling; and does not a want of discrimination, or rather does not that blindness which is inspired by prejudice, lead to that deficiency in candour which widens the difference? To profess opinions of which Scripture neither commands nor prohibits our belief, ought not to set at irreconcileable variance beings who are equally candidates for heaven. In that abode of perfect peace and perfect love, no small portion of the promised felicity may arise from our being of no party.

A difference in opinion on points on which the Holy Spirit has been silent, on which no declaratory sentence in Scripture has been pronounced, is surely no ground for the triumph of superiority in those who maintain them, nor for supercilious contempt in those who reject them. Is it not putting matters of minor importance in the place of essentials? while perhaps by the disputants on both sides, essentials are not always held with so firm a grasp, or at least are not debated with such unkind pertinacity.

We have hitherto alluded to difference of opinion between pious men, men who are in earnest in their religion. But are there not men of little piety to be found, who side with one or the other party, and become the hottest controvertists, while they take little real interest in vital religion; who oppose without belief, and defend without conviction, merely because they wish to be appended to that side which they happen to think most creditable, most popular, or most profitable?

Let us then love in each other now what God loves in us, and bear with the rest. The cultivation of this spirit of kindness would so sanctify the temper, that we should forgive and overlook those inferior matters in others, which might not exactly coincide with our own views and opinions.

These discrepancies in sentiment are perhaps permitted for mutual advantages; and the cultivation of a candid disposition may be carried to a wider extent, and a spirit of forbearance be kept in higher exercise, where there are some points to keep forbearance in action, than if there were no such thing as diversity of sentiment. By the constant and reciprocal operation of this spirit of Christian kindness, we shall be made more meet for that state where all will be of one mind, as well as one heart, where charity will have its full consummation, and forbearance its full reward.

Let us then prepare ourselves, and each other, by the exercise of the one for the fruition of the other. Let God be all in all now as He will be hereafter, and there will be no room left in the heart of a Christian for animosity, or unkindness towards his fellow Christians.

A cordial agreement in those essentials to which the Gospel has annexed salvation, should swallow up all the present petty, but dividing distinctions. Could this most desirable object be accomplished, then should we hope to see a renovation of that spirit which, in the early ages of the church, provoked even its enemies to exclaim with admiring wonder, *See how these Christians love one another!*

ON THE EXERTIONS OF PIOUS LADIES.

We are now about to tread, which we do with a fearful and timid step, on tender ground. It is with mingled respect and reluctance we venture to touch on certain delicate points which affect the sincerely pious; persons who equally avoid all eccentricity in doctrine, and negligence in practice; yet among whom little errors may hereafter creep in, the very consequence, perhaps, of that increasing and inestimable blessing, religious society. It is to be feared they may incur the hazard of raising in others objections against religion, by their honest zeal to promote it.

The persons to whom we presume to allude are of that sex, in which, perhaps, most piety is to be found, and who are in so many respects essentially advancing its cause. Their services are so materially useful, that it would be a subject of deep regret, if, by any slight inadvertence, their value should ever be diminished. We are too often led to complain of *deficiencies* in religion; we are now to speak — not of its excess, for we believe there is no such thing — but rather to guard the truly pious against the possibility of inconveniencies, which, should they arise, would be a diminution of their usefulness.

The thoughtless and dissipated indeed, who haunt unsocial crowds, and lay out their talents for that world which they have chosen for their portion, find their reward where they seek it, in the admiration of that world where they flutter and shine. The others patiently wait for theirs in that single sentence, " Well done, good and faithful servant." Yet though it is painful to say a syllable which might look like disapprobation when only caution is intended, may we hazard a few words, not of censure but of friendly intimation?

May not those large portions of time, and strength, and spirits, so generously spent abroad by zealous Christians, in the most noble exertions of religious charity, be sometimes suffered to entrench, in some measure, upon the imperious calls of domestic life, upon those pleasing and sacred duties for which HOME is a name so dear? May they not be so exhausted by external concerns, that they may be in danger of entering with diminished interest on the retired exercises of the closet. All business, even religious business, is apt to produce a hurry and bustle in the mind, and an agitation in the spirits, which the most serious persons lament, as being attended with some disqualification for personal improvement. — "My mother's children gave me their vineyards to keep, but mine own vineyard have I not kept," was the pathetic lamentation of the ancient church. They had engaged her in labours and difficulties which she feared had in some measure impeded the progress of her own spiritual concerns. It was in her own house, at Bethany, that Mary sat at the feet of Jesus.—We fully admit, however, not only the complete *compatibility*, but the expediency, of uniting what we owe to those abroad, and to ourselves and families at home; the highest characters are those who combine both. We are not combating, but applauding a zeal, which we fervently hope may never be suppressed, if it should ever require to be somewhat regulated.

There is no part of Christian duty which more requires us to look well to the motive by which our actions are set a-going. It is of importance to examine whether our most useful, if busy, pursuits, are not influenced by a natural fondness for bustle, an animal activity, a love of notice. Whether even the charitable labours grow not more from a restless spirit than from real piety. Let us observe, however, that though these defective motives may at first excite the zeal of some, yet by a perseverance in well-doing, assisted by humble prayer, the motive may at length become as pure as the act is undoubtedly right.

It is asserted, but we trust with more severity than justice, that there is a growing tendency in some truly excellent persons to introduce show and display in their religion; a tendency not quite consistent with the interior, spiritual nature of Christianity. It is not so much an evil *we* are guarding against, as the appearance of evil. Their sex, like their religion, is of a sober character; and the tendency to which we are alluding, may create a suspicion that religion, even among good people, is not so much considered as a thing between God and their own soul, as we know it really is; for we are far from suspecting that secret communion with their God and Saviour is not considered as their primary duty.

And we are willing to believe that the effect of this duty will always be visible in producing that sobriety and simplicity, which so conspicuously, and so beautifully distinguish the religion of the New Testament.

The religion of Jesus is utterly without parade, it affects no publicity. It is enough for his servants to believe that their Heavenly Father, who sees them in secret, sees them with an approving eye.

As they have got above acting from the fear of man, the next step is to get above acting for his praise;—the excessive applause and commendation of their Christian friends being, in reality, still more to be watched against than the reproach of the irreligious. The one teaches them to be circumspect, the other may in time induce them to believe that circumspection is no longer necessary. This negligence, if it do not make them do wrong, may lead them to be too much elated with doing what is right.

"But there are higher motives for the use of discreet reserve in the Christian's mind than what regards merely their personal character. However pure in motive, however innocent in action, they must be careful not to have their good evil spoken of. They must be scrupulously cautious of not bringing the least reproach on the cause dearest to their affections. Pious persons cannot but know, that with the utmost care to avoid adding to the offence which Christian truth, however discreetly exhibited, necessarily gives, that many are looking out for pretences to discredit not only the professor, but the profession itself. But if they should hereafter see any of those improprieties for which they are looking out; if any indiscretion should be found where it is sedulously sought, Christianity would suffer, and impiety triumph.

We sincerely hope that certain sharp-sighted observers, who are keenly on the watch for any thing that may discredit serious piety, who are peeping in at every crevice, through which they think they may detect any real or supposed ground of censure, may never be gratified with the discovery of what they so industriously seek. But it is obvious, that where they can detect no substantial fault, they take comfort in finding a foible; where there is no deformity they triumphantly carry away a blemish, and are ready to make the most of the slightest imperfection. And a speck which would not be perceived in an ordinary form, is conspicuous on that which is white and pure. This, by a little perversion, and not a little exaggeration, not only of fact but of conjecture, is propagated till it become a mischief. In the detection of the slightest flaw in characters of eminent piety, they go away rejoicing, as if they had found some hidden treasure. And it is well perhaps, even for the best Christians, that there are such critical inspectors; and the knowledge that they are watched will answer an excellent purpose, if it set them on watching themselves.

Am I then an enemy to Christian exertion? God forbid! It is the glory of our age, that among the most useful and zealous servants of our Divine Master, are to be found, of " devout and honourable women not a few." Ladies, whose own education not having been limited to the harp and the sketch-book, though not unskilled in either, are competent to teach others what themselves have been taught; who disdain not to be employed in the humblest offices of Christian charity, to be found in the poorest cottage, at the bed-side of the sick and dying; whose daughters, if not the best *waltzers*, are the best *catechisers*; whose houses are houses of prayer, whose closets are the scene of devout meditation; who, not contented with the stinted modish measure of a single attendance on public worship, so contrive to render the hours of repast subservient to those of duty, as to make a second visit to the temple of their God; and who endeavour to retain the odour of sanctity, shed on the sacred day, through the duties of the week.

But to pursue the subject in a different, though not distant direction, we cannot too much commend those valuable persons, whom neither fortune, rank, nor any temporal advantages, have been able to seduce to follow those vain pursuits, those light, and, in some cases, dangerous amusements, so eagerly sought by the votaries of pleasure. We cannot but admire, that all those energies which others are wasting in idle diversions, or employments little better than idleness, are, by these excellent persons, devoted to purposes of religion, and religious or useful charities.

If, indeed, like the females attached to the new school of theology, they deserted the established proprieties, and prescribed decorums, which have ever been considered as the safeguard, as well as the ornament, of their sex; if they assisted to propagate novel opinions; if they undertook to share the office of directors in spiritual concerns; if they diverted to public purposes, the talents given them for the more appropriate and subordinate, but not less useful offices of private life; if they attempted to clear difficulties in divinity, which the wisest and most learned men had approached with awe and reverence, and had receded, for fear of " darkening counsel by words without knowledge;"—if they undertook to decide between contending creeds while they considered the commandments as antiquated — new-modelling the one and rescinding the other without ceremony;—if they allowed themselves to determine the right and the wrong on points too abstruse, not only for female, but even for human intelligence, to decide upon, and to get rid of those they did not like or did not comprehend;—if they had quitted plain, practical, intelligible religion, for misleading theories, and, like the apostate Galatians, " removed from Him that called them into the grace of Christ unto another gospel;"—if all these things had taken place, then they would indeed deserve even more censure than they have incurred; then, though we should pity their error and lament their apostacy, we should be among the last to apologise for the one, or excuse the other.

It has been brought, as a charge, against the valuable ladies whose cause we are advocating, as if it were a departure from the delicacy of the sex, to attend at the annual meetings of certain religious and charitable societies; but we know not what reasonable objection can be made to their being modest and silent auditors on these occasions. They do not attend the resorts of the unemployed, or the ill employed —they do not attend to hear the idle news of the neighbourhood, but to hear "good news from a far country,"—news, which the angels in heaven stoop down to hear,—not the conversion of one sinner, but the conversion of many,—

to hear that best news, the extension of Christianity to the extremities of the globe,—to hear that

"All kingdoms and all princes of the earth
Flock to that light;"—

To hear

"That eastern Java to the farthest west,
And Ethiopia spreads abroad the hand
And worships!"

Compare now these inoffensive and quiet auditors, with the gay multitudes of their own sex which crowd the resorts of pleasure. Here, they are the peaceful listeners; there, they are the busy performers. The others are not, as here, passive recipients of entertainment, but the entertainers, but the exhibitors. Yet, who among the worldly censures one of these classes?—who, among the prejudiced, does not censure the other?

So much for the difference in the *act;* let us examine the difference in point of *time* ; for, as in our pleasurable pursuits, the consumption of time, that precious material of which life is made, forms a very considerable object, it cannot be thought unfair to compare the two classes on this ground.

Did the pursuits of both, in point of health, sobriety in dress, security of morals, preservation of delicacy, more nearly approach each other than the most strenuous advocate for dissipation can pretend; yet the prodigious inequality of the two, as to the waste of time, must settle the matter at once with those who know the value of this fugitive, this irretrievable talent.

Compare then the few hours in the day, and the very few days in the year, given up by the one to these serious pleasures, with the uncounted hours of the countless nights, spent by the other in the *anti-social* crowds of turbulent pleasure — spent, we will not say in the *midnight* parties, for that would give a false impression of the season of those amusements. The midnight hour was heretofore used proverbially to express *late* revelling. But from the present inversion of hours, that would give an idea not only of dulness and vulgarity, but it would also rather designate the hour when company met, than when they parted. Midnight was once the time which *closed* the scene of dissipation; it is now that of *commencing* it. And it is scarcely extravagant to say, that the morning frequenters of the charitable meetings join them not many hours after the others return from the scene of their unquiet pleasures. In the one case, no neighbourhood is kept awake by unseasonable noise and knockings, no servants are exposed to corruptions abroad, nor robbed of quiet rest at home.

To turn from the metropolis to the provinces. Compare the little absences from home of ladies who inspect the concerns, and give instruction to the poor, with the long and frequent desertion of another class, not of home only, but of country!

Upon the whole, though we would carefully guard against both, yet we must confess, in the present state of things, it is not so much a little excess in zeal in one quarter, as the visible growth of dissipation in another, which " has increased, is increasing, and ought to be diminished;" and truly happy should we be, if the pen of the ready writers, so frequently employed against the minor, would occasionally be exerted against the greater excess.

* * * * *

The opening of the nineteenth century has been a period for the display of extraordinary energies, exerted in every sort of direction. They had been powerfully exerted in bringing on the late revolution. All the energies of France, whether in science, talent, wit, or wealth, were combined in one huge engine for the establishment of atheism on the proposed ruins of Christ and his kingdom. We hope this grand device was partly foiled, even *there*. In the general assault some skirmishes were fought in this country; but here a counter-attack was made. " Michael and his angels fought against the dragon and his angels, and prevailed." — " The accuser of the brethren was cast down."

Afterwards the great human scourge of mankind in the same foreign country, by a singular energy of character, aided by an unprecedented combination of circumstances, to which the previous contempt of religion had led the way, projected the most exorbitant enterprises, and accomplished them by the most successful perseverance in every species of political and moral mischief. In imitation of one whom the enormity of his crimes would almost warrant us in calling his grand inspirer, his labours were perhaps more energetic, because " his time was short." Here again Michael made a counter-attack on the dragon. For it is to the same powerful energies, exerted in the contrary direction, that we may ascribe those numberless noble and beneficial societies at home, which promise to effect a moral change in the condition, not of one country, not of one Continent, but of the whole Globe, and by which we hope finally, through the Divine blessing, "to beat down Satan under our feet."

But this has not only been a period for exerting the energies of countries and communities. They have been exerted under different situations by different characters, and to opposite purposes, by individuals; they have been remarkably exhibited in private persons, in a sex where energy is less expected to break out into fearless action; in Charlotte Corday, in Madame Roland, and other political enthusiasts abroad, all acting with the spirit of the heroines of pagan Rome, and actuated by a religion much resembling theirs.

At home, the best energies of the human mind have been exerted to the best purposes, by private individuals also, and exerted without any departure from modesty, prudence, and simplicity, the sacrifice of which would ill repay the accomplishment of the most popular action.

It would be unpardonable in our remarks on well-directed energies, to pass over one instance, on which, we trust, there cannot be two opinions. If some of the novelties of the present period are its errors, others are its glory. It is cheering to the wearied pilgrim, in traversing the desert of this sinful world, to have the eye here and there refreshed with a verdant spot, yielding not only beauty, but fertility.

In alluding to certain recent undertakings which reflect honour on our country, it would be unjust to omit one which reflects honour on our sex. Justice, as well as gratitude, would be wounded, were no tribute to be paid to the most heroic of women.

The reader will have anticipated, that we allude to the female Howard. Hers is almost (her sex considered) a higher strain of Christian heroism. Unprotected and alone, she dared to venture into scenes that would appal the stoutest heart, and which the single principle alone by which she was actuated could have sustained her. With true Christian courage, she ventured to explore the dreary abodes of calamity and crime, of execration and despair. She took "the gauge of misery," not as a matter of curiosity, or philosophical speculation, but with the holy hope of relieving it. The favour of Him who stopped the mouths of the lions in the prophet's den, stopped those of these scarcely less savage beings. Her mild demeanour awed their rebellious spirits into peace.

Her visit was not the sudden ebullition of a charitable fit. It was the result of deliberate reflection, and doubtless of fervent prayer. She had long been projecting the means how to assist these most desperate and forlorn of human kind. She had conceived a hope, that what was flagitious might not be incorrigible; and adopted a well-digested plan for their religious instruction.

But she knew human nature too well, not to know that religious instruction would be very inefficacious, without correcting inveterately bad habits. Together with a few pious and able associates of her own sex*, she instituted a school of reform and industry, found manual employment for those who had never worked, and Christian instruction for those who had never been taught. The lips that had been seldom opened but to blaspheme their Maker, were taught to praise Him; the hands hitherto employed in theft were employed in honest labour. Infants, in a doubly-lamentable sense, born in sin, and bred in vice, were snatched from a destruction which had appeared inevitable, and put into a train of improvement. The gloomy mansion which had lately been a scene of horror,

---

* Among these Mrs. Steinkopff stands in the first rank.

only to be exceeded by those more dreadful future mansions to which it was conducting them, changed its face. The loathsome prison, which had witnessed nothing but intoxication and idleness; had heard no sounds but those of reviling and of imprecation, gradually became a scene of comparative decency, sobriety, and order.

If ever a charity of so extensive and public a nature could have been pleaded as some excuse for the remission of domestic duties, this might have been considered as the one exempt case, but it was not so. If she stole some hours from her family to visit the prison, she stole some hours from sleep to attend to her family.

Happily, goodness is contagious as well as sin. We may now say in a *good* sense, " Behold how great a matter a little fire kindleth!" Distant places have caught the flame. The bright example is already imitated by other ladies in some of our great towns, and will probably take a still more ample range.

May we conclude this part of our subject by observing, that ladies of other religious professions would do well to copy, in certain respects, the example of the females of the society to which this distinguished lady belongs;—giving into no habits of dissipation, they have time; addicted to little expense in personal decoration, they have money; and the time and money thus snatched from vain and frivolous purposes, are more wisely directed together into the same right channel of Christian benevolence.

HIGH PROFESSION AND NEGLIGENT PRACTICE.

There has seldom been a period in which there was more talk of religion, than that in which we live; and we are disposed to believe, that the abundance of the heart in this instance produces its usual effect upon the lips. But it must also be observed, that, in an age of much vital religion, as it must be acknowledged this is, there will naturally be not a little false profession, or, at best, in many professors, more external show than inward piety — a religion that is sometimes more distinguished by peculiar phrases, and hot contention about opinions, than by much devotedness of heart and life.

One of the causes to which the growth of crime amongst our poor has been assigned, is the growth of our population; and some have undertaken to prove, that it is not because they are worse, but because they are more. This same way of judging may, perhaps, be applied to the apparent growth of error in religion—that it is to be ascribed still to its well increase. If there is numerically a larger population, there may then also be naturally expected a larger proportion of error.

We now, therefore, offer a few remarks on another class of Christians, whose intentions, we hope, are not bad, though their charity is narrow, and their information small. We will distinguish them by the name of Phraseologists. These are persons, who, professing to believe the whole of the Gospel, seem to regard only one half of it. They stand quite in opposition to the useful and laborious class, when duly considered. None will accuse them of that virtuous excess, of that unwearied endeavour to promote the good of others, on which we there animadverted. There are assiduous hearers, but indifferent doers; very valiant talkers for the truth, but remiss workers. They are more addicted to hear sermons, than to profit by them.

Their religion consists more in a sort of spiritual gossipping, than in holiness of life. They diligently look out after the faults of others, but are rather lenient to their own. They accuse of being legal, those who act more in the service of Christianity, and dispute less about certain opinions. They overlook essentials, and debate rather fiercely on, at best, doubtful points of doctrine; and form their judgment of the piety of others, rather from their warmth in controversy, than in their walking humbly with God.

They always exhibit in their conversation the idiom of a party, and are apt to suspect the sincerity of those whose higher breeding, and more correct habits, discover a better taste. Delicacy with them, is want of zeal; prudent reserve, want of earnestness; sentiments of piety, conveyed in other words than are found in their vocabulary, are suspected of error. They make no allowance for the difference of education, habits, and society; all must have one standard of language, and that standard is their own.

Even if, on some points, you hold nearly the same sentiments, it will not save your credit; if you do not express them in the same language, you are in danger of having your principles suspected. By your proficiency or declension in this dialect, and not by the greater or less devotedness of your heart, the increasing or diminishing consistency in your practice, they take the gauge of your religion, and determine the rise and fall of your spiritual thermometer. The language of these technical Christians indisposes persons of refinement, who have not had the advantage of seeing religion under a more engaging form, to serious piety, by leading them to make a most unjust association between religion and bad taste.

When they encounter a new acquaintance of their own school, these reciprocal signs of religious intelligence produce an instantaneous sisterhood; and they will run the chance of what the character of the stranger may prove to be, if she speaks in the vernacular tongue. With them, words are not only the signs of things, but things themselves.

If the phraseologists meet with a well-disposed young person, whose opportunities are slender, and to whom religion is new, they alarm her by the impetuosity of their questions. They do not examine if her principles are sound, but "does she pray extempore?" This alarms her, if her too recent knowledge of her Bible and herself has not yet enabled her to make this desirable proficiency. "Will she tell her experience?" These interrogations are made without regard to that humility which may make her afraid to appear better than she is, and to that modesty which restrains a loud expression of her feelings. She does not, perhaps, even know the meaning of the term, in their acceptance of it.

Do we then ridicule experimental religion? Do we think lightly of that interior power of Divine grace upon the heart, which is one of the strongest evidences of the truth of Christianity? God forbid! But surely we may disapprove the treating it with flippancy and unhallowed familiarity; we may disapprove of their discussing it with as little reserve and seriousness, as if they were speaking of the state of the weather, or of the hour of the day; we may object to certain equivocal feelings being made the sole criterion of religion—feelings to which those who have them not may pretend,—which those who have them may fear to communicate, before they have acquired a strength and permanency which may make them more decisive; we may blame such injudicious questions to incipient Christians, who barely know the first elements of Christianity.

By the apparent depth of their views, and this cant in the expression, the stranger is led to think there is something unintelligible in religion — some mysterious charm, which is too high for her apprehension. They will not hold out to her the consoling hope of progressive piety; for, with them, growth in grace is no grace at all, — the starting-post and the goal are one and the same point. One of these consequences probably follows; she either falls into their peculiar views, or she is driven to seek wiser counsellors, or is led, by the hopelessness of attaining to their supposed elevation, to give up the pursuit of religion altogether.

These technical religionists are so far from encouraging favourable tendencies, and "the day of small things," that they have no patience with persons professing hope, and despise every advance short of assurance.

To judge of them by their conversation, they seem to have as firm a certainty of their own security, as of the danger of all the rest of the world; that is, of all those who do not see with *their* eyes, hear with *their* ears, and discuss in *their* language. You would suppose salvation a very easy attainment, to see them get so much above hopes or fears.

Surely eternal happiness is not so cheap a thing, as that any should plead their claim to it on slight grounds. Some who talk confidently of this certainty, do not give strong indications in their life, of their having entered in at "the straight gate" which leads to it. If it cost as few sacrifices, and required as little diligence, as some exhibit, there would not be so many who need doubt of their admission. Seek, strive, run, fight, labour, know thyself, humble thyself,—are imperatives not quite so easily or so generally obeyed, as to render "the narrow way" a very crowded avenue. Self-knowledge, self-denial, self-abasement, are safer symptoms than undoubting confidence and exulting security.

The desire of hearing and speaking much on religious subjects, though Christian duties, are less unequivocal marks of improvement, than whether we love money less, and our neighbour more; whether there is any abatement in our pride, any victory over our passions; whether we are more disposed to conquer our own will, and to submit to that of God. A growth in candour and charity, in kindness and forbearance, in meekness and self-distrust, will be the probable consequence of a close examination into our present deficiency in these amiable graces.

To these persons, the exclusive credit of their individual preacher is at least as valuable a consideration, as the glory of that God whom it may be *his* constant aim to glorify; and they do not think they exalt him sufficiently, if it be not done at the expense of others among his brethren, to whom he perhaps looks up with reverence. There is a wide difference between the kindness of praise, and the grossness of adulation; between affection and worship; between gratitude and idolatry.

Since the human mind is so constituted as sometimes to require remission from its stricter engagements; since it feels the need of relaxing into some intervals of pleasure; it is no unimportant object to enquire what pleasures are dangerous, what are safe, and what may even be made instructive, even where improvement is not the professed object.

The persons in question have little turn for books; might it not usefully fill many a vacant gap were they to devote a little of their leisure to rational reading? There is much valuable literature which occupies an intermediate space between strictly religious and frothy books. History, well-chosen travels, select biographical works, furnish not only harmless, but profitable reading. The study of these would improve their views; and by expanding their minds, furnish them with topics for general conversation and useful reflection. It would enlarge their charity, by letting them see that many authors are not wicked, though they do not confine their works to religious discussion.

Whatever invigorates our capacity of receiving knowledge, whatever adds new and sound ideas to our stock, is not to be despised as useless, or rejected as sinful. Be it observed, however, that general literature must not be allowed to absorb our time, nor interfere with what is of indispensable obligation; yet, if it be clear from every thing light, sceptical, or unsound, it safely fills up the otherwise idle intervals of a religious life, which without it is liable to sink into meaner recreations, and inferior pursuits.

Objects of the first importance cannot be exclusively pursued even by higher capacities than those we are considering. It is particularly necessary, therefore, for these last to supply their leisure with occupations which will furnish useful information, and matter of pleasing communication. For if the most elevated minds require the relief of change, much more does the ordinary and uncultivated intellect. It has but few images, which are soon exhausted, and must sink into weariness if it be not replenished by new ones. — Reading, such as we presume to recommend, might prevent the vacant mind from brooding over mysteries, which it has pleased the God of all wisdom, as well as all goodness, to hide from more enlightened minds than those we are contemplating. The want of something better to do, the want of resources of a higher order between the duties of the highest, reduces many persons to the most trifling ways of getting rid of time. They who allow of no intermediate reading between a sermon and a play, are often engaged in conversations, to which the most frivolous dialogues ever written would afford no adequate parallel; and they who would think it a sin to be studying the history of their country, are frequently, and perhaps eagerly enquiring into the gossip of their own village, and contributing new anecdotes to its idle annals.

Many books are useful, that are not professedly religious, for we have minds as well as souls. We may be well instructed for the purposes of this world, without invading on the more important business of another.

If then they would adopt sober literature, in exchange for indolent trifling, their minds would improve in vigour, and their tempers in cheerfulness and candour. Every unoccupied mind lays itself open to the incursion of more dangerous enemies than those it intends to avoid; such a mind takes refuge in what is more injurious than the supposed evil, into which it congratulates itself that it has not fallen. A lively "Spectator" of Mr. Addison, or a grave "Guardian" of Bishop Berkeley, would be a pleasing resource. An "Idler" or a "Rambler" of Dr. Johnson, might preserve them from realising those characters in their own persons. Such writers would teach them the knowledge of mankind, and let them into many a snug secret which lies unmolested in their own heart. Such books might correct their taste, without deducting any thing from their stock of piety, except perhaps the phrases which disfigure it; would give them a relish for better society, and thus turn their waste moments to some profit. Be it observed, we speak of persons who have much leisure; those who have little, should give that little to the one Supreme object.

These religionists delight to speak of themselves as a persecuted people; so that a stranger not accustomed to their dialect, and having been in the habit of hearing the term applied to imprisonment, anathema, and proscription, is rejoiced when he afterwards finds it means no more than a little censure, and not a little ridicule; the latter perhaps more frequently drawn on them by their quaint phrases, injudicious language, and oddity of manner, than meant to express any contempt of religion itself.

We do not pretend to say, that there is not still to be encountered that lighter species of persecution which consists in reproach, suspicion, and contempt; that there is not still an inferior kind of spiritual martyrdom, which those who would live godly in Christ Jesus must be content to suffer; a persecution which touches not the life but the fame: but this affects only Christians of a higher strain than those whom we are considering; persons who do not draw on themselves censure by their indiscretion, but by their strictness in principle, and their superiority in practice. This reproach, however, they esteem "a light evil," and are contented that as it was with the master, so it must be with the servant. It is well, however, if attack makes *even them* more discreet, and reproach more humble.

In short, the religion of the phraseologists is easy, their acquisitions cheap, their sacrifices few, their stock small, but always ready for production. This stock is rather drawn from the memory than the mind; it consists in terms rather than in ideas; in opinions rather than in principles; and is brought out on all occasions, without regard to time, place, person, or circumstance.

It has been triumphantly asserted, but probably with more confidence than truth, that the children of pious persons are not, in general, piously educated. We have known too many instances to the contrary to admit the charge.

Though a good man's religion cannot be always transmitted with his estate, yet much has been done, and is actually doing, towards this transmission: and if it is sometimes found that the fact is as has been asserted, it is, we suspect, chiefly, though perhaps not exclusively, to be found in the class we have been considering. It is perhaps in consistency with some tenets they maintain, that they neglect to prepare the ground, to sow the seed, and labour to eradicate the weeds; believing that education is of little use; trusting that whatever is good must come from above, and come in God's own time.

We, too, know that whatever is good must come from above; and that of whatever is good, God is the giver: but we know, also, that the ripening suns, and the gracious showers, and the refreshing dews, which descend from heaven, are not intended to spare the labour of cultivation, but to invigorate the plant, to fill the ear, to ripen the grain, and thus, without superseding, to reward and bless the labours of the cultivator.

AURICULAR CONFESSION.

There are certain topics which are almost too serious to be overlooked in an undertaking of this nature, and are yet almost too delicate to be touched upon.

Though we are far from thinking auricular confession the worst part of another church, yet we do not wish to see it introduced into our own, especially under the circumstances to which we are about to allude.—There are certain young ladies of good talents, and considerable cultivation, who have introduced, what we might be almost tempted to call the coquetry of religion. To the friendship of men of superior reputation for abilities and piety,—frequently to young men,— they insinuate themselves, by making a kind of false confidence. Under the humble guise of soliciting instruction and obtaining comfort, they propose to them doubts which they do not entertain, disclose difficulties which do not really distress them, ask advice which they probably do not intend to follow, and avow sensibilities with which they are not at all troubled.

This, it is to be apprehended, is a kind of pious fraud, a little stratagem to be thought better than they are, by the lowly affectation of appearing to be worse. They ask for consolation which they do not need, for they are really not unhappy; but it is gratifying to engage attention, and to excite interest. "These fanciful afflictions, these speculative discontents, after having, to the sympathising friend, appeared to be removed, are poured, with an air equally contrite, and a mind equally at ease, into the ear of the next pious, and polite listener; though the penitent had gone away from the first confessor more than absolved, the mourner more than comforted.

This confidential opening of the mind, this warm pouring forth of the soul, might be perfectly right and proper, were the communication confined to *one* spiritual director. For, here, the axiom is reversed; here, in the multitude of counsellors, there is not safety, but danger. If the perplexity be real, if the distress sincere, why not confide it to the bosom of some experienced female friend, of some able, and *aged* divine? There all would be right, and safe; there confession would bring relief, if relief and not admiration be wanted; and where the feeling of contrition is genuine, admiration will not be sought.

If the young persons in view were not really estimable, we should not have taken the liberty to guard them against this temptation to vanity and egotism. To vanity, because they go away not only with comfort, but exultation. To egotism, because they go away with an increased tendency to make self their subject!

A celebrated court *maxim-monger, who was deeply read in human nature, though he did not derive his knowledge from the best sources, nor always turn it to the best account, has however given a sound caution, from which communicative young persons might glean a lesson: "Never talk of *yourself*, neither of your good nor your bad qualities."

It is true the Christian will know the above admonition to be carried too far. He who considers that the soul is liable to diseases as well as the body, will allow the necessity for a spiritual as well as bodily physician. Now if a patient must, in order to obtain relief, tell his case to a practitioner for the body, is it to be forbidden that the languishing and dejected soul should lean for advice on a moral counsellor, "An interpreter, one of a thousand?"—But if the graces of

* Le Duc de la Rochefoucault.

the person or manner, or the hope of attracting undue attention, add nothing to the skill or worth of the adviser in one case, let us take care they do not influence our choice of the confidant in the other.

The writer has been induced to hint at the abuse of this practice, from actual instances, in which unsound confidence, and a piety too artificial, by exciting kindness and awakening sympathy, have led to ill-assorted connections, formed on a misconception of the real state of mind of the confessing party.

These remarks are by no means intended to apply to that Christian communion at once so profitable and so delightful. When the intention is simple, the heart sincere, the motive pure, and the parties suitable, such intercourse cannot but be warmly recommended. The advantage is reciprocal. The doubting and distressed spirit receives the counsel and the consolation it seeks; while the pious counsellor gains a deeper knowledge of the human mind in its varieties, by the communication of the wants, the difficulties, and the sense of sin in the contrite heart. In other religious intercourse, where there is a nearer approach of character, the heart is warmed by the expansion, and improved by the interchange of pious sentiments. The prophet even annexes to it a reward: "They that feared the Lord spake often one to another; and the Lord hearkened and heard it, and a book of remembrance was written before Him for them that feared the Lord, and that thought upon His name."

UNPROFITABLE READING.

We have already ventured to allude to the disproportionate quantity of human life which is squandered in the ever multiplying haunts of public dissipation: but as this is an evil too notorious to require any fresh animadversion, we shall not stop to insist on the excess to which it is carried, but shall advert to another, which, if less ostensible, is scarcely less mischievous—we allude to the increased and increasing prevalence of idle reading.

For whether a large proportion of our probationary being—time, that precious talent assigned us for providing for the treasures of eternity,—be consumed in unprofitable reading at home, or in frivolous diversions abroad, the effect on the state of the mind is not very dissimilar. The difference between private excess and public intoxication, is not very material as to its effects on the individual: the chief difference lies in the example and the expenses; for the mind is nearly as much unfitted for sober duties by the one, as by the other.

It is the same principle which influences the inveterate novel reader, and the never-wearied pursuer of public dissipation; only its operation is different in different tempers. The active and lively trifler seeks to lose reflection in the bustling crowd; while the more indolent alienates her mind from what is right, without any exertion of the body. In one it is the imagination which is acted upon; in the other, the senses. In one sense, indeed, the domestic idleness is the worst; because it wraps itself up in its own comparative merit, and complacently reposes on its superior sobriety; for, if the spirits are more agitated in the one case, in the other they sink into a more perilous indolence. The scenes acted over by the imagination in private, have also a superiority in mischief over those of actual, busy gaiety in others, as being more likely to be retained and repeated. Instances, however, are not rare, in which a thorough manager contrives to make both meet. In this union the injury is doubled.

But it will be urged by the too ready advocates, that *all* these books are not wicked. It is readily granted. Many works of fiction may be read with safety, some even with profit; but the constant familiarity even with such as are not exceptionable in themselves, relaxes the mind that wants hardening, dissolves the heart which wants fortifying, stirs the imagination which wants quieting, irritates the passions which want calming, and, above all, disinclines and disqualifies for active virtues, and for spiritual exercises. The habitual indulgence in such reading is a silent, mining mischief. Though there is no act, and no moment, in which any open assault on the mind is made, as in the instances previously noticed, yet the constant habit performs the work of a mental atrophy; it produces all the symptoms of decay, and the danger is not less for being more gradual, and, therefore, less suspected.

The general manners are becoming more and more relaxed. Even the old restraints, which had a regard to appearances, were not without their use. The writer remembers to have heard Dr. Johnson reprove a young lady in severe terms, for quoting a sentiment from Tom Jones — a book, he said, which, if a modest lady had done so improper a thing as to read, she should not do so immodest a thing as to avow.

Many instances might be adduced to prove, that the age is gradually grown less scrupulous. We will give only one. Another young lady, independent and rich, about the same time was tempted to send for Rousseau's Heloise. A very little progress in the work convinced her, that it was neither safe for her to read, nor, having read it, could she either modestly confess it, or conscientiously deny the perusal, if questioned. Her virtue conquered her curiosity; she sent away, unread, a book which may now be seen lying openly on the tables of many who would be shocked at the slightest imputation on the delicacy of their minds, or the scrupulousness of their morals.

But to limit the evil of idle reading to the single article of *time*:—It is, perhaps, not too much to assert, that if the hours spent by the higher and middle classes in this profitless perusal could be counted, they would, probably, far exceed in number those spent by the gay in more ostensible and public dissipation. Nay; we are almost tempted to say, that if, to the account of time dissipated by the latter, were added the hours spent by both classes in acts of devotion and serious reading, perhaps the total aggregate would be exceeded in number by the hours thrown away in the retirement of idle readers.

We are the more earnest on this subject, from being in possession of some facts which evince, beyond any persuasions, which confirm beyond any arguments, the perils which we may be thought too warm in deprecating. Among the overflowing number of fictitious writings, not a few are there in the English, and still more and worse in the French and German schools, in which the intrigue between the already married hero and heroine is opened by means so apparently innocent, and conducted so gradually, and with so much plausibility, as, for a time, to escape detection. Vicious scenes are artfully kept out of sight, while virtuous principles are silently, but systematically undermined, till the imagination, that notorious corrupter of the heart, has had time to prepare the work of destruction. Such fascinating qualities are lavished on the seducer, and such attractive graces on the seduced, that the images indulged with delight by the fancy, carry on the reader imperceptibly to a point which is not so far from their indulgence in the act as some imagine. Such soothing apologies for an amiable weakness, that is, in plain English, for the breach of the seventh Commandment, are made by the writer, that the reader begins to think her judgment is convinced, as well as her inclination gratified; and the polluted mind, brought into the state, of all others, the least willing, and the least able, to resist practical crime, is ready to exclaim, with the satyrist of political vices,

That *not* to be corrupted is the shame.

Thus the violation of as awful a prohibition as any in the decalogue, is softened down into a pardonable weakness. The stabbing the peace and honour of the husband, and the barbarous desertion of the innocent babes, or the still deeper wound given to the grown up daughters, is reduced to a venial fault, for which the irresistibleness of the temptation is shamelessly, but too successfully pleaded.

In tracing the effect, almost exclusively, of the unrestrained indulgence in these soothing pictures of varnished corruption, we could, were it prudent, produce actual instances of this breach of solemn vows, this total abandonment of all the proprieties, and all the duties of life: and it is too probable, that, besides the known instances to which allusion is here made, others might be adduced as having imbibed from the same sources the rudiments of moral misery, which has alarmingly swelled the recent list of divorces, and thus render it more than probable, that the circulating library is no unfrequent road to Doctors' Commons.

There are distinctions and gradations maintained by the squanderers of time in their several ways, of which the well-employed do not perceive the difference.

Many who would turn with contempt from the card-table, think little of giving days and nights to these pernicious, or, at best, unimproving fictions — an exchange without being an improvement; for the volumes do not, like the cards, confine the mischief to the time they are in the hands, but, as we have observed, often leave impressions behind them when the others are forgotten.

How gladly should we limit these observations to persons whose time is turned to little account, and spent with little scruple, in *any* amusement which is not obviously corrupt! But it is with real reluctance we take the liberty to animadvert on the same error, though not carried to the same excess, in persons of a higher strain of character, persons of correct manners and considerable attainments. Do not many such tolerate in their families abundance of reading which, to say the least, is not improving, and of which, frequently, this would be too gentle a censure? Even where the books contain little that is coarse or corrupt, still it must be repeated, the prodigious quantity of life they consume must exceedingly deduct from that which would otherwise be allotted to more wholesome studies.

And this is not all.—We hear passages, not the most pure in point of delicacy, and quite unequivocal in point of impiety, repeated with enthusiasm by young ladies, from the works of a noble, but profligate and infidel poet: a poet rich in abused genius, and abounding in talents, ungratefully employed to dishonour Him who gave them.—But from the same fair lips, we hear little of Milton and of Spenser, of Cowper and of Young, of Thompson and of Goldsmith, of Gray and of Beattie, names once dear to every lover of enchanting song. Nor need we look back exclusively to departed genius, for the innocent and refreshing delights of poetry. The muses have living votaries, who pour forth strains at once original, mellifluous, and chaste.

What shall we presume to say to sober-minded parents, even to grave clergymen, who not only do not prohibit the authors of the school in question; who not only do not restrain their daughters from being students in it, but who not unfrequently introduce, as part of the family reading, poetry, which if it contain not the gross expressions, and vulgar wickedness of the wits of Charles's days, is little less prophane in principle, or corrupt in sentiment? There is some knowledge which it is a praise not to know; and the vice in this case being somewhat refined through certain strainers, furnishes at once a temptation and an apology.

It may be urged, in vindication of this remissness, that as soon as young persons get out of their parents' hands, they will naturally choose their books for themselves. This is granted. — But is not every year which prolongs their precious innocence, a year gained? May not, within that period, the nascent libertinism be checked, the ardent imagination fixed to other pursuits, the sentiment of virtue kindled, the taste for purity confirmed, and the habit and love of prayer established? And, above all, is it not a pity that they should be able hereafter to plead as an apology for their intimacy with such books, that they were introduced to them by a fond and careful parent?

May we not take the liberty to ask of worthy, but, in this instance, injudicious parents, is this practice quite consistent with the command given to fathers, even under a darker dispensation, that they should not limit the improvement of their children to any set hours, but that they should "teach them diligently, sitting in the house, and walking by the way, rising up, and lying down?"

THE BORDERERS.

Religion, and the world, used formerly to be considered as two different regions, situated separate and apart from each other. They seldom maintained much unnecessary intercourse. One party shuddered at the strictness and severity of the other; which, in its turn, kept aloof from a communication which it feared might contaminate its own purity. Between them lay a kind of neutral ground, which, though it divided them, was however occasionally passed during any short interval of peace, for offices of necessity, of business, or of kindness; offices which, nevertheless, produced at no time entire reconciliation.

This neutral territory has been lately seized upon and occupied by a third party, a civil, obliging, and accommodating people, who are so perfectly well-bred, as to be desirous of keeping well with their neighbours on both sides the boundary. They are invited to intimacy by the gratifications held out by the one, and the reputation conferred by the other; present indulgence tempts on the left, future hope on the right. The present good, however, is generally too powerful a competitor for the future. They not only struggle to maintain their own interest in both countries, but are kindly desirous of accommodating all differences between the belligerent powers. Their situation, as borderers, gives them great local advantages on both sides. Though they keep on the same good terms with both, they have the useful and engaging talent, of seeming to belong exclusively to that party in which they happen to find themselves.

"Their chief difficulty arises when they happen to meet the inhabitants of both territories together; yet so ingenious are they in the art of trimming, that they contrive not to lose much ground with either.

"When alone with one party, they take care never to speak warmly of the absent. With the worldly they smile, and perhaps good-naturedly shake their head at some little scruples, and some excess of strictness in the absent party, though they do not go the length of actual censure.

"When with the religious colony, they tenderly lament the necessity imposed on them of being obliged to associate so much with neighbours from whom, they confess, there is not much to be learned, while they own there is something to be feared; but, as they *are quite sure* their inclination is not of the party, they trust there is no great danger. They regret, that as they *must* live on terms with the world, they cannot, without a singularity to which ridicule would attach, avoid adopting some of their manners and customs. Thus they think it prudent to indulge in the same habits of luxury and expense, to conform to many of the same practices, doubtful at the best, and to attend on some places of diversion, for which, indeed, they profess to feel no great relish, and which, for the sake of propriety, are rather submitted to than enjoyed. "One would not be particular, one does no good by singularity."

By an invariable discretion, they thus gain the confidence and regard of both parties. The old settlers on the fashionable side are afraid of losing them, by opposition to their occasionally joining their enemies; while the religious colonies are desirous of retaining them, and rendering them service by courtesy and kindness, still charitably hoping their intentions are right, and their compliances reluctant. — Thus their borders are every day extending, and their population increasing. As they can speak, as occasion requires, the language of both countries, they have the advantage of appearing to be always at home with each, who never suspect that the same facility in the dialect of the other, equally secures their popularity there.

In one respect, they carefully comply with the Apostle's injunction, applying to it, however, a meaning of their own, "They let their moderation be known unto all men." They scrupulously avoid extremes. They keep a kind of debtor and creditor account with religion and the world, punctually paying themselves for some practice they renounce, by adopting some other which is a shade or two lighter: between these shades they discriminate nicely; and the pride they feel in what they have given up, is more sincere than the gratification at what they retain.

Thus, though hovering on the borders of both countries, they do not penetrate into the depths of either. The latitude they happen to be cast in varies according to circumstances. An awakening sermon will drive them, for a time, beyond the usual geographical degree; an amusing novel, or a new Canto of Childe Harold, will seduce them to retreat. Their intentions however, they flatter themselves, are generally on the right side, while their movements are too frequently on the other.

But though their language can accommodate itself to both parties, their personal appearance is entirely under the direction of one of them. In their external decorations, they are not behind the foremost of their fashionable friends; and truth obliges us reluctantly to confess, that their dress is as little confined within the bounds of strict delicacy, as that of women the rest of whose conduct is more exceptionable. The consequence is not unnatural; for to those who must *do* like other people, it is also necessary to *look* like other people. It does, however, seem a little incongruous, to hear the language of one of the countries spoken, even with a strong accent, by ladies in the full costume of the other.

These borderers are frequently disposed to be benevolent, partly from a warm temperament, partly from a conviction that charity is a duty. They profess to give whatever they can spare, but of that proportion they allow vanity, and not piety, to be the arbiter. If personal ornament, if habits of luxury, did not swallow up their money, charity would have it. Charity is the next best thing to self-gratification.

Should they continue their present course, and their numbers increase, or, as is commonly the case, should continual motion accelerate progress, the landmarks of separation between the several countries will insensibly be lost, and it will be difficult to define the exact limitations of the invading neighbours.

It has frequently been regretted that an amicable accommodation between the adverse parties could not be accomplished by the interference of this intermediate region. But whenever it has been attempted, it has not always been successful. The coalition, it has been found, could not readily be brought about. Prejudices on the one part, and rigorous demands on the other, have hitherto perpetuated the separation.

Terms of peace, indeed, cannot easily be made where one side expects so many sacrifices, and where the other has so much that must be parted with. The worldly territory having, beyond all comparison, the larger population, is of course the stronger, and therefore most likely to hold out.

But though no actual flag of truce has yet been sent out for a general peace, yet alliances are frequently contracted between individuals of the hostile countries, but on very unequal terms; for it unfortunately happens that the party from the more correct side, "who come out to visit the daughters of the land," have been seduced by the cheerful music, splendid banners, and gay attractions of the other; and have been prevailed upon to settle in the enemy's camp. To them it more frequently happens that they gradually forget all they learnt in their father's house, and insensibly adopt the manners of the strange country, than that they bring over the other party to their side. It may, therefore, perhaps be safer not to contract these *unholy alliances*, till there is a conquest obtained by the small territory over the great one; an event which, if we may judge by the present state of the parties, seems at a very considerable distance.

But enough, and perhaps the scrupulous Christian will say, too much, of this light manner of treating a serious subject. We acknowledge the charge; we bow to the correction: confessing that we scarcely knew how to approach this important and interesting class of persons, without the thin veil of something between fiction and fact, between allegory and true history. We felt an almost sinful reluctance to say any thing which might seem revolting to those pleasing characters who have shown some disposition to religion, who love its disciples, without having courage to imitate them. But real concern for their best interests will not allow those who assume to advocate the cause of Christianity, to conceal the distance at which they at present appear to stand from its constraining power, and from its practical consequences.

Perhaps your creed is not very erroneous. Probably the rectitude of your religious friends, whose doctrines are sound, and the indifference of your fashionable friends, who " care for none of these things," have preserved you pretty clear from errors of opinion. Whilst the occasional society of the pious has kept your sentiments in order, the amusements of the worldly have indemnified you for the severities of the other quarter. But opinions do little till they are ripened into principles. It is reputable to say with one party, "straight is the gate and narrow is the way;" but the company of the other lets you see that it is not so easy to enter in at that gate, and to walk in that way, as you had flattered yourself you should have found it.

To you the *world* is by far the most formidable foe of the triple alliance, of the three confederate enemies, which the Scripture tells us war against the soul. We have presumed that your opinions may not be very erroneous, but there are moral as well as speculative heresies, of which worldliness is the originating principle, and in which it is the practical operator. The WORLD is the grand heresiarch. There are many more who " love the world, and the things of the world," than who care whether doctrines are true or false. While they themselves are let alone to follow their own devices; while they are left undisturbed to their own pursuits; you may propound, or controvert, or adopt any opinion, sound or heretical, with equally little danger, with equally little benefit to them.

To the devotee of pleasure there is something harsh and repulsive in doctrines and dogmas; to take part with them would be going out of the way; while to those who can contrive to make right opinions live on friendly terms with wrong practices, it would be a gratuitous folly to add to the faults of conduct the errors of speculation.

In this affectionate remonstrance, we allude not to what might be called palpable and tangible offences; these the decorums of their condition set them above any temptation to commit. We speak not of any disbelief or contempt of religion; these are not the immediate perils of their position: it is not infidelity but indifference — a disinclination to Christianity, not as opposed to unbelief, but as it contradicts the maxims, the manners, the habits of their associates. Their danger consists in a supreme attachment to present objects, and a neglect of such as are future; it consists in preferring the pleasures and the interests of the world to the service of Him who made it. They are governed by other principles than those of that gospel which has proclaimed that "the friendship of the world is enmity against God." They are influenced by its opinions, misled by its example, enslaved by its amusements; they fear lest any deviation from its prescribed code should bring their good sense and good taste in question; lest withdrawing from its practices should bring on them the imputation of narrowness or enthusiasm. In short, they go with "the multitude that keep holiday," not, indeed, in the scriptural sense, but in direct conformity to the vulgar acceptation of that term.

Worldly allurements find in the unrenewed heart a willingness to meet them, a disposition accommodated to them by temperament, a readiness to pursue them, increased by habit. The natural heart is already on the world's side. Before the world has time to begin its attack, the citadel is disposed to yield. Before the assault is made, there is a mutual good understanding, a silent connivance between the besiegers and the besieged. As soon as the trenches are opened, the disposition to parley and to submit is nearly the same act.

You appeared, however, to take the first step in what is right, by occasionally joining religious society, and by the pleasure you expressed in it. By that introduction you seemed not undesirous of ranging yourself partly on that side. Having broken through that first obstruction, it was hoped that every subsequent step would have become less irksome.

That religion has its difficulties, we do not pretend to deny; but, with a hearty concurrence of the will, nurtured by cordial prayer, strengthened by a full reliance on the Saviour, and sustained by the aid of His Spirit, which is offered you, the difficulties will daily diminish. Rest not, then, in that low state of religion which is satisfied with the hope of escaping punishment; calculate not how small a measure may suffice to effect that escape. Search not out for an imaginary intermediate state between the children of wrath and the children of God. Rest not till you have attained that entire consecration of heart, whose object, aim, and end, is eternal life. Forget not that they who run in a race, though they may come closer to the goal, yet, if they come short of it, fail of the prize as completely as those competitors whose distance is greater; and, if we come short of heaven, whether we lose it by more or fewer steps, the failure is equally decisive, the loss equally irreparable.

Those worldly persons with whom you associate are intrenched on every side by numbers; they therefore act as if they thought that the evil, supposing it to be evil, which is shared among so many, cannot be injurious to the individual; forgetting that every man must bear his own burden, and suffer for his own sin; for, though multitudes may give countenance to your errors here, they will not answer for you hereafter.

Do not follow those who have no settled course of their own — who are hurried to and fro by every breath of custom — whom fashion leadeth whithersoever it listeth. The persons against whom we would guard you, though confident, are not without their fears; but it is worth observing, that their fears seldom lie on the same side with their dangers. They fear not great practical errors; these they soften down and treat with complacency; these are tenderly mentioned as the infirmities of nature — weaknesses to which we are all liable. Almost every excess in personal gratification is thus kindly palliated: "Why did God give us both the disposition and the means to indulge it, if indulgence were a sin?" There is but one excess they guard against — an excess, indeed, of which they are in little danger,—we mean a high degree of religion; for surely excess is little to be feared, where the thing has not yet even been entered upon!

Be assured, that whatever serves to keep the heart from God, is one and the same spirit of irreligion, whether it appear in the shape of coarse vice, or whether it is softened by the smoothness of decorum, and the blandishments of polished life. We are far from comparing them together, as if they were equally injurious to society, or equally offensive to decency; but we *must* compare them together as equally drawing away the heart from the worship and the love of God. Courteousness, which is unaccompanied by principle, will stand the most courteous in no stead, with Him who is a discerner of the thoughts and intents of the heart.

Some of these well-bred persons, who exercise this large and liberal candour towards practical offences, and treat with tenderness certain vices, not thought disreputable by the world, and who even put a favourable construction on things very unjustifiable in the sight of God, lose all their kindness, put no favourable interpretation, when sound religion is in question. They are, indeed, too discreet to reprobate it under its own proper name, but the ready appellation of enthusiasm presents itself—is always at hand to vindicate the hastiest judgment, and the most contemptuous construction.

But though we think far better things of you, whom we are addressing, yet may you not, in this society, be tempted to disavow, or, at least, to conceal, even the measure of piety you actually have, for fear of exciting that dreaded suspicion, of " being righteous over much?" May not this fear, strengthened by this society, keep you back till your pious tendencies, by being suppressed, may gradually come to be extinguished?

We are ready to acknowledge, and

to love, all that is amiable in you; but we must not forget, that the fairest and most brilliant creature, the most engaging manners, and the most accomplished mind, stands in the same need of repentance, forsaking of sin, redemption by the Son of God, and renovation by His Spirit, as the least attractive. The more engaging the manners, and the more interesting the acquirements, the more is it to be lamented, that those very attractions, by your complacency in them, may have stood between you and heaven,—may, by your resting in them, have been the cause of your not pressing towards the mark for the prize of your high calling of God in Christ Jesus.

Bear then in mind, that you may be pleasing to others, while you have an unsanctified heart; that politeness, though it may put on the appearance of humility, is but a poor imitation of that prime grace; that good breeding, though the beautiful decoration of a pious mind, is but a wretched substitute for the want of it.

Be assured, however, at the same time, that true religion will in no wise diminish your natural or acquired graces; so far from it, those graces will be more estimable; they will be even more admired, when they are known not to be the best things you have. When you set less value on them yourself, they will be more pleasing to others; who, though they will not estimate them above their worth, will not depreciate them below it.

We are persuaded that you are too reasonable to expect that Christianity will change its character, or lower its requirements, or make the straight gate wider, or the narrow way broader, or hold out false colours, in order to induce you to embrace it. It is not that easy and superficial thing which some suppose, as requiring little more than a ceremonious attendance on its forms, and a freedom from the gross violation of its commands. This may be nominal, but it is not saving Christianity. It is not that spiritual, yet practical religion, for which the Son of God endured the cross, that He might establish it in the hearts of His followers,—which He is pleading with His Heavenly Father to establish in your heart. He did not suffer that His children might be excused from self-denial; nor that, because He was holy, they might be negligent. He suffered, that " the women that are at ease might rise up; that the careless daughters might hear His voice, and give ear unto His word."

If you are disposed to think that what you must give up is great, compare it with what you will gain, and you will be ashamed of your miscalculation; you will think the sacrifice as small as the objects sacrificed were worthless; for Christianity, though a self-denying principle, yet denies you nothing which, even now, adds to your real happiness. It only disenchants you from an illusion, and gives you substantial peace in exchange. It will rob you of nothing which good sense and sound reason do not condemn, as well as the New Testament.

Perhaps you have just religion enough to render you occasionally uneasy. The struggle between the claims of the world and your casual convictions, is far from being a happy state. The flattery which delights, misleads; the diversions which amuse, will not console: the prospect, which promises, disappoints. Continue not, then, " working in the fire for very vanity." Labour not to reconcile two interests, which, spite of your endeavours, will ever remain irreconcileable.

A life governed by Christianity differs in every thing from the worldly system. It is free from the turbulence and the agitation of its pursuits: it has none of the anxieties and jealousies of its competitions; consequently none of the lassitude and the vexation of its disappointing results. The further you proceed in its paths of pleasantness, the pleasanter they become. Its difficulties diminish, its delights increase. It has pleasures of its own, higher and better; satisfactions which depend not on human admiration, but on His favour, whom to know is eternal life.

Continue not, then, to live as if the great end for which you were sent into the world, was already accomplished. Continue not to act as if you thought you had done all for which God gave you an intelligent mind, reasoning faculties, aspiring thoughts, capacities for endless happiness. Let not those powers which were meant to fit you, not only for the society of angels, but for the vision of God, be any longer wasted on objects the most frivolous; on things which, at best, must end when this world ends. Oh! renounce pursuits, some of them below a rational, unsuited to an accountable, and altogether unworthy of a never-ending being! Renounce them for objects more becoming a candidate for an inheritance among the saints in light, better adapted to an immaterial, immortal spirit, and commensurate with eternity.

REFLECTIONS

ON

PRAYER,

AND

ON THE ERRORS WHICH MAY
PREVENT ITS EFFICACY.

ON THE CORRUPTION OF HUMAN NATURE.

THE most original French writer of our own time, but who employed his powerful talents to the most pernicious purposes, abruptly begins his once popular work on education with this undeniable truth, — " All is good as it comes out of the hands of God, all is corrupted in the hands of man."

In his first position, this sceptic bears a just testimony to the goodness of his Creator; but the second clause, his subsequent application of it, though also a truth, is not the whole truth. He ascribes all the evils of man to the errors of his institution.

Now, though it cannot be denied that many of his faults are owing to a defect in education, yet his prime evil lies deeper, is radical, and must be traced to a more remote and definite cause.

Had the writer been as enlightened as he was ingenious, he would have seen that the principle of evil was antecedent to his education; that it is to be found in the inborn corruption of the human heart. If then, from an infidel, we are willing to borrow an avowal of the goodness of God in the creation of man, we must look to higher authorities to account for his degeneracy, even to the sacred oracles of God himself.

The subject of man's apostacy is so nearly connected with the subject of prayer, being indeed that which constitutes the necessity of this duty, that some mention of the one ought to precede any discussion of the other. Let, then, the conviction, that we are fallen from our original state, and that this lapse furnishes the most powerful incentive to prayer, furnish an apology for making a few preliminary remarks on this doctrine.

The doctrine is not the less a fundamental doctrine, because it has been abused to the worst purposes; some having considered it as leaving us without hope, and others, as lending an excuse to unresisted sin. — It is a doctrine which meets us in one unbroken series throughout the whole sacred volume; we find it from the third of Genesis, which records the event of man's apostacy, carried on through the history of its fatal consequences in all the subsequent instances of sin, individual and national, and running in one continued stream from the first sad tale of woe, to the close of the sacred canon in the Apocalyptic Vision.

And, to remove the groundless hope, that this quality of inherent corruption belonged only to the profligate and abandoned, the Divine Inspirer of the sacred writers took especial care, that they should not confine themselves to relate the sins of these alone.

Why are the errors, the weaknesses, and even the crimes of the best men recorded with equal fidelity? Why are we told of the twice repeated deceit of the father of the faithful? Why of the single instance of vanity in Hezekiah? Why of the too impetuous zeal of Elijah? Why of the error of the almost perfect Moses? Why of the insincerity of Jacob? Why of the far darker crimes of the otherwise holy David? Why of the departure of the wisest of men from that piety, displayed with sublimity unparalleled in the dedication of the Temple? Why seems it to have been invariably studied, to record with more minute detail the vices and errors of these eminent men, than even those of the successive impious kings of Israel, and of Judah; while these last are generally dismissed with the brief, but melancholy sentence, that they did that which was evil in the sight of the Lord; followed only by too frequent an intimation, that they made way for a successor worse than themselves? The answer is, that the truth of our universal lapse could only be proved by transmitting the record of those vices, from which even the holiest men were not exempt.

And as these affecting details unanswerably establish the truth of the doctrine, so they are not recorded for barren doctrinal information. They are recorded to furnish Christians of every age with salutary caution, with awful warning.

Surely the best man among us will hardly venture to say, that he is more holy than Abraham, Moses, David, or Peter. If, then, these saints exhibited such evidences of not having escaped the universal infection, will not every reflecting child of mortality yield to the conviction, that this doctrine is as true as the history which has recorded it? Will he not proceed further to say, " How then shall I be high-minded? How shall I not fear? How shall I deny the cause of the evil tendencies of my own heart, the sins of my own life, the thoughts of foolishness, and the actings of iniquity within myself?" And will not such serious enquiry, by God's grace, acting on the study of the characters of these highly eminent, but not perfect worthies of old times, patriarchs, prophets, and saints, lead the enquirer, through the redemption wrought for all, and faith in the operation of the blessed Spirit, to that effectual repentance, and fervent prayer, to which, in this same Divine history, such gracious promises are made?

Had the Holy Scriptures kept back from man the faithful delineations of the illustrious characters to which we have referred, the truth of the doctrine in question, though occasionally felt, and in spite of his resistance, forced upon him, would not have been believed; or, if believed, would not have been acknowledged.

It is, then, one great end of the oracles of Divine truth, to humble man, under a sense of his inherent and actual corruptions. The natural man feels it repugnant to his pride to suppose this doctrine is addressed to him.

It is very true, that this all-important doctrine of human corruption, is, like many other truths, both in the natural, moral, and spiritual world, liable to certain speculative objections, and metaphysical difficulties. Laying hold on these, which, often, a child might discover, and no philosopher be able to answer, even upon merely philosophical subjects, we excuse ourselves altogether from studying the Divine book; and fearful, in secret, of the discoveries we should make, pretend that its Author has left truth so obscure, as to be impervious to human eyes; or so lofty, as to be above human reach.

But is it not making God unjust, and even the author of that sin which he charges on ourselves, to suppose that he had put truth and knowledge out of our reach, and then threatened to punish us for failing in that which he himself had made impossible? Is it probable that He, whose eyes you say are so pure, that he cannot look upon iniquity, should tolerate it, by tying our hands, and blinding our eyes, and thus abandon us to the unrestrained dominion of that which he hates?

The only real question which concerns us in our present imperfect and probationary state, is this:— Are the statements of revelation sufficient to establish this or that doctrine? And is the doctrine so established a sufficient ground for the duties required? If this be answered in the affirmative, then to ask for fewer difficulties, clearer light, or stronger motives to action, is only to enter a vain contest with Almighty wisdom, and Divine supremacy. Our present disobedience proves that more light would only increase our guilt, stronger motives would only render us more inexcusable. We should reject then what we neglect now. To refuse what we now have, is not for want of light, but of eyes: not for want of motives, but of faith; not for want of rules, but of obedience; not for want of knowledge, but of will. Let us then pity those blind eyes which do not see, and especially those wilful eyes which will not see.

The Christian revelation, as far as respects its professed practical purpose, is brought within the reach of the plainest understanding. We speak of the Gospel itself, and not of those metaphysical perplexities with which the schools have endeavoured to meet metaphysical objections; we speak of the fundamental truths on which God has made salvation to depend. The unlettered Christian lays hold on those truths which the philosopher misses. The former looks to the Holy Spirit for his teacher, the latter to his own understanding. The one lives holily, and thus, " by doing the will of

God, he comes to know of the doctrine whether it be of God."

Christianity hangs on a few plain truths; " that God is, and that he is the rewarder of all that seek him;" that man has apostatised from his original character, and by it has forfeited his original destination; that Christ came into this world and died upon the cross to expiate sin, and to save sinners; that after his ascension into Heaven, he did not leave his work imperfect. He sent his Holy Spirit, who performed his first office by giving to the Apostles miraculous powers. His offices did not cease there; he has indeed withdrawn his miraculous gifts, but he still continues his silent but powerful operations, and that in their due order,—first, that of convincing of sin, and of changing the heart of the sinner, before he assumes the gracious character of the Comforter. What need, then, of heresies to perplex doctrines, or of philosophy to entangle, or of will-worshippers to multiply them?

We do not deny that there are, in Christianity, high and holy mysteries; but these " secret things," though they " belong to God," have their practical uses for us; they teach us humility, the prime Christian grace; and they exercise faith, the parent attribute of all other graces.

This religion of facts, then, the poorest listeners in the aisles of our churches understand sufficiently, to be made by it wise unto salvation. They are saved by a practical belief of a few simple, but inestimable truths.

By these same simple truths, martyrs and confessors, our persecuted saints, and our blessed reformers, were saved. By these few simple truths, Locke, and Boyle, and Newton, were saved; not because they saw their religion through the glass of their philosophy, but because theirs was not " a philosophy, falsely so called;" nor their science, " a science of opposition;" but a science and a philosophy which were made subservient to Christianity, and because their deep humility sanctified their astonishing powers of mind. These wonderful men, at whose feet the learned world is still satisfied to sit, sat themselves at the feet of Jesus. Had there been any other way but the cross by which sinners could be saved, they, perhaps, of all men, were best qualified to have found it.

The wise and the weak, the illiterate and the learned, cannot, indeed, equally discuss or expound these doctrines, but they are equally saved by them. In view of the simple means of salvation, talents lose their superiority, learning its dignity, and power its pre-eminence. While the sober Christian keeps on his safe, because prescribed course; the wise, and th disputer of this world, by deserting it fall into absurdities which plain men escape; they make the difficulties they do not find, and wander in the endless mazes of presumptuous deviation.

To return, then, to the particular doctrines under consideration:—Let us believe man is corrupt, because the Bible tells us he is so. Let us believe that such were so by nature, even the best, since we learn it from the Divine source. Let us, from the same authority, trace the disorder to its source from a fallen parent, its seat in a corrupted heart, its extent through the whole man, its universality over the entire race.

All are willing to allow that we are subject to frailties, to imperfections, to infirmities; facts compel us to confess a propensity to crimes, but worldly men confine the commission of them to the vulgar. But to rest here would lead us to a very false estimate of the doctrine in question, contrary to the decisive language of Scripture; it would establish corruption to be an accident, and not a root. It would, by a division of offenders into two classes, deny that all offences are derived from one common principle.

Among the higher ranks there is little temptation to the commission of certain sins; murder is rare, fraud uncommon, robbery not found, yet the inborn principle is the same in all. Circumstances, rank, education, example, reputation, give advantages to one class, which, had they changed places, might have led to the vices so common in the other; while, had the notorious offenders against the laws and the Divine law-giver, changed situations with their superiors, we should then have heard only of *their* imperfections, *their* infirmities, their *frailties*.

Temptation does not make the sin, it lies ready in the heart. Accident does not create the propensity, it only brings it into action. It destroys the plea of exemption from natural corruption, but it does not put that corruption *into* the heart. It was there before, ready, without the grace of God, ready, without the restraint of religion, ready, without the bridle of an enlightened conscience, to break out into any excess. Yet there are many flagrant offences against God and against human laws, which the high-born and the high-bred frequently commit with as little scruple as the lowest. The frequency of duelling, the breach of the seventh commandment, two offences frequently found in the same company, gaming, the violation of the Sabbath, with other enormities, would alone sufficiently prove the principle to exist, independently of rank, education, or fortune. Are not what, by way of distinction, we may call the metaphysical or spiritual sins, which are cherished without loss of character — is not ambition, which knows no bounds — envy, which knows no rest — avarice, which destroys all feeling — jealousy, which is its own tormentor — ill-temper, which is the tormentor of others — ungoverned anger, which is murder in its first seed; are not all these equally to be found in the high-born and the low-bred? Again, is not sensuality in the great, which, in the case of the poor, might have produced unfair means to indulge it — is not the love of splendour and ostentation, which are thought to add dignity to the rich, the very principle which leads the necessitous to forgery, the crime for which so many are now suffering capital punishment?

If then men would examine their own bosoms as closely, as they censure the faults of others loudly, we should all find there the incipient stirrings of many a sin, which, when brought into action, by the temptations of poverty, of ignorance, of unresisted passion, produce consequences the most appalling. Let us then bless God, not that we are better than other men, but that we are placed by Providence out of the reach of being goaded by that temptation, stimulated by that poverty, which, had they been our lot, might have led to the same termination.

Let then the fear of God, the knowledge of his word, and the knowledge of ourselves, teach us that there is not, by nature, so wide a difference between ourselves and the men we abhor as we fondly fancy; that there is not, by nature, a great gulf fixed, that they who are on this side might not have passed over to the other. Let us not look to any superior virtue, to any native strength of our own, but let us look with a lively gratitude to that mercy of God which has preserved us from such temptations; to his unmerited goodness, which has placed us in circumstances that have put us above necessity — "the devil's plea." But, above all, let us look to that preventing and restraining grace which is withheld from none who ask it, and we shall not be so very forward to say, contemptuously, to the worst of our fellow-creatures, "stand by, I am holier than thou." A thorough belief in this doctrine would lead us to pray more fervently to be delivered in "all time of our wealth, as in all time of our tribulation."

It is not enough that God has *revealed* the way of salvation, he must also incline us to *accept* it. It is this gift, and this acceptance, which makes the distinction between the best men and the worst. Without this all-powerful grace, Latimer might have led Bonner to the stake;

with it, Bonner might have ascended the scaffold a martyr to true religion. Without this grace, Luther might have fattened on the sale of indulgences; and with it, Leo the Tenth might have accomplished the blessed work of the reformation.

FALSE NOTIONS OF THE DIGNITY OF MAN, SHEWN FROM HIS HELPLESSNESS AND DEPENDENCE.

MAN is not only a sinful, he is also a helpless, and therefore a dependent being. This offers new and powerful motives for the necessity of prayer, the necessity of looking continually to a higher power, to a better strength than our own. If that Power sustain us not, we fall; if He direct us not, we wander. His guidance is not only perfect freedom, but perfect safety. Our greatest danger begins from the moment we imagine we are able to go alone.

The self-sufficiency of man, arising from his imaginary dignity, is a favourite doctrine with the nominal Christian.

He feeds his pride with this pernicious aliment. The contrary opinion is so closely connected, indeed is so intimately blended, with the subject of the preceding chapter, that we shall have the less occasion to extend our present observations to any length.

We hear much, and we hear falsely, of the dignity of human nature. Prayer, founded on the true principles of Scripture, alone teaches us wherein our true dignity consits. The dignity of a fallen creature is a perfect anomaly. True dignity, contrary to the common opinion, that it is an inherent excellence, is actually a sense of the want of it; it consists not in our valuing ourselves, but in a continual feeling of our dependence upon God, and an unceasing aim at conformity to his image.

Nothing but a humbling sense of the sinfulness of our nature, of our practised offences, of our utter helplessness, and constant dependence, can bring us to fervent and persevering prayer. How did the faith of the saints of old flourish under a darker dispensation, through all the clouds and ignorance which obscured their views of God. "They looked unto Him and were enlightened!" How do their slender means and high attainments reproach us!

David found that the strength and spirit of nature which had enabled him to resist the lion and the bear, did not enable him to resist his outward temptations, nor to conquer his inward corruptions. He therefore prayed, not only for deliverance "from blood guiltiness," for a grievously remembered sin, he prayed for the *principle* of piety, for the *fountain* of holiness, for "the creation of a clean heart," for "the renewing of a right spirit," for "truth in the inward parts," that the "comfort of God's help might be granted him." This uniform avowal of the secret workings of sin, this uniform dependence on the mercy of God to pardon, and the grace of God to assist, render his precatory addresses, though they are those of a sovereign and a warrior, so universally applicable to the case of every private Christian.

One of our best poets—himself an unsuccessful courtier—from a personal experience of the mortifying feelings of abject solicitation, has said, that if there were the man in the world whom he was at liberty to hate, he would wish him no greater punishment than attendance and dependence. But he applies the heavy penalty of this wish to the dependants on mortal greatness.

Now, attendance and dependence are the very essence both of the safety and happiness of a Christian. Dependence on God is his only true liberty, as attendance on Him is his only true consolation. The suitor for human favour is liable to continual disappointment;—if he knock at the door of his patron, there is probably a general order not to admit him. In the higher case, there is a special promise, that " to him that knocks it shall be opened."

The human patron hates importunity; the Heavenly Patron invites it. The one receives his suitor, according to his humour, or refuses his admission from the caprice of the moment; with the other, " there is no variableness nor shadow of turning :" " Come unto me," is his uniform language.

The man in power has many claimants on his favour, and comparatively few boons to bestow. The God of Power has all things in His gift, and only blames the solicitor for coming so seldom, or coming so late, or staying so little a while. He only wishes that His best gifts were more earnestly sought.

When we solicit an earthly benefactor, it is often upon the strength of some pretence to his favour — the hope of some reward for past services: even if we can produce little claim, we insinuate something like merit. But when we approach our Heavenly Benefactor, so far from having any thing like claim, any thing like merit to produce, our only true, and our only acceptable plea, is our utter want both of claim and merit — is the utter destitution of all that can recommend us; yet we presume to ask favour, when we deserve nothing but rejection; we are encouraged to ask for eternal happiness, when we deserve only eternal punishment. Though we have nothing to produce but disloyalty, we ask for the privilege of subjects; though nothing but disobedience to offer, we plead the privileges of children — we implore the tenderness of a father.

In dependence on God there is nothing abject; in attendance on Him, nothing servile. He never, like the great ones of the world, receives the suitor with a petrifying frown, or, what is worse, never dismisses him with a cruel smile and a false promise.

Even if the petitioner to human power escape the vexation of being absolutely rejected; even if his suit be granted, the grant, it may be, is accompanied with a mortifying coldness, with an intelligible hint that the donor expects to be no further troubled. The grant may be attended with such a tedious delay, as may make it no benefit. The boon granted does not, perhaps, prove so valuable as the applicant expected; or he finds he might have spent the long season of his attendance, his watching, and his waiting, to better purpose; or he might have employed his interest in another quarter, in obtaining something more important; or, after all, he may have received it too late in life to turn it to the profitable account he had expected.

But the Almighty Donor never puts off His humble petitioner to a more convenient season. His Court of Requests is always open. He receives the petition as soon as it is offered; He grants it as soon as it is made; and, though He will not dispense with a continuance of the application, yet to every fresh application

He promises fresh support. He will still be solicited, but it is in order that He may still bestow. Repeated gifts do not exhaust His bounty, nor lessen His power of fulfilment. Repeated solicitation, so far from wearying His patience, is an additional call for His favour.

Nor is the lateness of the petition any bar to its acceptance: He likes it should be early, but He rejects it not though it be late.

With a human benefactor, the consciousness of having received former favours, is a motive with a modest petitioner for preventing his making an application for more; while, on the contrary, God even invites us to call on Him for future mercies, by the powerful plea of His past acts of goodness—" even mercies which have been ever of old." And as past mercies on God's part, so, to the praise of His grace be it said, that past offences on our own part are no hindrance to the application of hearty repentance, or the answer of fervent prayer.

The petitioner to human power, who may formerly have offended his benefactor, contrives to soften his displeasure, by representing that the offence was a small one. The devout petitioner to God uses no such subterfuge. In the boldness of faith, and the humility of repentance, he cries, " Pardon my iniquity, for it is *great*."

It is no paradox, then, to assert that dependence on God is the only true safety; dependence upon Him, the only true freedom — freedom from doubt, and fear, and sin; freedom from human dependence; above all, freedom from dependence on ourselves. As pardoned sinners, through the redemption wrought for them, find, in the renewed nature, a restoration to that dignity they had forfeited, so those who are most destitute of the dignity which arises from this dependence, missing the reality, deceive themselves with the shadow.

He who does not believe this fundamental truth, on which the other doctrines of the Bible are built,—even he who does nominally profess to assent to it as a doctrine of Scripture; yet, if he does not experimentally acknowledge it; if he does not feel it in the convictions of his own awakened conscience, in his discovery of the evil workings of his own heart, and the wrong propensities of his own nature, all bearing their testimony to its truth—such a one will not pray earnestly for its cure—will not pray with that feeling of his own helplessness, with that sense of dependence on Divine assistance, which alone makes prayer efficacious.

Of this corruption he can never attain an adequate conception, till his progress in religion has opened his eyes on what is the natural state of man. Till this was the case, he himself was as far from desiring the change, as he was from believing it necessary. He does not even suspect its existence, till he is in some measure delivered from its dominion.

Nothing will make us truly humble, nothing will make us constantly vigilant, nothing will entirely lead us to have recourse to prayer so fervently or so frequently, as this ever abiding sense of our corrupt nature,—as our not being able to ascribe any disposition in ourselves, to any thing that is good, or any power to avoid, by our own strength, any thing that is evil.

THE OBLIGATION OF PRAYER UNIVERSAL — REGULAR SEASONS TO BE OBSERVED. — THE SCEPTIC AND THE SENSUALIST REJECT PRAYER.

AMONG the many articles of erroneous calculation, to which so much of the sin and misery of life may be attributed, the neglect or misuse of prayer will not form the lightest. The prophet Jeremiah, in his impassioned address to the Almighty, makes no distinction between those who acknowledge no God, and those who live without prayer. "Pour out thy fury, O Lord, upon the heathen, and upon the families that call not upon thy name."

Some duties are more incumbent on some persons, and some on others; depending on the difference of talents, wealth, leisure, learning, station, and opportunities; but the duty of prayer is of imperative obligation; it is universal, because it demands none of any of the above requisites; it demands only a willing heart, a consciousness of sin, a sense of dependence, a feeling of helplessness. Those who voluntarily neglect it, shut themselves out from the presence of their Maker. " I know you not," must assuredly be the sentence of exclusion on those who thus " know not God." Nothing, it is true, can exclude them from His inspection, but they exclude themselves from his favour.

Many nearly renounce prayer, by affecting to make it so indefinite a thing, as not to require regular exercise. Just as many, also, unhallow the Sabbath, who pretend they do nothing on week-days, which they should fear to do on Sundays. The truth is, instead of sanctifying the week-days by raising them to the duties of Sunday — which is, indeed, impracticable, let men talk as they please,—they desecrate the Sunday to secular purposes, and so contrive to keep no Sunday at all.

Stated seasons for indispensable employments, are absolutely necessary for so desultory, so versatile a creature as man. That which is turned over to any chance time is seldom done at all; and those who despise the recurrence of appointed times and seasons, are only less censurable than those who rest in them.

Other duties and engagements have their allotted seasons; why, then, should the most important duty in which an immortal being can be employed, by being left to accident, become liable to occasional omission, liable to increasing neglect, liable to total oblivion?

All the other various works of God know their appointed times;—the seasons, the heavenly bodies, day and night, seed-time and harvest,—all set an example of undeviating regularity. Why should man, the only thinking, be the only disorderly, work of Almighty power?

But whilst we are asserting the necessity of seasons of prayer, let us not be suspected of attaching undue importance to them; for all these are but the frame-work, the scaffolding, the mere mechanical and subsidiary adjuncts; they are but the preparation for Christian worship; they remind us, they intimate to us, that an important work is to be done, but are no part of the work itself.

They, therefore, who most insist on the value of stated devotions, must never lose sight of that grand, and universal prime truth, that wherever we are, still we are in God's presence; whatever we have is His gift; whatever we hope is his promise; feelings which are commensurate with all time, all places, and limited to no particular scenes or seasons.

There is in some, in many it is to be feared, a readiness to acknowledge this general doctrine, which miscalled natural religion teaches; but who are far from including in their system the peculiarities, the duties, the devotions of Christianity. These are decorous men of the world, who, assuming the character of philosophical liberality, value themselves on having shaken off the shackles of prejudice, superstition, and system. They acknowledge a Creator of the universe, but it is in a vague and general way. They worship a Being, " whose temple is all space ;" that is, every where but in the human heart. They put Him as far as possible from themselves. Believing that He has no providential care of them, they feel no personal interest in Him. God and nature are with them synonymous terms. That the creation of the world was His work, they do not go the length of denying; but that its government is in His hands, is with them very problematical.

In any case, however, they are assured that a Being of such immensity requires not the littleness of superstitious forms, nor the petty limitations of stated seasons, and regular devotions; that he is infinitely above attending to our paltry concerns, though he himself anticipated this objection, when he condescended to declare, " He that offereth me thanks and praise, he honoureth me."

One says, *he* can adore the Author of nature in the contemplation of his works; that the mountains and the fields are *His* altar for worship. Another says, that his notion of religion is to deal honestly in his commerce with the world; both insist that they can serve God any where, and every where. We know they can, and we hope they do; but our Saviour, who knew the whole make of man, his levity, instability, and unfixedness, and who was yet no friend to the formalist or the superstitious, not only commands, at the hour of prayer, our entering into the closet; but our shutting the door, a tacit reproof perhaps of the indevotion of the Sadducean, as well as the publicity of the Pharisaic religion, but certainly, an admonition of general obligation.

This, indeed, is not the place to enter on that mass of concurring evidence which so irresistibly confirms the especial truth of Christianity. But is it not extraordinary that these men, who overlook, or rather enquire not into, that accumulation of evidence in the exhibition of miracles, and the fulfilment of prophecy,—that is, who do not read the Bible,—should not at least attend to one species of evidence more immediately within their reach, and more intelligible to common observation; we mean the confirmation derived to the proofs of Scripture, from the history of the world, from their avowal of moral evil, their careful cultivation, where it suits them, of habits of an opposite nature, their practical and prudential maxims, where they have an end to pursue, an interest to gain. Do not similar rules, applied to Christian principles, and delivered in the Divine record, prove clearly that our

Divine teacher " knew what was in man?"

In treating of prayer, it would be a superfluous labour to address unbelievers with the same arguments or persuasions which we would humbly propose to such as aver, with whatever degree of conviction, their belief in Christianity. It would be folly to address them with motives drawn from a book which they do not believe, or do not read. With those who are ignorant of the first principles of religion, or those who reject them, we have no common ground on which to stand. St. Paul, with his usual discrimination, has left us an example in this as well as in all other cases. With the philosophical Athenians he confined his reasonings to natural religion. To the Jewish king, Agrippa, who "believed the prophets," in telling the story of his own conversion, he most judiciously introduced the great doctrines of remission of sins and justification by faith.

If the Pyrrhonist in question were to

see a genuine christian character delineated in all its dimensions, marked with its fair lineaments, and enlivened by its quickening spirit, such, for instance, as is exemplified in the character of St. Paul, he would consider it as a mere picture of the imagination; and would no more believe its reality than he does that of Xenophon's Prince, the Stoic's Wise Man, Quintilian's Perfect Orator, or any other Platonic or Utopian representation. Or could he be brought to believe its actual existence, he would set such a man far above the necessity of prayer; he would emancipate him from any such humbling practice; he would enthrone him in his own independent worth; for how should he ever suspect that such a man would ever pray at all, much less would be in prayer more abundant, in humiliation more profound, in self-renunciation more abased?

Is it not probable that some of those enquiring minds, who adorned the porch and the academy, as well as those more favoured men who saw the future, through the dim and distant perspective of prophecy, would have rejoiced to see the things which you see, and have not believed?

How gratefully would many of these illustrious spirits have accepted advantages which you overlook! How joyfully would they have received from Him who cannot lie, the assurance that if they would seek of Him that truth after which they "were feeling," they should find it! How gladly would that sublime and elegant spirit, whose favourite theme was pure spiritual love, have listened to the great apostle of love; to him who caught the flame, as he leaned on the bosom of his affectionate master!

How would this same exalted genius, who taught the immortality of the soul to the bright, yet blind, Athenians—he, whose penetrating mind rather guessed, than knew what he taught—whose keen eye caught some glimpses of a brighter state through the darkness which surrounded him — how would he have gloried in that light and immortality which the gospel revelation has brought to light! — but with what unspeakable rapture would he have learned that He who revealed the life could give it, that He who promised immortality could bestow it! With what obedient transport would he have heard this touching apostrophe, at once a strong reproof and a tender invitation — "Ye will not come unto me that ye might have life!" Ye philosophising cavillers, who live in the meridian splendour of this broad day, how will *you* escape, if you neglect so great salvation?"

But if pride, the dominant intellectual sin, keeps the sceptic aloof from the humiliating duties of devotion; the habitual indulgence of the senses, in another class, proves an equal cause of alienating the heart from prayer.

The man absorbed by ease and enjoyment, and sunk in the relaxing softnesses of a voluptuous life, has a natural distaste to every thing that stands in opposition to the delights of that life. It is the smoothness of his course which makes it so slippery. He is lost before he feels that he is sinking. For whether we plunge at once from a precipitous height, or slide down from it on an inclined plane, still, while there is a yawning gulf at the bottom, our destruction is equally inevitable.

The systematic but decorous sensualist is one whose life is a course of sober luxury, of measured indulgence. He contrives to reconcile an abandonment of sound principle with a kind of orderly practice. He enquires rather what is decent than what is right, what will secure the favourable opinion of the world, especially his own class, rather than what will please God. His object is to make the most of this world. Selfishness has established its throne in his heart. His study is to make every thing and every person subservient to his own convenience, or pleasure, or profit, yet without glaringly trespassing on the laws of propriety or custom.— Self is the source and centre of all his actions; but though this governing principle is always on the watch for its gratification, yet, as part of that gratification depends on a certain degree of reputation, it frequently leads him to do right things though without right motives; for the main-spring sometimes sets the right a-going as well as the wrong.

He goes to church on all public occasions, but without devotion; gives alms without charity; subscribes to public institutions without being interested in their prosperity, except as they are frequently succeeded by a pleasant dinner and good company, and as the subscription list of names he knows will be published. He lives on good terms with different, and even opposite classes, of men, without being attached to any; he does them favours without affection, knowing that he shall have occasion to solicit favours in return, for he never does a small kindness without a view to asking a greater.

He deprecates excess in every thing, but always lives upon its confines.

Prayer enters not into his plan—he has nothing to ask, for he has all in himself—thanksgiving is still less his practice, for what he has he deserves.

He has read that "to enjoy is to obey," and he is always ready to give this cheerful proof of the most unlimited obedience. He respects the laws of the country, especially such as guard property and game, and eagerly punishes the violators of both. But as to the laws of God, he thinks they were made to guard the possessions of the rich, to punish the vicious poor, and to frighten those who have nothing to lose. Yet he respects some of the commandments, and would placard on every post and pillar that which says "thou shalt not steal;" whilst he thinks that which says "thou shalt not covet" might be expunged from the decalogue.

If you happen to speak of the helplessness of man, he thinks you are alluding to some paralytic; if of his dependence, to some hanger-on of a great man; if of his sinfulness, he adopts your opinion, for he reads the Newgate calender. But of sin, as an inherent principle, of the turpitude of sin, except as it disturbs society, he knows nothing; but religion as a principle of action, but prayer as a source of peace or a ground of hope, he neither knows nor desires to know. The stream of life glides smoothly on without it; why should he ruffle its placid flow? why should he break in on the course of enjoyment with self-imposed austerities? He believes himself to be respected by his fellow-men, and the favour of God is not in all his thoughts. His real character the great day of decision will discover. Till then he will have two characters.

"Soul take thine ease, thou hast much goods laid up for thee," is perhaps the state of all others which most disqualifies and unfits for prayer. Not only the apostrophe excites the bodily appetite, but the SOUL is called upon to contemplate, to repose on, the soothing prospect, the delights of that voluptuousness for which the "much goods are laid up." Thou fool! that soul which thou wouldest quicken to such base enjoyment, that soul shall this night be required of thee.

Thus we see what restrains prayer in these two classes of character. The sceptic does not pray, because he does not believe that God is a hearer of prayer. The voluptuary, because he believes that God is such a one as himself, and because he has already gotten all that he wants of Him. His gold, and the means of gratifying his sensuality, would not be augmented by the dry duties of devotion; and with an exercise which would increase neither, he can easily dispense.

ERRORS IN PRAYER, WHICH MAY HINDER ITS BEING ANSWERED.—THE PROUD MAN'S PRAYER.—THE PATIENT CHRISTIAN.—FALSE EXCUSES UNDER THE PRETENCE OF INABILITY.

ALL desire the gifts of God, but they do not desire God. If we profess to love him, it is for our own sake: when shall we begin to love him for himself? Many who do not go the length of omitting prayer, but pray merely from custom, or education, frequently complain that they find no benefit from prayer; others, that they experience not the support and comfort promised to it. May not those who thus complain, and who perhaps are far from being enemies to religion, find, on a serious examination of their own hearts and lives, some irregularity in desire, similar to that just mentioned, to be the cause of their discontent, and alleged disappointment?

We are more disposed to lay down rules for the regulation of God's government, than to submit our will to it as he has settled it. If we do not now see the efficacy of the prayer which he has enjoined us to present to him, it may yet be producing its effect in another way. Infinite wisdom is not obliged to inform us of the manner, or the time of his operations; what he expects of us is to persevere in the duty. The very obedience to the command is no small thing, whatever be its perceptible effects.

Under the apparent failure of our prayers, the source of our repinings must be looked for in the fact of our own blindness and imperfection; for the declarations of the gospel are sure; their answer must be found in the grace of God in Christ Jesus, for his mercies are infallible. Wherever there is disappointment we may be assured that it is not because he is wanting to us, but because we are wanting to ourselves.

The prophet's expression, "the iniquity of our holy things," will not be thoroughly understood except by those who thus seriously dive into the recesses of their own heart, feel their deficiences, mark their wanderings, detect and lament their vain imaginations and impertinent thoughts. It is to be regretted that these worldly trifles are far more apt to intrude on us in prayer, than the devout affections excited by prayer are to follow us into the world. Business and pleasure break in on our devotions; when will the spirit of devotion mix with the concerns of the world?

You who lament the disappointment of your requests, suffer a few friendly hints.— Have you not been impatient because you receive not the things that you asked at your own time? How do you know that if you had persevered God might have bestowed them in His time? He certainly would, had He not in His wisdom foreseen they would not have been good for you; and, therefore, in His mercy withheld them. Is there not some secret, unsuspected infidelity lurking behind such impatience? Is it not virtually saying there is no God to hear, or that He is unfaithful to his promises? For is it not absolute impiety to insinuate an accusation, that the Supreme Judge of men and angels is capable of injustice, or liable to error? God has pleasure in the prosperity of His children. He neither grants nor denies any thing which is not accurately weighed and measured; which is not exactly suited to their good, if not to their request.

If we pray aright it may please God not only to grant that for which we pray, but that for which we do not pray. Supplicating for the best things, we may receive inferior and unrequested things, as was the case with Solomon in his prayer for wisdom. God will not forget our labour of love. If he does not seem to notice it at present, he may lay it by for a time when it may be more wanted.

In prayer we must take care not to measure our necessities by our desires; the former are few, the latter may be insatiable. A murmuring spirit is a probable cause why our petitions are not granted. The certain way to prevent our obtaining what we desire, or enjoying what we have, is to feel impatient at what we do not receive, or to make an improper use of what has been granted to our prayers.

Or you may perhaps address God with sinister and corrupt views; as if you had left his omniscience out of his attributes; as if you thought Him such an one as yourself; as if He might be entrapped with the "secret ambush of a specious prayer." Your design in the application of the boon you solicit may not be for his glory. It may be the prayer of ambition, cloked under the guise of more extensive usefulness; it may be the prayer of covetousness, under the pretext of providing for your family. It may be the prayer of injustice, a petition for success in some undertaking for yourself, to the circumvention of another's fairer claim. God, in mercy to our souls, refuses the gift which would endanger them.

Thus, then, if we ask and receive not, because we ask deceitfully or blindly, we must not wonder if our prayers are not answered. Or, if we obtain what we solicit, and turn it to a bad account, or to no account at all, we must not be surprised if Divine grace is withheld, or withdrawn.

The same ill results may be expected if we ask formally, or carelessly. Who has not felt, that there is a kind of mechanical memory in the tongue, which runs over the form, without any aid of the understanding, without any concurrence of the will, without any consent of the affections? For do we not sometimes implore God to hear a prayer, to which we ourselves are not attending? And is not this presumptuously to demand from Him that attention, which we ourselves are not giving to our own requests, even while we are in the act of making them?

A mere superficial form, by lulling the conscience, hardens the heart. The task is performed, but in what manner, or to what result, is not enquired. Genuine prayer is the homage of the soul to God, and not an expedient to pacify Him.

If you observe the form, but forget the dispositions it is intended to produce, it is evident the end of such prayer is not answered. Yet be not so far discouraged by feeling no sensible effect from prayer as to discontinue it; it is still a right thing to be found in the way of duty.

But, perhaps, you neglect to implore the Spirit of Christ towards the direction of your prayers, and His intercession for their acceptance. As there is no other name through which we can be saved, so there is no other through which we can be heard: we must not sever his mediation from his atonement. All His divine offices are not only in perfect harmony, but in inseparable union *. Or, perhaps you have used the name of the Redeemer for form'-sake, or as an accustomed close to your petitions, without imploring his efficacious grace in changing your heart, as well as in pardoning your sins.

Perhaps you think it a sufficient qualification for acceptable prayer, that you are always forming good intentions; now, though these make up the value of good actions, yet good intentions, not acted upon, when occasion invites and duty calls, will not lessen, but inflame the reckoning. For does it not look as if you had resisted the offer of that Holy Spirit, which had originally prompted the intention? And may it not induce him to withdraw his blessed influences,

---

* We observe with regret, that, in many forms of prayer, the aid of his mediation is much more frequently implored, than the benefits of his death and merits. He is, indeed, our divine Intercessor, but his mere intercession is not the whole source of our dependence on him.

when they have been both invited and rejected?

Do you never, by unwholesome reading, fill the mind with images unfavourable to serious exercises? The children of the pure and holy God should feed on the bread of their father's house, and not on the husks of the prodigal.

Do you never use prophanely or lightly, that name which is above every name? He who made the ear, shall he not hear; and if he has heard, during the day, his awful name used by the thoughtless as an expletive, or by the impious as an interjection, or an imprecation, will he in the morning be called on as a saviour, and in the evening as an intercessor?

But no profession of faith however orthodox, no avowal of trust in Christ however confident, no intreaty for the aid of the Spirit however customary, will avail, if it be not such an influential faith, such a practical trust, such a living devotedness, as shall be productive of holiness of heart and life, as shall tend to produce obedience to the commands, and submission to the will of God. This is an infallible test, by which you may try every doctrine, every principle of the gospel. We do not mean the truth of them, for that is immutable; but your own actual belief, your own actual interest in them. If no such effects are visible, we deceive ourselves, and the principles we defend, are not those by which we are governed.

Prayer is so obviously designed to humble the proud heart of the natural man, by giving him a feeling sense of his misery, his indigence, and his helplessness, that we should be unwilling to believe, that even the proudest man can carry his pride to the Throne of Grace, except to supplicate deliverance from it; yet such a character is actually drawn by him who knew the thoughts and intents of the heart of man, and a little consideration will teach us, that the "two men who went up into the temple to pray," were not intended as individual portraits, but as specimens of a class.

The proud man does not perhaps always thank God that he is not guilty of adultery, or extortion, to which vices he may have little temptation; nor does he glory in paying tithes and taxes, to which the law would compel him. Yet is he never disposed, like the Pharisee, to proclaim the catalogue of his own virtues? to bring in his comparative claims, as if it were a good thing to be better than the bad? Is he never disposed to carry in his eye, (as if he would remind his maker of his superiority,) certain persons who are possibly less the objects of Divine displeasure, than he, by his pride and selfishness, may have rendered himself; although his regularity in the forms of devotion may have made him more respectable in the world, than the poor, reprobated being whom he praises God he does not resemble. It is the abasement, the touching self-condemnation, the avowed poverty, the pleaded misery of the destitute beggar that finds acceptance. It is the hungry whom God's mercy fills with good things, it is the rich in his own conceit, whom his displeasure sends empty away.

Whenever you are tempted to thank God that you are not like other men, compare your own condition with that of the afflicted and the bereaved among your own friends; compare yourself with the paralytic on his couch, with the blind beggar by the way-side, with the labourer in the mine; think on the wretch in the galleys; on the condemned in the dungeons of despotic governments; on the miserable beings in our own prisons, those loathsome abodes of sin and wretchedness. Above all, think, and this is the intolerable acmé of sin in the inflictor, and of misery in the sufferer; think on the wretched negro chained in the hold of a slave ship! Think seriously on these, and put pride into your prayer if you can. Think on these, not to triumph in your own superiority, but to adore the undeserved mercy of God, in giving you advantages to which you have no higher claim, and let your praise of yourself be converted into prayer for them.

For there are no dispositions of the heart which are more eminently promoted by prayer, than contentment and patience. They are two qualities of the same colour, but of different shades, and are generally, when found at all, found in the same breast. Both are the offspring of genuine religion, both nurtured by cordial prayer. The cultivation of the one, under easy circumstances, prepares for the exercise of the other under more trying situations. Both emanate from the same divine principle, but are drawn out by different occasions, and varying circumstances.

Content is the tranquillity of the heart, prayer is its aliment; it is satisfied under every dispensation of Providence, and takes thankfully its allotted portion, never enquiring whether a little more would not be a little better; knowing, that if God had so judged, it would have been as easy for him to have given the more as the less. That is not true content, which does not enjoy as the gift of infinite wisdom what it has, nor is that true patience, which does not suffer meekly the loss of what it had, because it is not his will that it should have it longer.

The contentment of the irreligious man is apathy, his patience either pride or insensibility. The language of the patient man under trials is, it is the Lord.—Shall a living man complain, is his interrogation? "A good man," says Solomon, " is satisfied from himself." Here the presumptuous might put in *his* claim to the title. But his pretension arises from his mistake, for his satisfaction is *with himself*, that of the Christian with Providence; it arises from the grace of God shed abroad in his heart, which is become a perennial spring of consolation and enjoyment; and which, by persevering prayer, is indented into his very soul. Content knows how to want and how to abound; this is the language of equanimity: "shall I not receive evil from the hand of the Lord, as well as good," this is the language of patience in speaking of providence. Content is always praising God for what she possesses; patience is always justifying Him for what she suffers. The cultivation of the one effectually prepares us for the exercise of the other. But these dispositions are not inherent in the human heart. How are they generated? by the influences of the Holy Spirit. How are they kept alive? by heart-felt devotion.

The prosperous man of the world, exulting in any recent success, may acknowledge, "the Lord gave," but it is only Christian patience can say, "the Lord taketh away," and even bless Him for the resumption of His gift. The contented, patient Christian, has the same keen feelings, the same fond attachments with other men, for, though his passions are regulated by religion, they are not totally extinguished.

Under the pressure of any affliction, *thy will be done*, as it is the patient Christian's unceasing prayer, so is it the ground of his unvarying practice. In this brief petition he finds his whole duty comprized and expressed. It is the unprompted request of his lips, it is the motto inscribed on his heart, it is the principle which regulates his life, it is the voice which says to the stormy passions, "Peace! be still!" Let others expostulate, he submits. Nay, even submission does not adequately express his feelings. We frequently submit, not so much from duty as from necessity; we submit, because we cannot help ourselves. Resignation sometimes may be mere acquiescence in the sovereignty, rather than conviction of the wisdom and goodness of God; while the patient Christian not only yields to the dispensation, but adores the dispenser. He not only submits to the blow, but vindicates the hand which inflicts it; "the Lord is righteous in all his ways." He refers to the chastisement as a proof of the affection of the chastiser. "I know that in very faithfulness thou hast caused me to be afflicted." He recurs to the thoughtlessness of his former prosperity. "Before I was afflicted I went astray," and alludes to the trial less as a punishment than a paternal correction. If he prays for a removal of the present suffering, he prays also that it may not be removed from him, till it has been sanctified to him. He will not even part from the trial till he has laid hold on the benefit.

Perhaps the impediment which hinders the benefit of prayer in characters apparently correct, may be the fatal habit of indulging in some secret sin, the private cherishing of some wrong propensity, the entertaining of some evil imagination. Not being accustomed to control at other times, it intrudes, when you would willingly expel it; for a guest which is unreservedly let in at other seasons, and cordially entertained, will too frequently break in when you desire to be alone.

The Scriptures are explicit on this subject. It is not merely the committing actual sin that ruins the comfort growing out of prayer; the divine prohibition runs higher; its interdiction is more intimately interior; it extends to the thoughts and intents of the heart. The door of heaven is shut against prayer under such circumstances. "If I regard iniquity in my *heart*, the Lord will not hear me." A cherished corruption in the mind is the more likely to interpose between God and the soul, because it does not assume the shape and bulk of crime. A practical offence, the effect of sudden temptation, is more likely to be followed by keen repentance, deep self-abasement, and fervent application for pardon; whereas to the close bosom-sin, knowing that no human charge can be brought against it, the soul secretly returns with a fondness, facilitated by long indulgence, and only whetted by a short separation. Vain, covetous, malignant, impure thoughts, habitually fostered by the imagination, are more likely to start out into action, are a more probable preparation for a bolder sin, than many who indulge them believe or intend.

It was, perhaps, this acute, experimental feeling which led David to pray to be delivered from "secret sins;" these, he was probably conscious, had led to those "presumptuous sins," which had entangled his soul and embittered his life; and whose dominion he so frequently and fervently deprecates. This, it is to be feared, may be the case with some, whose language and exterior cause them to be ranked with the religious; these are, at least, the dangers to which they are most exposed. It is, therefore, that our Lord connects, in indissoluble union, watching with prayer.

Perhaps, when the conscience is more than usually awakened, you pray with some degree of fervour to be delivered from the guilt and punishment of sin. But, if you stop here, your devotion is most imperfect. If you do not also pray to be delivered from its power and dominion over your heart and life, you do not go much further than the heathens of old. They seem to have had a strong feeling of guilt, by their fond desire of expiating it by their sacrifices and lustrations.

Of their terror of its punishment we have many intimations in their fables; for what is fable to us, was probably to them obscure history, or wild tradition worked up into an absurd but amusing mythology. The eternity of their punishments is strongly implied in the insatiable thirst and ungratified appetites of Tantalus; his misery augmented by that flowing water and those tempting fruits which hung in his sight and mocked his appetites, not unlike the anguish of Dives, which was rendered more intolerable by beholding the blessedness of those on the other side of the great gulf. The profitless toils of Sisyphus, and of the daughters of Danaus, whose ever-failing efforts prove their labours to be infinite and their punishment eternal. The wheel of Ixion, which, as it was to be perpetually in motion, so the punishment was to have no end; a doctrine not so strongly held by many Christians, as it seems to be implied in this blind mythology.

Will you not then be most unweariedly fervent in prayer to the God of mercy, for deliverance from the dominion of that sin which, if not forsaken as well as lamented, will be inevitably followed by that punishment which you deprecate, and which will never end? But such is the love of present ease, and the desire of respite, that you think, perhaps, it is better not "to be tormented before the time." How many now in a state of irreversible misery wish they had been tormented sooner, that they might not be tormented for ever! But with you it is not yet too late. With you the day of grace, which to them is over, is not yet past. Use it then without delay, instead of persisting in laying up fresh regrets for eternity.

But too many deceive themselves, by imagining that when they have pronounced their prayer the duty is accomplished with the task, the occult medicine being taken, the charm is to work of itself. They consider it as a duty quite distinct and unconnected with any other. They forget that it is to produce in them a principle which is to mix with all the occurrences of the day. Prayer, though not intended as a talisman, is yet proposed as a remedy. The effect of its operation is to be seen in assisting to govern the temper, in bridling the tongue, in checking, not only calumny but levity, not only impure, but vain conversation.

But we have a wonderful talent at deceiving ourselves. We have not a fault for which we do not find an apology. Our ingenuity on this head is inexhaustible. In matters of religion men complain that they are weak, a complaint they are not forward to urge in worldly matters. They lament that their reluctance to pray arises from being unable to do what God, in his word, expects them to do. But is not this virtual rebellion, only with a smooth face and a soft name? God is too wise not to know exactly what we *can* do, and too just to expect from us what we *cannot*.

This pretence of weakness, though it looks like humility, is only a mask for indolence and a screen for selfishness.

We certainly *can* refuse to indulge ourselves in what pleases us, when we know it displeases God. We *can* obey his commandments with the aid of the infused strength which He has promised, and which we *can* ask. It is not He who is unwilling to give, but we who are averse to pray. The temptations to vice are strengthened by our passions, as our motives to virtue are weakened by them.

Our spiritual enemy would not be so

potent, if we ourselves did not put arms into his hands. The world would not be so powerful an enchantress, if we did not assist the enchantment, by voluntarily yielding to it; by insensibly forsaking Him who is our strength. We make apologies for yielding to both by pleading their power and our own weakness. But the inability to resist is of our own making. Both enemies are indeed powerful, but they are not irresistible. If we assert the contrary, is it not virtually saying " greater are they that are against us than He that is for us?

But we are traitors to our own cause; we are conquered by our own consent; we surrender, not so much because the conqueror is powerful, as because the conquered is willing.

Without diminishing any thing of *His* grace and glory, to whom every good thought we think, every victory over sin we obtain, is owing — may it not add to our happiness, even in heaven, to look back on every conflict we maintained with our grand spiritual enemy, every triumph over the world, every victory over ourselves? Will not the remembrance of one act of resistance then, far surpass every gratification now, which the three confederated enemies of our souls may present to us?

It is not merely by our prayers that we must give glory to God. Our Divine Master has expressly told us wherein His Father is glorified; it is "when we bring forth much fruit." It is by our works we shall be judged, and not by our prayers. And what a final consummation is it that obedience to the will of God, which is our duty here, shall be our nature hereafter! What is now our prayer shall then be our possession; there the obligation to obey shall become a necessity, and that necessity shall be happiness ineffable.

The various evils here enumerated, with many others not touched upon, are so many dead weights on the wings of prayer; they cause it to gravitate to earth, obstruct its ascent, and hinder it from piercing to the throne of God.

GOD OUR FATHER.—OUR UNWILLINGNESS TO PLEASE HIM.—FORMS OF PRAYER.—GREAT AND LITTLE SINS.—ALL SIN AN OFFENCE AGAINST GOD.—BENEFIT OF HABITUAL PRAYER.

The distinction between the personal nature of Faith, and the universal character of Charity, as it is exercised in prayer, are specifically exhibited in the two pronouns which stand at the head of the Creed and of the Lord's Prayer. We cannot exercise faith for another, and therefore can only say *I* believe. But when we offer up our petitions, we address them to *our* father, implying that He is the author, governor, and supporter, not of ourselves only, but of his whole rational creation. It conveys also a beautiful idea of that boundless charity which links all mankind in one comprehensive brotherhood. The plural *us*, continued through the whole prayer, keeps up the sentiment with which it sets out, tends to exclude selfishness, and to excite philanthropy, by recommending to God the temporal as well as spiritual wants of the whole family of mankind.

The nomenclature of the Divinity is expressed in Scripture by every term which can convey ideas of grandeur or of grace, of power or of affection, of sublimity or tenderness, of majesty or benignity; by every name which can excite terror or trust, which can inspire awe or consolation.

But of all compellations by which the Supreme Being is designated in his holy word, there is not one more soothing, more attractive, more endearing, than that of FATHER; it includes the idea of reconcilement, pardon, acceptance, love.

It swallows up His grandeur in His beneficence. It involves also the inheritance belonging to our filial relation. It fills the mind with every image that is touching, and the heart with every feeling that is affectionate. It inspires fear softened by love, and authority mitigated by gratitude. The tenderest image the Psalmist could select from the abundant storehouse of his rich conceptions to convey the kindest sentiment of God's pity towards them that fear Him, was that it resembles the pity of a " father for his *own children*." In directing us to pray to our Father, our Divine Master does not give the command without the example. He every where uses the term He recommends. " I thank Thee, Oh Father, Lord of heaven and earth!" and in the 17th of St. John he uses this endearing name no less than seven times.

" Lord shew us the Father and it sufficeth," was the ill-understood prayer of the inquiring disciples. To us this petition is granted before it is made. Does He not shew himself to all as a Father, in the wonders of his creation, in the wonders of our being, preservation, and support? Has he not, in a more especial manner, revealed Himself to us as a Father in the sublime wonders of his word, in the unsearchable riches of Christ, and the perpetuated gift of the Holy Spirit? Does He not shew Himself our Father, if, when we have done evil, He withholds His chastening hand; if, when we have sinned, He still bears with us; if, when we are deaf to his call He repeats it; if, when we delay, He waits for us; if, when we repent, He pardons us; if, when we return, He receives us; if, when in danger, He preserves us from falling; and if, when we fall, He raises us?

We have a beautiful illustration of the goodness of God as a merciful and tender Father in the deeply affecting parable of the Prodigal Son. Though the undone spendthrift knew that he had no possible-claim on the goodness he had so notoriously offended, yet he felt that the endearing name of Father had an eloquence that might plead forgiveness of his offence, though he feared not for a restoration to affection and favour. But while he only meekly aspired to a place among the servants, while he only humbly pleaded for a little of their redundant bread, he was received as a pardoned, reconciled, beloved child.

Yet the human heart is not easily warmed into gratitude, or softened into love, or allured to imitation, because it takes only slight and transient views of the divine benignity. What God has done for us, and what we have really done against ourselves, will, in the great day of decision, crown Him with glory, and ourselves with shame. What we think we do for our own benefit in temporal concerns is so animated, so earnest, so unremitted—what we are called to do for God—which ultimately, indeed, would be done for ourselves—is so little, so reluctant, so heartless, as to bear no sort of comparison. In the former case, every thing is a gratification; in the latter, every thing is a sacrifice.

We think much of the smallest instance of self-denial if it be for God; if it be an act of acknowledgment to the most gracious of all Fathers; if it be a tribute of homage to the King of Kings, however large or lasting the promised recompence. But we think little of any present privation of our own, if it insure to us a longer subsequent enjoyment, though but for a season.

In speaking of the manner in which we should address our Heavenly Father, it is to be observed there may be evident differences in the state, both of the mind and circumstances, for which the best written forms of prayer can make no provision. We ourselves can alone know those varieties, and the petitions which expressly belong to them. We are sometimes under the influence of particular tempers, which we wish to cultivate and improve; in this case, we shall naturally use addresses very different from those which the prevalence of unfavourable tempers or wrong dispositions require.

As to the outward events in which we are concerned — for *accident* is a term which has no place in the Christian's vocabulary — God in every dispensation is at work for our good. In more prosperous circumstances He tries our gratitude; in mediocrity our contentment; in misfortunes our submission; and as every new situation calls into exercise some new virtue, by consequence it calls for some alteration in the mode of our devotions. The prayers of yesterday and to day will consequently be as different as the circumstances — these are some of the advantages of private, over public prayer.

The great and general topics are, however, of a fixed, unalterable nature, on which, though we may be more or less diffuse, according to the state of the mind, yet the term and spirit will require little variation. This is more especially the case with respect to praise and thanksgiving; and to express these, the use of stated forms may occasionally come in with much advantage, as the cardinal points to be expressed here must be ever the same. Invariably must the glory and honour of whatever is good be ascribed to the great source of light and life, the giver of every good and perfect gift; and the addition in secret of particular clauses of praise for personal mercies will not be difficult to find where gratitude is really felt.

A deep sense of his corruptions will powerfully draw the real penitent to an humbling avowal of sin in prayer; but it is to be feared that some, who, because they cannot charge themselves with flagrant offences, do not consider a contrite confession of the sins of the heart, and of the daily life, an indispensible part of their devotions. But God will charge many with sin who neglect to charge themselves. Did they attend to the remonstrances of a conscience not laid asleep by neglect, or quieted by palliatives, they would find that were the daily *omissions* alone, of even their best days, registered and presented to them, they would form no inconsiderable catalogue for repentance.

There are too many who do not consider that all sins are equally a breach of the Divine law. Without pretending to bring all sins, small and great, to one common level, we should remember that *all* sin is an offence against a gracious father.

In that profoundly self-abasing prayer of David, after the commission of the two black offences which disgraced his otherwise exemplary life; though he deeply felt his barbarous treatment of his brave general, in first dishonouring his wife, and then exposing him to meet inevitable death in the fore-front of the hottest battle—yet, in praying to be delivered from this blood-guiltiness, he bequeathed an important lesson to posterity, when in his lowly prostration at the throne of God, his first cry was, "against *Thee, Thee* only, have I sinned, and done this evil in *Thy* sight," plainly declaring, that all sin is, in the first instance, a sin against God.

While the most worldly are ready enough to exclaim against notorious sins, or against any sins carried to the greatest excess, to smaller offences they contrive to be tolerably reconciled. They think the commission of these not inconsistent with the profitable use of prayer in their formal way of using this customary exercise.

They are also sufficiently lenient to certain degrees of great sins; and various are the modifications and distinctions in their logic, and not over-correct the gradations in their moral scale of degrees. They do not consider that it is the extirpation, and not merely the reduction, of any sin, which is to procure them that peace and comfort for which they sometimes pray, and which they wonder they do not receive as an answer to their prayers.

They forget that the evil of sin is not to be measured by its magnitude only, but by the spirit of disobedience which it indicates towards a generous Father, —a Father whose commands are all founded in mercy and love, and who considers every voluntary fault as no light offence when committed against supreme authority, exercised with perfect tenderness.

But it is their reluctance to part with the remaining degrees, their wish to retain these modified sins; it is their favourite reserves to which they still cling, that prevent that peace which is promised to the victory, I had almost said to the omnipotence, of prayer.

For it is not so much the nicely measured quantity, as the nature of sin which constitutes its malignity, and obstructs the benefit of prayer. The inferior degree which is cherished, will, without earnest supplication to God, be ready to become the excess which is deprecated, whenever the appropriate temptation shall present itself. For, however our compassionate Father may pardon the unpremeditated fault, yet how can we expect Him to forgive any degree of sin that is allowed, that is even, in a certain measure, intended to be committed? Diminution, however, is a favourable step, if, by perseverance in prayer, it lead gradually to extirpation.

Habitual prayer may prove a most effectual check to any doubtful or wrong action, to which circumstances may invite us during the day on which we are entering — the very petition to our Heavenly Father, — "deliver us from evil," forcibly felt and sincerely expressed, may preserve us from being seduced into it. And is not the praying Christian less likely to "fall into temptation," than they who neglect to pray that they may not be led into it?

The right dispositions of the heart, and the fervour of devotion reciprocally excite each other. A holy temper sends us to prayer, and prayer promotes that temper. Every act of thanksgiving tends to make us more grateful, and augmented gratitude excites more devout thanksgiving.

The act of confession renders the heart more contrite, and deeper contrition induces a more humbling avowal of sin. Each, and all, send us more cordially to the Redeemer: the more fervent the prayer, the more entire is the prostration of the whole man at the foot of the cross.

THE DOCTRINE OF IMPUTED SANCTIFICATION, NEWLY ADOPTED.—THE OLD ONE OF PROGRESSIVE SANCTIFICATION NEWLY REJECTED.—BOTH DOCTRINES INJURIOUS TO PRAYER.—ST. PAUL'S CHARACTER.

We have hitherto spoken of errors in prayer. We come now to errors of opinion, which supersede the necessity of prayer itself. There are moral as well as speculative corruptions gaining ground amongst us, and there is an involution of one in the folds of the other. When men once indulge themselves in any deviation from the course so plainly marked out, in that only unerring *road-book*, the gospel of Jesus Christ, they can never be sure where the first turning off may lead them.

When a man, with more ingenuity than sober judgment, wishes to introduce a novel error; in order to work successfully, and prevent the suspicion of his design, he commonly seizes on some acknowledged truth for his basis. On this truth he raises his own fanciful superstructure, but with little departure at first from the avowed design; so that his gradual deviation from it makes the error continue still to look so much like truth, that ordinary observers will not easily detect where the old truth ends, or where the new fabrication totally changes the character of the original edifice.

The great and glorious doctrine of the New Testament was to exalt the Saviour and to humble the sinner; the new doctrine is to exalt the sinner also, and in that proportion to establish and secure him in sin. For if the Saviour's righteousness by transfer becomes so far the believer's righteousness, as to become, in the new language, his own personal holiness, he has in his own person "whereof to glory," and any further attainment is anomalous; or at best this transfer is even less rational, and evidently more removed from common sense as well as from charity, than the doctrine of supererogation itself; for that only teaches that some men were rich in good works enough and to spare; but this, instead of the friendly disposal of such superfluous wealth, teaches that we have none worth keeping, and that if we had, there is a provision made for rendering it utterly useless.

A distorted truth then, is worse than an original falsehood, because it deceives the injudicious and ill-informed by retaining some little vestige of the truth they had been taught to venerate. Thus, they who pretend to add new glory to the character and offices of Christ, are in effect dishonouring by misrepresenting him. It is a fearful fact, that the holiest doctrine may be perverted, till, instead of its being the source of salvation, it becomes a fountain of impiety. Instead of humbling the sinner, it confirms him in sin; instead of purifying, it corrupts; instead of sobering, it inebriates; and lands him on a daring and presumptuous confidence. Instead of promoting the cause of God, as it professes, it advances that of Satan. It is a false light which leads to utter darkness, for "if the light which is in thee be darkness, how great is that darkness!"

This error is so much worse than any other sin, as by fair and legitimate deduction it renders all virtue anomalous, and consequently all prayer ridiculous. Virtue cannot be needed, where to be like minded with Christ is replaced, or made synonymous with having his holiness substituted for our own; and prayer cannot be upheld in any one of its essential qualities, where no room is left in the heart for self-distrust, meekness, lowliness of spirit, the fear of offending God, and the sense of dependence on him for "more grace."

Much has also been advanced in favor

of another kindred doctrine, a doctrine with which St. Peter must have been utterly unacquainted, when he exhorted his converts to " GROW in grace and in the knowledge of Jesus Christ." The preceding opinion having encouraged the new proselytes, for they can create as well as destroy, has called another into existence, *that there is no such thing as progressive sanctification.* This novel doctrine, if practically adopted, would not fail to contribute its full share to the extermination of any remains of moral goodness, which its precursor might have left behind. It may indeed deserve some little toleration, when its founder shall have been able to produce one individual child of Adam, who is already as good as he ought to be, or even as he might have been.

If this doctrine be true, a large portion of Scripture must be abandoned to the clippers and mutilators of the sacred volume; for what becomes of the gracious promise of being " renewed from day to day?" what of the precept "to increase and abound more and more?" what of the incessant inculcation of this command, repeated in all the various forms which language could supply; a command of which neither the variety of the illustration, nor of the language which conveys it, ever alters the idea, an idea which, like a golden thread, runs through the whole fabric of the New Testament.

We have been accustomed to hear that fervent prayer, through the influence of the Divine Spirit, is the grand instrument of this renewal; and it is on this ground that we have ventured to introduce the subject here, as connected with the general design of these pages. But the present doctrine completes what the former had commenced, and renders prayer wholly inapplicable to all spiritual ends: it leaves us nothing to implore, but merely temporal advantages; to ask for things only which will end when this life ends. It would abolish the necessity of every petition in the Lord's prayer, except that for our daily bread.

Why will not those who profess to make the Bible the only rule of their faith and practice, learn from that Bible, that diffidence and reverential awe, a frank avowal of their own ignorance, a humble withholding from intruding into unrevealed things, and devout gratitude for the glorious things which are revealed, best become blind, ignorant and dependent creatures?

If this newly invented doctrine were true, what would become of the useless interval of life, useless as to all possibility of improvement, which is the great end of life, the interval between the decisive moment of complete sanctification and our closing scene?

The unanswerable argument in favor of progressive holiness, is the progress itself. The man to whom it was asserted, that there was no such thing as motion, made the most definitive answer,— he got up and walked.

Every advance of the Christian inclines him to push on to still further advances. But under the influence of this stationary principle the busy current of life would become a stagnant pool. It is motion which gives the sense of spiritual, as well as natural life. It is progress which gives the sustaining feeling, not of independent, but of infused strength. Hope, which is the pulse of spiritual life, would not only intermit, but stand still. " Is this all," would the disappointed Christian say? " Shall I never be more holy than I now am? I do not find the right sort of rest in being a fixture." Torpor is not ease, numbness is not relief. It is exercise, not indolence, which induces safe and wholesome repose.

New difficulties, fresh trials, unknown temptations may yet assail us in our mortal journey, which will require new applications to the Throne of Grace for support. With that support promised to prayer, though " Alps on Alps arise," we need not be discouraged. For if our progress be an upward, it is an onward path, and the acclivity diminishes the higher we ascend. Difficulties may be great, but with the grace of God they will not be insuperable. God is not only strong, but Strength. Yet let us not aim at an ascent above our promised support. In aspiring to reach a visionary elevation, we lose the height we had actually gained.

It is curious to observe, how naturally one invention involves another. We find an instructive illustration of this truth in a Pagan fable. Dædalus was not only made a prisoner himself in the labyrinth of his own projecting, but like the projectors of the new theological metaphysics, he was no sooner involved in its mazes, than he went on to study a new and still wilder contrivance. But his next invention, his wings of wax, in which he trusted to secure his flight, in their ultimate result betrayed their insufficiency. His incautious companion, by mounting above the prescribed region of safety, exposed his artificial wings to be melted by the sun, as a punishment for approaching it too nearly. His fate was the inevitable consequence of his temerity.

If we were completely and instantaneously sanctified, such a state would boldly contradict the character of our human condition, every where described in Scripture, namely, that life is to the end a journey, a conflict, a race, a warfare, whereas in the new scheme all would be peace; the Christian would have no more to tempt, no more to fear, no more to resist, in short, earth would be heaven.

Every thing that is great is progressive. The noblest things are the longest in attaining their perfection. This analogy subsists in nature, and in grace. Surely, then, there is no assignable period, when our virtues will be incapable of addition; when our duties will be finished; when our piety will have soared to such a pitch as to render a higher elevation impossible, as to render prayer, not only unnecessary, but absurd.

Saint Paul's conversion was indeed instantaneous, but it was miraculous. Yet, though it was attended with circumstances peculiar to itself; though the shining light from heaven surrounded him; though, to evidence the miracle, he heard the voice of the Lord Jesus himself; though his natural sight was taken from him, preparatory to the opening of his spiritual eyes; though his change was of this distinguished character, yet did he stop short there? So far from it, he only began to cry out, " Lord, what wilt thou have me to *do?*" Thus we see, that the instantaneous conversion was prayer; practical prayer; prayer which involved doing; prayer which denoted progress.

If ever progressive sanctification was exhibited in the life, as well as writings, of any one man more than another, it was in this heroic champion of divine truth. If ever one man more than another had a right to depend on his own safe state, it was the divinely illuminated Saint Paul.

Yet did *he* spend his after-life in self-satisfaction and indolent security? Did *he* ever cease to watch, or pray, or labour? Did *he* ever cease to press the duty of prayer on his most established converts? Did *he*, in the confidence of supremely eminent gifts, ever cease himself to pray? Were *his* exertions ever abridged; *his* self-denial ever diminished? Did *he* rest satisfied with present, though supernatural attainments? Did *he* remember the things which were behind? Did *he* live upon the good he had already done, or the grace he had already received? Did *he* count himself to have attained? Did he stop in the race set before him? Did not he press forward? Did not his endeavours grow with his attainments? Did not his humility, and sense of dependence outstrip both? If *he* feared being a castaway, after the unutterable things he had seen and heard, and after the wonders he had achieved, shall the best man on earth be contented to remain as he is? If it were attempted, the most sanguine man on earth would find it to be impossible; nothing either in nature or in grace "continueth in one stay." He who does not advance, is already gone back. This glorious, because humble Apostle, went on in progressive sanctification, he continued to grow and to pray, till he at length attained to the measure of the stature of the fulness of Christ.

But what enabled this unparalleled man to maintain, to the end, this painful conflict? It was the same support which is still offered to the meanest Christian. It was humble, fervent, persevering prayer. It was the spirit of supplication, infused and sustained by "the renewing of the Holy Ghost," and presented through the divine Mediator.

And what the Apostle did in his own

person, we repeat, he unweariedly pressed upon all his converts. He exhorted them to pray for themselves, and for each other, in the same spirit in which " he bowed his own knees unto the Father of our Lord Jesus Christ, that they might be strengthened with might by his spirit in the inner man;—that Christ might dwell in their hearts by faith;—that they might be rooted and grounded in love;—that they might know the love of Christ, which passeth knowledge;— that they might be filled with all the fulness of God."

It is obvious why God does not give us the full measure of his grace; it is in order that we may be induced to pray for it; and that prayer which we are commanded continually to repeat for greater degrees of grace, is a standing proof of that imperfection in us which requires it; is a perpetual intimation, that we stand in need of fresh supplies, and larger measures of this superinduced strength than we have yet attained.

A sincere Christian must know, because he must feel, that he is an imperfect Christian; and to rest satisfied in a state of imperfection is not " fighting the good fight," is not " finishing our course" in the way our beginning promised. As we advance, Providence assigns us new employments, new trials. Sanctification will never have reached its ultimate point, without that persevering progress which the Scriptures every where inculcate. Do we not rob ourselves of the reward promised to those who strive to go on unto perfection, if we are stopped short by the fatal delusion, that we have already reached it?

There is a fearful denunciation in the Apocalypse, and it is made the closing passage of the sacred canon; it is made a fence, as it were to shield divine truth from the additions and mutilations of bold intruders; no less than a tremendous menace, that " to him who adds unto these things, God shall add to him the plagues written in this book. To him that takes away, God shall take away his part out of the book of life."

CHARACTER OF THOSE WHO EXPECT SALVATION FOR THEIR GOOD WORKS. — OF THOSE WHO DEPEND ON A CARELESS NOMINAL FAITH. — BOTH THESE CHARACTERS UNFAVOURABLE TO PRAYER. — CHRISTIANITY A RELIGION OF LOVE WHICH DISPOSES TO PRAYER, EXHIBITED IN A THIRD CHARACTER.

We proceed now to make some observations on two different classes of Christians, who, without neglecting prayer, obstruct its efficacy by certain opinions in immediate connection with their practice; opinions, which, though in direct opposition to each other, yet, if Christianity be true, are neither of them safe.

The one, with a pretence of faith, profess to know God; but in works, in a great measure, deny Him; the other are working out their own salvation, but it is without fear or trembling; they work in their own strength, without looking unto God to enable them " to will and to do of His good pleasure."

While multitudes are ruining themselves by a fatal reliance on the merit of their own works, it is, perhaps, not saying too much to assert that more are undone by a loose, traditional, unexamined dependence on the Saviour. If many are wrong who think to purchase heaven by their own industry, more err by this cheaper mode of an indefinite and careless reliance on the ill-understood promises of the Gospel. If we cannot, of these two evils, determine which is greatest, it would not be difficult to prove that both are equally unfavourable to fervent prayer.

The careless liver who trusts in an unfounded hope, deceives himself, because he thinks his trust, though he never enquires into it, looks more like grace.

Good works are rather less likely to deceive always, because those who maintain their superiority as a doctrine, cannot but see how far they fall themselves in practice, short of their profession; so far as to render it evident, that good works are with much greater sedulity performed by that sound class of Christians, who utterly reject any confidence in the performance of them. The former make salvation the easiest possible acquisition; the other believe it to be difficult, but fancy that the difficulty is to be overcome by a few more good deeds; which, shall we say, is the more misleading opinion?

Yet it must be confessed, that in this age of speculative religion, many do not sufficiently insist on these indispensable indications of a true and lively faith. For, after all, are not the right actions of a consistently holy life, the most unequivocal outward signs of an inward and spiritual grace? Not to insist on them, is to despise the value of those substantial evidences which our Lord himself made the criterion by which to judge of men, — " by their fruits ye shall know them." The tree of life is no barren tree; it bears all manner of fruits.

There is indeed less necessity than ever to decry good works. Men are not so violently addicted to them, as, by the warnings given against them, one might be led to suppose. To exalt good works as the procuring cause of salvation, is to put them in the place of Christ. To depreciate good works, is to depreciate such a life as Christ has given us both the command, and the example to lead; that command, of which the language was always one, " if ye love me keep my commandments;" and that example which presents such a tissue of holy actions, as nothing but Divinity could exhibit, yet enlightened and assisted humanity may and must aspire to imitate.

With this command and this example,

devotion was always indissolubly connected. Previously to giving his Divine pattern for the due performance of prayer, he alluded to the actual duty as already well understood and regularly practised; for doubtless he had habituated them to the duty, before he said, " *when* ye pray," — " After this manner therefore pray you."

Faith is the principle which first led the sinner to apply for grace and mercy to the Redeemer of sinners. It is the same principle, which, by its gradual operation, leads to the renewing of his nature, the purifying his heart, and the sanctifying his conduct. This faith, with its practical consequences, must be sought for, by the only means through which it can be obtained, the influence of the Holy Spirit on humble, fervent, spiritual prayer.

But there is another, and, it is to be feared, a large class, who do good without being good. Though this may be too frequently the case; though it is the motive which determines on the quality of the action, yet, if the best action will not save the best man, there is little hope of its efficacy towards the salvation of a bad one.

Perhaps the man in question is charitable; but his charity may be stimulated by his vanity — a too common, but most misleading motive. Perhaps he does a deed of bounty from the too usual hope that this good action may be thrown into the opposite scale against a bad one; perhaps he hopes that his acts of benevolence may atone for the irregularities of a disorderly life — but, be this as it may, do not discourage his giving, let him continue to give, the act may improve the principle, he may in time detect the difference of his internal feelings in the performance of a good and a bad action. Perhaps the repetition of his good deeds may lead to a diminution of his bad ones. The passion of shame sometimes operates usefully, and every passion being under the control of God, may eventually be made the instrument of good.

And who does not remember instances in which the frequently repeated bounty was the unprompted feeling of a compassionate and liberal heart, of a heart tender and kind, though yet unsanctified by religion?

Yet who would restrain the right action? Who would forbid the gentle deed of charity? Who would wish to aggravate his, perhaps awful account, by witholding his hand? Who would willingly add this omission of what is right to his aggregate sum of what is wrong? Who would not even hope that it may prove a leading step to what is better? Who would not hope that, as good principles naturally tend to good actions, yet though it is reversing the usual order, for the stream to lead back to the fountain, yet who knows but the repetition of good actions may not only deter him from such as are bad, but may put his mind into such a frame as may lead him to examine the true principle of action, and thus to find, that though he has unhappily begun at the wrong end, that the right end is not even yet unattainable? Who can say that he may not be brought to examine his own heart, and be thus brought to the exercise of cordial prayer; by that he will be taught to know that "if any man will do the will of God, he shall know of the doctrine whether it be of God."

Our compassionate Redeemer cherished every hopeful appearance. When he saw some symptoms of goodness in the young Ruler " He loved him." But his amiableness was not religion. Though his obedience to the commandments was less defective than that of many a high professor; like others, who confidently trust in their own merit, he enquired not it is to be feared, so much for improvement, as from a sense of conscious integrity and the hope of commendation — he enquired what was yet wanting to the perfection of his character.

He who knew all things, already knew that his love of money was greater than his love of God. Here he saw that this promising character was vulnerable. The one thing he wanted was more than the many things he possessed. He failed in the trial. He had some concern about his soul, but more about his money; "he went away sorrowing," because he could not secure the one without the sacrifice of the other.

This is, with *us*, as much a test of character now, as it was then. It is not until we see a man acting in direct opposition to his predominant sin that we can venture to hope that he is renewed in the spirit of his mind, that he is even got on right ground. Zaccheus, who probably set out worse than the ruler, obtained this grand victory which the other missed.

This promising young man, in proclaiming his obedience to the commands, did not, however, boast of his devotion; yet, in so moral a character, we cannot suppose that prayer was altogether neglected — but it must have been that prayer of which our Lord says "this people draweth nigh unto me with their mouth, and honoureth me with their lips, but their heart is far from me." Had it been sincere prayer, it would have been influential prayer. No slave to avarice *can* worship God in spirit and in truth, and it is such that the Father seeketh to worship him. While the heart remains unchanged, the temper unsanctified, and the life unfruitful, the prayer has not been "the effectual fervent prayer which availeth much."

But there is a third character, who, thinking both the others lately noticed to be wrong, is determined himself to be right. He divides the difference, and adopts half of the scheme of each. He approves of works, but doubts their unassisted efficacy to obtain salvation. He honours the Redeemer, and places confidence in His sacrifice; but it is not a full, entire, unmeasured, confidence. He thinks the Saviour so far competent towards effecting part of his salvation that he cannot be saved without him, but dares not trust Him with the whole. So, without intending to be profane, he enters into a kind of partnership with Him whose blood was made a full, perfect, and sufficient oblation, and satisfaction for the sins of the whole world. He proposes to contribute his own share to a contract of his own making, trusting that, as the Saviour knows he is not perfect, He will graciously supply whatever is deficient in his services, and make up what is lacking to their perfection, he himself continuing to be the working partner.

But, if he be a thinking and a feeling character, if he be sincere in his desire after divine truth, though ignorant of its true nature, he at length begins to find that the plan, which he once thought so admirably contrived, does not answer.

He finds that his spiritual interests do not advance. He begins to discover that his faith is cold, even his work is sluggish, and its progress unsatisfactory. His exertions want the inspiring principle, they want a genuine faith. He begins to discover, that even his good actions, on which he had been accustomed to rest half his salvation, are exceeded by those persons who do more, and put no trust in them.

He at length, through the influence of divine grace, begins to discover, or rather to feel, that while one party is exclusively exalting faith and the other works, both seem to have forgotten, or rather not to have known, that there is a third, a heavenly principle, a sacred cement without which their separation might be eternal, and even their junction would be imperfect. This sacred principle is LOVE. He now knows, experimentally, that Christianity is a religion of the affections, a sentiment of the heart—that it demands and confers that charity without which faith is dead, and works are vain. It is that heavenly sentiment, the love of God in Christ shed abroad in the heart, without which he that liveth is counted dead — that principle without which the gift of prophecy, of mysteries, and all knowledge were unavailing — without which, giving all the goods to the poor, and even the body to be burned, will not profit — it is that indestructible attribute, which, when prophecies shall fail, and tongues shall cease, and knowledge vanish away, will *never fail* — it is that perfect thing which shall subsist when " that which is in part shall be done away." Love will survive when faith shall become sight, and hope shall be fruition. It shall constitute our happiness when we shall know God " even as we are known." We shall possess it in its plenitude, when we shall awake up after His likeness. For love, like every other holy disposition, is but an emanation of the perfections of God, a spark from the original flame, an assimilation to his nature; since God is love.

In faith there may be fear; in works there may be constraint; but the inspiring, invigorating, endearing, principle of love changes the fearful slave into the affectionate child; transforms *Him* whom we had degraded as a hard master into a tender father.—This love makes labour light, service freedom, dependence safety, duty delight, sufferings easy, obedience pleasure, submission choice. By the warmth with which he now cultivates this "Unction from the Holy One," he will be rendered more meet for that fulness of joy which is at His right-hand for evermore.

He has now completely found his own utter insufficiency for this great work. He is in the situation of the newly converted apostle, who had doubtless previously exercised a regular but formal devotion, but it never would have been said of him before—"behold he prayeth!" He begins with lowly prostration to besiege the throne of grace; he now prays with a fervour he never felt before. He goes on to feel, not only its necessity, but its efficacy; gradually acknowledges its transforming power, and in time becomes sensible that its consolations are neither few nor small.

He now sees objects with other eyes, the visual ray is purged; to his rectified optics — " trees are become men." He now exclaims, " not of works, lest any man should boast." But though he has left off boasting, he is so far from having left off working, that he is far more active in good deeds, than when he trusted they would carry him to heaven; superinduced humility, has completely let him into the secrets of his own heart. He feels wants and desires of which he was never before sensible; and wants felt readily find a tongue, readily suggest unbidden prayer, unprompted praise. Prayer is become the very breath of his being; praise is so much his delight, that he almost forgets it is his duty. It is no longer his task, but his refreshment. What lately seemed a necessary drudgery, the severe injunction of a hard master, is now the pleasant service of an affectionate child.

He is deeply grieved at the time he has lost, but he is no less disposed to retrieve than to lament the past. He has found that the soul will not be saved where the heart is not renewed. Of that renewal, by the influence of the Divine Spirit, he is become more and more sensible in his devotional exercises. With a deeper sense of imperfection as he becomes less imperfect, he is yet sensible of new dispositions, of new energies, of a heart to trust, and a will to obey. He feels an increasing desire of conformity to his Divine Saviour, and such a growth in grace, that with him to will and to do is almost become the same thing.

All the faculties which God has given him are filled with the idea of God—

He retains Him in his *memory* by the recollection of His mercies — he retains Him in his *understanding*, by meditating on His perfections. By this intelligent faculty he reflects on what God is in himself, in His word, and to His own soul. In his *will*, he loves God, and laments that he ever loved any thing in comparison of Him. Thus all his intellectual powers, voluntarily as it were, press into the worship of God, or, in the fewer and better words of the Psalmist, he summons them all to assist in his devotions, saying, " Let all that is within me praise the Lord."

PRAYER. — THE CONDITION OF ITS ATTENDANT BLESSINGS. — USELESS CONTENTION ABOUT TERMS.

Men contend more about words than about things. A misunderstanding respecting them causes more disputes than the subjects of which they are the signs. In speaking, for instance, of the connection between prescribed duties and promised blessings, are there not certain inoffensive and well-meaning words which seem to have brought more reproach on those who use them than their harmless, if not legitimate, character, may be thought to deserve. One of them, indeed, might expect more gentle treatment on the single ground that it is very frequently to be found in the Holy Scriptures.

The obnoxious terms to which we here allude are *rewards* and *conditions*. We have, in general, avoided the use of them, not for any harm discoverable in them when used and understood in the scriptural sense, but for fear of creating an idea contrary to what was intended to be conveyed. In the legal sense they are very exceptionable, for in the one case we deserve nothing from God, and in the other we can do nothing of ourselves.

We do not presume to make conditions with God, but He condescends to propose them to us. In this latter case, it is free grace imposes the reasonable condition: his free grace bestows the unmerited reward. Are not all the promises of the Gospel conditional? The beatitudes include both the condition and the reward. Our blessed Saviour, in his sermon, multiplies, and individualizes his promises. He gives us a string of articles of blessedness and recompence; the specific recompence to the specific duty; amongst others, mercy to the merciful; the kingdom of heaven to those who are persecuted for righteousness' sake; the vision of God to the pure in heart.

The Holy Spirit consecrates the doctrine of *rewards*, by teaching the Apostle to connect it even with the very being of Omnipotence. "God *is*," and it immediately follows, that " he is a *rewarder* of them that seek him." Surely this is a condition, as much as the threat that he will punish those " who know not God." Every where, and particularly in the Psalms, prayer is made the condition of obtaining. In asking, seeking, and knocking, the condition and the reward most appropriately meet.

To those who come to the Redeemer, he has declared that " they shall in no wise be cast out." Their coming is the condition of their being accepted. "Rest," again, is the consoling promise which he makes to " the heavy laden" who come to him. " He that honoureth me, I will honour," is both a condition and a reward. What is the promise of pardon to repentance, but a condition? The negative denunciation is a condition. "Ye will *not* come to me, that ye might have life." "Without holiness no man shall see the Lord; without faith it is impossible to please God." Do not these imply the blessings attending the contrary temper? State the question thus: Shall we be heard, if we do not pray? Shall we be pardoned, if we do not repent?

"Eye hath not seen, nor ear heard, the things which God hath prepared for them that love him." It is the love of God then, which is the condition of obtaining those things which the heart of man cannot conceive.

All the promises made to faith are conditions, as are those made to Holiness. The good and faithful servants who well employed their ten and five talents, were rewarded by having their talents doubled; the punishment of their unprofitable companion was a conditional punishment. He had made no use of what was committed to him.

Why is that bright variety of promises, "to him that overcometh," repeated with such unwearied iteration, in the sublime visions of the saint at Patmos? What is it but a beautiful concatenation of conditions and rewards, closed with that joyful climax, "he that overcometh shall be a pillar in the temple of the Lord, and shall go no more out." If language more clear can be found, if assurances more explicit can be given, if promises more distinct can be produced, we confess we know not where to look for them. Did not Moses himself, the most disinterested of men, look to the recompense of the reward? And did not a greater than Moses, "for the joy that was set before him endure the cross, despising the shame?"

Promises like these were the support, and joy, and triumph, of his immediate apostles, and of their remotest successors;

of Ridley, of Latimer, and Cranmer. They will still be the consolation of the Christian sufferer for righteousness' sake to the end of time. Let us not then forfeit our inheritance by slighting the promise.

"This is a reward wholly of grace in respect of our deserving, but of justice, on account of the purchase of it by the sacred treasure of Christ's blood, and the unchangeable tenor of the Gospel, wherein God promises heaven to all obedient and true believers."

The things may be called by other names, but they amount to the same meaning. There is a proud disinterestedness which would seem to intimate, that, because we deserve nothing we expect nothing. Our expectation, it is true, arises entirely from God's goodness, and not at all from our merit. It arises especially from his fidelity, which leads him to make good his own engagement. He has Himself said, "faithful is He that has promised."

This view of the subject deducts nothing from that free salvation purchased for us by the death of the Redeemer. We repeat, it deducts nothing from the sovereignty of God. All the promises are the gracious offers of an amnesty by an insulted King, who condescends to offer a treaty to his rebellious subjects. We deserve nothing at his hands. He owes us nothing. Punishment we do indeed deserve " if He were extreme to mark what is done amiss;" yet He declares that punishment is his strange work. He has reversed the attainder, by the sacrifice of his Son. The attainted rebel, instead of disputing about the terms of reconciliation, instead of proposing terms of his own, thankfully accepts what the king offers. Though our pardon hangs on a firm belief in the great truths he has revealed, let us not so explain these as to hazard or neglect the duties he has enjoined us to perform. If our faith, though sincere, is often weak, let us remember, that our obedience is even more imperfect than our faith; and let us, by fervent and unremitting prayer, labour at once to build up our faith which is weak, and to perfect our obedience which is defective.

God not only pardons as a merciful king, He enacts laws as a wise legislator; still the old revolutionary principles are continually breaking out; to check which, the sovereign proposes *terms* as proofs of our allegiance. He does by no means annex salvation to them, but He requires them as marks of our repentance, as confirmations of our loyalty. He requires them as evidences, both of our faith and of our submission. By the infusion of a new spirit of life consequent on His pardon, the acquitted rebel adopts a new set of principles which shew themselves by overt acts, suggested and nourished by fervent prayer.

We are aware that the term " evidences" used above, is to many no less revolting, than those which we have previously noticed, but by this excessive affectation of disinterestedness and refining on the promises, we shall come to do away all moral obligation, we shall attenuate the substantial realities of Christianity into a meagre theory, reduce the fruitful principle of practical religion, to a dry and unproductive speculation, a barren thing to which nothing that is perceptible, palpable, tangible, and practical, is necessarily appended.

On the other hand, it is but too notorious, that the terms here humbly attempted to be vindicated and restored to their true signification, are too frequently made the sum and substance, the whole of religion, till the spirituality of the Gospel, and the great peculiarities of the religion of Jesus, are smothered in the heap of frigid human ethics.

It is by the promises annexed to these conditions, that the Christian is gradually brought to consider prayer, not merely as a duty, but to value it as a privilege; and the more earnestly he cultivates this spirit of supplication, the more deeply will it enable him to penetrate into the recesses of his own heart. The more he discovers the evils which he there finds, he will be so far from being deterred by the discovery, from approaching to the fountain of mercy, that it will lead him to be more diligent as well as more fervent, in his application there. Nothing so faithfully discovers to us our spiritual exigencies, nothing can quicken our petitions for their relief so powerfully, as the conviction of their actual existence. In this full conviction, in this earnest application, the Christian at length feels the efficacy of prayer in its consolations, its blessedness, in its transforming power,

VAIN EXCUSES FOR THE NEGLECT OF PRAYER.—THE MAN OF BUSINESS.— CASE OF NEHEMIAH.—PRAYER AGAINST THE FEAR OF DEATH.— CHARACTERS TO WHOM THIS PRAYER IS RECOMMENDED.

There are not a few, who offer apologies for the neglect of spiritual duties, by saying they believe them to be right, but that they are tempted from the exercise of them by idleness, or business, by company, or pleasure. This may be true, but temptations are not compulsions. The great adversary of souls may fill the fancy with alluring images of enjoyment, so as to draw us away from any duty, but it is in our own choice to indulge, and through grace to repel them. He may act upon the passions through outward objects, which introduce them to the mind through the senses, but the grace of God enables all who faithfully ask it, to withstand them.

If we were not at liberty to reject temptation, sin would be no sin. It is the offer of the grace of resistance not used, which makes the offender to be without excuse. All the motives and allurements to sin, would be ineffectual, would we keep up in our minds what are its " wages "—death; death spiritual, death eternal!

Of all the excuses for the neglect of prayer, the man of business justifies his omission to himself, by the most plausible apologies. Many of this class, active for themselves, and useful to the world, are far from disputing either the propriety, or the duty of prayer; they are willing however, for the present, to turn over this duty to the clergy, to the idle, to women and children. They allow it to be an important thing, but not the most important. They acknowledge, if men have time to spare, they cannot spend it better; but *they* have no time. It is indeed a duty, but a duty not to be compared with that of the court, the bar, the public office, the counting-house, or the shop.

Now, in pleading for the importance of the one, we should be the last to detract from that of the other. We only plead for their entire compatibility.

We pass over the instance of Daniel, a man of business and a statesman, and of many other public characters, recorded in Scripture, and confine ourselves to the example of Nehemiah. He was not only an officer in the court of the greatest king of the East, but it was his duty to be much in the royal presence. He was, on a particular occasion, under deep affliction; for Jerusalem was in ruins! On a certain day his sadness was so great, as to be visible to the king, at whose table he was attending.

The monarch enquired the cause of

his sorrow, and what request he had to make. He instantly "prayed to the God of heaven," doubtless to strengthen him, and then made his petition to the king for no less a boon, than to allow him to rebuild the walls of the sacred city. His prayer preceded his request. It was that prayer, which gave him courage to present that petition, and which perhaps induced the sovereign to grant it. What a double encouragement is here given to the courtier, both to pray to God, and to speak truth to a king!

Though the plea of the man of business, for his own particular exemption, can by no means be granted; yet it is the sense he entertains of the value of his professional duties, which deceives him. It leads him to believe, that there can be no evil in substituting business for devotion. He is conscious that he is industrious, and he knows that industry is a great moral quality. He is rightly persuaded, that the man of pleasure has no such plea to produce. He therefore imposes on himself, with the belief that there *can* be no harm in substituting a moral for a religious exercise; for he has learned to think highly of morality, while he assigns to religion only an inferior degree in his scale of duties.

He usually goes to church once on the Sunday; but it does not at all infringe on his religious system to examine his accounts, to give a great dinner, or to begin a journey on that day.

Now it is a serious truth, that there is no man to whom prayer is more imperatively a duty, or more obviously a necessity, than to the man of business; whether in the higher or the middle classes of society. There is no man who more stands in need of quieting his anxieties, regulating his tempers, cooling his spirits by a devout application for the blessing of God; none to whom it is more necessary to implore the divine protection for the duties, or preservation from the dangers of the scene in which he is about to engage; none to whom it is more important to solicit direction in the difficulties which the day may produce; none on whom it is more incumbent to solicit support against the temptations which may be about to assail him; none to whom the petition for an enlightened conscience, an upright intention, a sound probity, and an undeviating sincerity, is of more importance.

What is so likely as prayer to enable him to stand prepared to meet the accidental fluctuations in his affairs, to receive without inebriation, a sudden flow of prosperous fortune, or to sustain any adverse circumstance with resignation?

Even persons in more retired situations, even those who have made considerable advances in religion, cannot but acknowledge how much the ordinary and necessary cares of daily life, especially, how much any unexpected accession to them, are likely to cause absence and distraction in their devotions:—how much then ought they, whose whole life is business, to be on their guard against these dangers, to double their vigilance against them, and to implore direction under them.

Were the Christian soldier accustomed never to engage in the moral battle of daily life, without putting on this panoply, the shafts of temptation would strike with a feeble and erring blow; they would not so deeply pierce the guarded heart. And were fervent humble daily prayer once conscientiously adopted, its effects would reach beyond the week-day engagements. It would gradually extend its benign influence to the postponing of settling accounts, the festive dinner, and the not absolutely necessary journey, to one of those six days in which we are enjoined to labour. It would lead him to the habit of doing " no manner of work" on that day, in which the doing of it was prohibited by the great Lawgiver in his own person.

We have more than once alluded to the diversities of character, occasional events, difference in the state of mind, as well as of circumstances, which may not only render the prayer which is suitable to one man unsuitable to another, but unsuitable to the same man under every alteration of circumstances.

But among the proper topics for prayer, there is one which, being of universal interest, ought not to be omitted. For by whatever dissimilarity of character, capacity, profession, station, or temper, the condition of man, and, of course, the nature of prayer, is diversified — there is one grand point of union, one circumstance, one condition, in which they must all meet; one state, of which every man is equally certain; one event which happeneth to all, — "it is appointed unto every man once to die." The rugged road of sorrow, the flowery path of pleasure, as well as

"The paths of glory lead but to the grave."

In praying, therefore, against the fear of death, we do not pray against a contingent but a certain evil; we pray to be delivered from the overwhelming dread of that house which is appointed for all living — we are put in mind that all who are born must die!

"The end of all things is at hand." To what purpose does the apostle convert this awful proclamation? Does he use it to encourage gloomy tempers, to invite to unprofitable melancholy? No: he uses the solemn admonition to stir us up to moral goodness — therefore, "be sober" — he does more, he uses it to excite us to religious vigilance, — "and watch unto prayer."

Some men, and they are not the best men, talk boldly of death, especially while they suppose it to be at a distance; but this boastful heroism is a very equivocal symptom of their being in a proper state to meet it. Others of a less confident, but not more serious cast of mind, take pains to keep it as far as possible from their thoughts, lest the indulging such gloomy reflections should make them uneasy, and embitter their present enjoyments. They banish it, indeed, from their thoughts, as they do other unpleasant subjects; but it is no proof that we do not fear a thing, because we manage to keep it out of sight; on the contrary, the effort betrays the very fear which it denies.

There is an inconsistency in the character of man, so preposterous, that we should not believe it, if we did not feel as well as see it. We continue eagerly to catch at the things which are always sliding from us, and which no grasp of ours can retain, whilst we forget the things that are not only hastening to meet us, but which will remain with us, not through time only, but eternity.

Others are afraid to think of death for the same reason that they are afraid to make their will, lest it should bring it nearer: but we know that it will keep up the remembrance without accelerating the approach; familiarity with the thought is the best means of conquering the fear. It is not pusillanimity, bu prudence, so to fear death as to fear to meet it in an unprepared state of mind; and that fear will always be safe and salutary, which leads to the preparation.

Prayer against the fear of death, by keeping up in us a constant remembrance of our mortality, will help to wean us from a too intimate attachment to the things we are so soon to quit. By this habitual preparation to meet our Judge, we shall be brought to pray more earnestly for an interest in the great Intercessor; and to strive more effectually against every offence which may aggravate the awfulness of that meeting.— Above all, such prayer will more emphatically remind us that it was sin which brought death into the world; which introduced that original principle and first act of sin, from which all our natural, evil, and practical offences are derived.

But let us not be accustomed to think of death as a detached and separate object, as the mere insulated circumstance of its closing our eyes for ever on all we have been accustomed to cherish; let us not think of it only as a consignment to the narrow chambers of the tomb, but let us ever connect with the idea of death, the consoling assurance that, to the real Christian, its sting is drawn out; this will fill the heart with boundless love and endless gratitude to Him who has extracted it. This thought of death, though it will keep up in the mind the anticipation of that night, which, as to this world shall know no morning, will also keep up the glorious prospect of that eternal day which shall know no night.

Fervent prayer, that divine grace may prepare us for death, will, if cordially adopted, answer many great moral purposes. It will remind every individual of every class that "the time is short"—that "there is no repentance in the grave."

To the *man of opulence*, who heapeth up riches and cannot tell who shall gather them, prayer will be a constant memento:

it will remind him that he walketh in a vain shadow, and disquieteth himself in vain; it will remind him of laying up treasures where thieves cannot enter, nor rust corrode.

The habit of praying against the fear of death would check the pride of youthful *beauty*, by reminding her how soon it must say to the worm, thou art my father, and to corruption thou art my mother and my sister.

The *man of genius*, he who thought that of making many books there would be no end; who, in his zeal to write, had neglected to pray; who had thought little of any immortality but that which was to be conferred by the applause of dying creatures like himself; who, in the vanity of possessing talents, had forgotten that he must one day account for the application of them; if happily he should be brought to see the evil of his own heart, to feel the wants of his own soul, how intense will be his repentance, that he had loved the praise of men more than the praise of God! how fervently will he pray that his mercies may not aggravate the account of his sins; that his talents may not become the instrument of his punishment! How earnestly will he supplicate for pardon, how devoutly will he " give glory to God before his feet stumble on the dark mountains!"

The *man of business*, to whom we have already adverted, who thought his schemes so deeply laid, his speculations so prudently planned, that nothing could frustrate them; who calculated that the future was as much in his power as the present, forgot that death, that grand subverter of projects, might interpose his *veto*. This man, who could not find time to pray, must find time to die — he may at length find — happy if he ever find it, that he cannot meet his end with a peaceful heart, and a resigned spirit, without the preparation of prayer for support in that awful period, " when his purposes shall be broken off and all his thoughts perish."

The *man of pleasure,* alas! what shall we say for *him?* He is sunk to the lowest step of degradation in the moral scale; he has not even human supports; he has robbed himself even of the ordinary consolations resorted to by ordinary men. He has no stay on which to lay hold, no twig at which to catch, no pretence by which to flatter himself into a false peace; no recollection of past usefulness; he has neither served his country, nor benefited society — what shall we say for him? If he pray not for himself, we must pray for him — with God all things are possible.

The *patriot,* indefatigable in the public service, distinguished for integrity, but neglecting the offices of Christianity; whose lofty character power had not warped, nor cupidity debased, but whose religious principles, though they had never been renounced, had not been kept in exercise; a spirit of rare disinterestedness; a moralist of unblenched honour, but who pleaded that duty had left him little time for devotion! Should divine grace incline him at last to seek God, should he begin to pray to be prepared for death and judgment, he will deeply regret with the contrite cardinal, not that he served his king faithfully, but that his highest services had not been devoted to their highest object. In this frame of mind, that ambition which was satisfied with what earth could give, or kings reward, will appear no longer glorious in his eyes. True and just to his king, devoted to his country, faithful to all but his God and himself, he now laments that he had neglected to seek a better country, neglected to serve the King Eternal, the blessed and only Potentate; neglected to obtain an interest in a kingdom which shall not be moved. He feels that mere patriotism, grand as is its object, and important as is its end, will not afford support to a soul sinking at the approach of the inevitable hour, at the view of final judgment.

The *hero*, who, in the hot engagement, surrounded with the " pride, pomp, and circumstance of war," bravely defied death, forgot all that was personal, and only remembered — nobly remembered, his country, and his immediate duty;— animated with the glory that was to be acquired with his arm, and almost ready to exclaim with the Roman patriot;

" ——————— What pity
That we can die but once to serve our country!"

yet this hero, if he had never made a conscience of prayer, may he not hereafter find, that the most successful instrumentality is a distinct thing in itself, and will be different in its results, from personal piety? May he not find that, though he saved others, himself he cannot save?

If, however, in after-life, in the cool shade of honourable retirement, he be brought through the grace of God, to habituate himself to earnest prayer, he will deeply regret that he ever entered the field of battle without imploring the favour of the God of battles; that he had ever returned alive from slaughtered squadrons, without adoring the Author of his providential preservation. If his penitence be sincere, his prayer will be effectual. It will fortify him under the more depressing prospect of that death which is soon to be encountered in the solitude of his darkened chamber, without witnesses, without glory, without the cheering band, without the spirit-stirring drum; without the tumultuous acclamation; with no objects to distract his attention; no conflicting concerns to divide his thoughts; no human arm, either of others or his own, on which to depend. This timely reflection, this late, though never *too* late prayer, may still prepare him for a peaceful dying-bed; may lead him to lean on a stronger arm than his own, or that of an army; may conduct him to a victory over his last enemy, and thus dispose him to meet death in a safer state than when he despised it in the field, may bring him to acknowledge, that while he continued to live without subjection to the Captain of his salvation, though he had fought bravely, he had not yet fought the good fight.

THE CONSOLATIONS OF PRAYER—ITS PERPETUAL OBLIGATION.

In addition to what has already been observed, as to convenient seasons for prayer, we cannot but remark, that many Christians have been enabled to convert their trials into blessings, by gradually bringing themselves to devote the hours of wakeful and even painful nights to devout meditation and prayer. By doing at first some violence to their inclinations, they have afterwards found in it both profit and pleasure. The night has been made to them a season of heart-searching thought and spiritual consolation. Solitude and stillness completely shut out the world; its business, its cares, its impertinences. The mind is sobered, the passions are stilled, it seems to the watchful Christian as if there were in the universe only God and his own soul. It is an inexpressible consolation to him to feel that the one Being in the universe, who never slumbereth nor sleepeth, is the very Being to whom he has free access, even in the most unseasonable hours. The faculties of the mind may not, perhaps, be in their highest exercise, but the affections of the heart, from the exclusion of distracting objects, more readily ascend to their noblest object. Night and darkness are no parasites: conscience is more easily alarmed. It puts on fewer disguises. We appear to ourselves more what we really are. This detection is salutary. The glare which the cheerful daylight, business, pleasure, and company, had shed over all objects, is withdrawn. Schemes which, in the day had appeared plausible, now present objections. What had then appeared safe, now, at least, seems to require deliberation. This silent season of self-examination, is a keen detector of any latent evil, which, like the fly in the box of perfume, may corrupt much that is pure.

When this communion with God can be maintained, it supplies deficiencies of devotion to those who have little leisure during the day; and, by thus rescuing these otherwise lost hours, it snatches time from oblivion, at once adds to the length of life, and weans from the love of it.

If the wearied and restless body be tempted to exclaim "would God it were morning," the very term suggests the most consoling of all images. The quickened mind shoots forward beyond this vale of tears, beyond the dark valley of the shadow of death; it stretches onward to the joyful morning of the Resurrection; it anticipates that blessed state where there is no more weeping and no more night—no weeping, for God's own hand shall wipe away the tears; no night, for the Lamb himself shall be the light.

If disqualifying pain, or distressing languor, prevent the utterance of supplication, patience is itself a prayer, and a prayer which will not fail to be heard. We have a striking instance of an answer to silent prayer, in the case of Moses. In a situation of extreme distress, when he had not uttered a word, "the Lord said unto him, I have heard thy crying."

The tender mercy of our compassionate Father will make sense, and find meaning in a prayer which is almost unintelligible to the languid sufferer who offers it. God wants not to be informed, he wants only to be remembered, to be loved, to be sought.

If, however, in the conduct of this nightly watching, and this nightly prayer, your own stock of thought or expression is absolutely deficient, prophets and apostles will not only afford you the most encouraging examples, but most profitable assistance. More especially the royal treasury of king David lies open to you; and whatever are your wants, there your resources are inexhaustible.

What joyful appeals does the psalmist make to Him to whom the darkness and the light are both alike! "Have I not remembered Thee in my bed, and thought upon Thee when I was waking?" "In the night," he again exclaims, "I commune with my own heart, and search out my spirit." And of this holy practice was he so little weary, that he resolves to persevere in it. "As long as I live will I magnify Thee in this manner." Similar to this is the apostrophe of the evangelical prophet — "With my soul have I desired Thee in the night."

The Psalms of David exhibit the finest specimen of experimental religion in the world. They are attended with this singular advantage and this unspeakable comfort, that in them God speaks to us and we speak to Him. This delightful interlocution between the King of saints and the penitent sinner; this interchange of character, this mixture of prayer and promise, of help implored and grace bestowed, of weakness pleaded and strength imparted, of favour shown and gratitude returned, of prostration on one part and encouragement on the other, of abounding sorrow, and overflowing mercy, this beautiful variety of affecting intercourse between sinful dust and infinite goodness, lifts the abased penitent into the closest and most elevating communion with his Saviour and his God.

Yet, inestimable as are the Psalms of David, in every point of view, and especially for the purpose here recommended, as a refuge for the suffering body, the wakeful mind, the praying spirit, and the oppressed heart — that very sanctity, and depth of devotional feeling, which is their life-blood, may lead to a dangerous misapplication in the mouth of the irreligious. Holy expressions in prayer, and ebullitions of grateful praise, are more easily committed to the memory, than impressed upon the heart. And is there not some danger, that not only the mere formalist, but even the immoral man may apply to himself sentiments, declarations, assurances, and comforts, which can only belong to the real Christian? For instance; the arrogant man, as if, like the dervise in the Persian fable, he had shot his soul into the character he assumes, repeats with complete self-application, " Lord, I am not high-minded;" the trifler says, " I hate vain thoughts;" the irreligious, " Lord, how I love thy law." He who seldom prays at all, confidently repeats, " All the day long I am occupied in thy statutes." The covetous, in the words of Paul or David, with as much self-complacency deprecates avarice, as if the anathema against it had ever opened either his heart or his purse.

On the other hand, as the hardest substances, by continual attrition, are at length penetrated, it is the pleasing task of charity to hope, that the habitual repetition of such feelings, sentiments, and principles may sink into the hard heart, may lead its possessor to look into himself, to compare what he feels with what he reads, and by discovering the discrepancy between his life and his prayers, may open his eyes on his own danger, till by the grace of God the holy vehicle of his hypocrisy may be made that of his conversion.

Perhaps you are a doubting, weak, and trembling penitent; not indeed doubting of the mercies of God, but of your own interest in them. This feeling may arise from a deep and humbling sense of your own sins and infirmities, rather than from any criminal unbelief. Here comes into your relief a whole host of gracious promises, peculiarly adapted to your case. The tender images of "the smoking flax," and "the bruised reed," the promised acceptance of "the contrite spirit, and the broken heart." But beyond all praise is the consoling assurance of our great High Priest, that "he is touched with the feeling of our infirmities." Touched with them, not only when he was "a man of sorrows and acquainted with grief," but now when he is even "ascended to the glory which he had with his Father before the world began."

How soothing is this expression of the Divine compassion! It is not barely the hearing or the seeing, it is the *feeling* of our infirmities. He was in all points tempted like as we are. This is the most exquisite touch of sympathy; he not only suffered but was tempted; here indeed the resemblance has its limitation: for he was without sin. He knew the condition of " being tempted," but not that of yielding to it. It is this feeling of being tempted, which gives him such an intimate concern in the feeble, fearful Christian. He sends the angel of his presence, and saves them. What a striking confirmation of the blessed truth, that in all our afflictions he is afflicted, is the awful interrogation, " Saul, Saul, why persecutest thou," — not my church, but " *me ?*"

It is a further encouragement to the dejected spirit, that the Almighty was not contented to shew his willingness to pardon by single declarations, however strong and full. He has heaped up words, he has crowded images, he has accumulated expressions, he has exhausted language, by all the variety of synonymes which express love, mercy, pardon, and acceptance. They are graciously crowded together, that the trembling mourner who was not sufficiently assured by one, might be encouraged by another. And it is the consummation of the Divine goodness, that this message is not sent by his ambassador, but that the King of kings, the blessed and only Potentate, condescends Himself to pronounce this royal proclamation, "The Lord, the Lord God, merciful and gracious, long-suffering and abundant in goodness and truth, keeping mercy for thousands, forgiving iniquity, transgression, and sin!" Forgiving indeed; but in consonance with his just demand of repentance and reformation, "who will by no means clear the guilty."

The ardent and affectionate Apostle of the Gentiles, within a very few verses, has also represented the Almighty under every character that is endearing and consoling. He denominates him "the God of patience and of comfort," "the God of hope and of peace:" titles which are peculiarly addressed to all the exigencies of man, and graciously expressive of God's will and power to supply them. There is an appropriation of the terms to the state of the fallen children of mortality, caculated to take away all fear, and to fill the vacant room with love, and peace, and gratitude unspeakable.

Refuse not then to take comfort from the promises of God, when perhaps you are easily satisfied with the assurance of pardon from a frail and sinful creature like yourself whom you had offended. Why is God the only being who is not believed? who is not trusted? O Thou that hearest prayer, why unto Thee will not all flesh come?

But though God's pardoning grace knows no bounds, his sanctifying grace is given by measure, is given as we use what we have already received. God seems to reserve in his own hands a provision for our humility, and thus keeps prayer in full exercise. The one is progressive in its operation, the other is full and free, bestowed, not for any righteousness in the receiver, but for that full and perfect oblation once made for sin. Is it not a most fallacious trust to expect that our sins will be blotted out without that habitual repentance annexed to the promise? It is vain to offer the bribe of burnt offerings, the thousands of rams, or the rivers of oil. God desires not to be paid for our pardon, nor profited by our offerings. He never sells his favours. The riches of the universe, which are indeed already his, could not procure the pardon of a single sinner, but he prescribes the duty, when he promises the pardon. "Repent, that your sins may be blotted out."

It would therefore supply ample matter for habitual prayer, had we only the sins of our nature to lament; but when to these we add our practical offences, oh, how great is the sum of them! Yet though they are more than we can express, they are not greater than God can forgive; not more than the blood which was shed for them can wash out.

But he to whom the duty of prayer is unknown, and by whom the privilege of prayer is unfelt, or he by whom it is neglected, or he who uses it for form and not from feeling, may probably say, Will this work, wearisome even if necessary, never know an end? Will there be no period when God will dispense with its regular exercise? Will there never be such an attainment of the end proposed, as that we may be allowed to discontinue the means?

To these interrogatories there is but one answer, an answer which shall be also made, by an appeal to the enquirer himself.

If there is any day in which we are quite certain that we shall meet with no trial from Providence, no temptation from the world, any day in which we shall be sure to have no wrong tempers excited in ourselves, no call to bear with those of others, no misfortune to encounter, and no need of Divine assistance to endure it, on that morning we may safely omit prayer.

If there is any evening in which we have received no protection from God, and experienced no mercy at his hands; if we have not lost a single opportunity of doing or receiving good, if we are quite certain that we have not once spoken unadvisedly with our lips, nor entertained one vain or idle thought in our heart, on that night we may safely omit praise to God, and the confession of our own sinfulness, on that night we may safely omit humiliation and thanksgiving. To repeat the converse would be superfluous.

When we can conscientiously say, that religion has given a tone to our conduct, a law to our actions, a rule to our thoughts, a bridle to our tongue, a restraint to every wrong passion, a check to every evil temper, then, some will say we may safely be dismissed from the drudgery of prayer, it will then have answered all the end which you so tiresomely recommend. So far from it, we really figure to ourselves, that if we could hope to hear of a being brought to such perfection of discipline, it would unquestionably be found that this would be the very being who would continue most perseveringly in the practice of that devotion, which had so materially contributed to bring his heart and mind into so desirable a state, who would most tremble to discontinue prayer, who would be most appalled at the thought of the condition into which such discontinuance would be likely to reduce him. Whatever others do, he will continue for ever to "sing praises unto Thee, O Thou most Highest; he will continue to tell of Thy loving kindness early in the morning, and of thy truth in the night season."

It is true that while he considered religion as something nominal and ceremonial, rather than as a principle of spirit and of life, he felt nothing encouraging, nothing refreshing, nothing delightful in prayer. But since he began to feel it as the means of procuring the most substantial blessings to his heart; since he began to experience something of the realization of the promises to his soul, in the performance of this exercise, he finds there is no employment so satisfactory, none that his mind can so little do without; none that so effectually raises him above the world, none that so opens his eyes to its empty shadows, none which can make him look with so much indifference on its lying vanities; none that can so powerfully defend him against the assaults of temptation, and the allurements of pleasure, none that can so sustain him under labour, so carry him through difficulties; none that can so quicken him in the practice of every virtue, and animate him in the discharge of every duty.

But if prayer be so exhilarating to the soul, what shall be said of praise? Praise is the only employment, we had almost said, it is the only duty, in which self finds no part. In praise we go out of ourselves, and think only of Him to whom we offer it. It is the most purely disinterested of all services. It is gratitude without solicitation, acknowledgement without petition. Prayer is the overflowing expression of our wants, praise of our affections. Prayer is the language of the destitute, praise of the redeemed, sinner. If the angelic spirits offer their praises exempt from our mixture of infirmity or alloy, yet we have a motive for gratitude, unknown even to the angels. They are unfallen beings; they cannot say as we can,

"Worthy the Lamb, for he was slain for us." Prayer is the child of faith, praise of love. Prayer is prospective. Praise takes in, in its wide range, enjoyment of present, remembrance of past, and anticipation of future blessings. Prayer points the only way to heaven, "praise is already there."

ON INTERCESSORY PRAYER.

THE social affections were given us, not only for the kindliest, but the noblest purposes. The charities of father, son, and brother, were bestowed, not only to make life pleasant, but to make it useful; not only that we might contribute to the present comfort, but to the eternal benefit of each other.

These heaven-implanted affections are never brought into exercise more properly, nor with more lively feelings, than in intercessory prayer. Our friends may have wants which we cannot remove, desires which we cannot gratify, afflictions which we cannot relieve, but it is always in our power to bring them before God; to pray for them whenever we pray for ourselves. This, as it is a most pleasant and easy, so it is an indispensible obligation. It is a duty which brings the social affections into their highest exercise, and which may be reciprocally paid and received.

The same Scriptures which expressly enjoin that supplication, prayers, intercession, and giving of thanks be made for all men, furnish also numerous examples of the efficacy of intercessory prayer. We need not dwell on the instance of the rain obtained by the prayers of Elijah, or the earlier availing intercessions of Moses, with other public deliverances effected in the same manner.

Though the perseverance of Abraham's prayer did not prevent the extermination of the polluted city, yet doubtless the blessing he solicited for it returned into his own bosom, and the successive promises made by the Almighty Judge to the successively reduced number of the righteous, for whose sake the petition for preservation was offered, afford a proof of the Divine approbation and a striking encouragement to persist in the duty of intercessory prayer. The promise of God was not withdrawn. The prayer was conditional, and could the petitioner have made up his very lowest complement, the city had been saved. The interceding heart in any event is sure to gain something for itself.

Prayer is such an enlarger of the affections, such an opener of the heart, that we cannot but wonder how any who live in the practice of it, should be penurious in their alms; or if they do give, should do it "grudgingly or of necessity." Surely if our prayer be cordial, we shall be more ready to assist as well as to love those for whom we are in the habit of making supplication to God. It is impossible to pray sincerely for the well-being of others, without being desirous of contributing to it. We can hardly conceive a more complete species of self-deception than that practised by an avaricious professor of religion, one who goes on mechanically to pray for the poor, whilst his prayer has neither opened his heart nor his purse. He may value himself on this, as on other instances, of his ingenuity, in having found out so cheap a way of doing good, and go on contentedly, till he hear those tremendous words of exclusion, " Inasmuch as ye did it not to one of the least of these, ye did it not to me."

There is a generosity in religion. The same principle which disposes a Christian to contribute to the temporal interests of those he loves, inclines him to breathe his earnest supplication for their spiritual benefit. Not only does prayer for others promote natural affection, not only does it soften the heart of him who intercedes, but it is hoped that they for whom the intercession is made, may reap the benefit.

But our intercessions must neither dwell in generalities for the public, nor in limitations to the wants of our particular friends. The Christian is the friend of every description of the children of mortality. In the fulness of our compassion for the miseries of mankind, we pour out our hearts in prayer for the poor and destitute, and we do well. But there is another and a large class who are still more the objects of our pity, and consequently, should be of our prayers. We pray for those who have no portion in this world, but do we not sometimes forget to pray for those who have their whole portion in it? We pray for the praying servants of God, but perhaps we neglect to pray for those who never pray for themselves. These are the persons who stand most in need of the mercy of the Almighty, and of our Christian importunity in their favour.

Is it not affecting, that even into our devotions we are disposed to carry the regard we too highly indulge of the good things of this life, by earnestly imploring mercy upon those who want them; and by forgetting to offer our supplications in favour of those who are blinded by the too full enjoyment of them. If the one duty be done, should the other be left undone?

Happily we live in an age presenting many instances, where neither high station, nor great riches impede piety, or obstruct devotion. Yet, it is to be feared, that the general tendency of rank, and especially of riches, is to withdraw the heart from spiritual exercises, more than the hand from pecuniary bounty.

Let us then fervently include among the objects of our supplication that very pitiable and very necessitous class among the rich and great, if such a class there be, who live without any sensible feeling of the presence of God as acknowledged in prayer:—for those persons who never entertain a doubt of their own deserts, even if they do not deny Him who is the giver of the boundless blessings which lead them to forget Him. Strange! that the very overflowing cup which ought to ensure gratitude should induce forgetfulness! Strange! that prayer to

God should be neglected in proportion to the magnitude of His bounties.

May the writer be permitted to enrich the penury of her own meagre composition with a beautiful extract from one whose unequalled rhetoric was always warmed by a deep sensibility, and occasionally tinctured with religious feeling — the eloquent and almost prophetic author of Reflections on the Revolution in France:—

"The English people are satisfied, that to the great, the consolations of religion are as necessary as its instructions. They too are among the unhappy. They feel personal pain and domestic sorrow. In these they have no privilege, but are subject to pay their full contingent to the contributions levied on mortality. They want this sovereign balm under their gnawing cares and anxieties, which being less conversant about the limited wants of animal life, range without limit, and are diversified by infinite combinations in the wild and unbounded regions of imagination. Some charitable dole is wanting to these our often very unhappy brethren, to fill the gloomy void that reigns in minds which have nothing on earth to hope or fear; something to relieve in the killing languor and over-laboured lassitude of those who have nothing to do; something to excite an appetite to existence in the palled satiety which attends on all pleasures which may be bought, where nature is not left to her own process, where even desire is anticipated, and therefore, fruition defeated by meditated schemes and contrivances of delight; and no interval, no obstacle, is interposed between the wish and the accomplishment."

O you great ones of the earth, whom riches ensnare and prosperity betrays — be largely liberal, even from self-interest. Not, indeed, expecting to make the liberality you bestow a remuneration for the devotions you withhold. Scatter your superfluities, and more than your superfluities, to the destitute, if not to vindicate Providence, yet to benefit yourselves. Not, indeed, to revive the old pious fraud of depending for salvation on the prayers of others; yet still you may hope to be repaid, with usurious interest, from the pious poor, by the very tender charity of their prayers for you. Their supplications may possibly be so heard, that you may, at length, be brought to the indispensable necessity, and the bounden duty of praying for yourselves.

As to the commanded duty of praying for our enemies, the most powerful example bequeathed to us in Scripture, next to that of his Divine master on the cross, is that of St. Stephen. Even *after* the expiring martyr had ejaculated " Lord Jesus receive my spirit;" he kneeled down and cried with a loud voice " Lord lay not this sin to their charge." Let every instance of Roman greatness of mind, let every story of Grecian magnanimity be ransacked, and produce, who can, such another example. Theirs is tumour, this is grandeur; theirs is heroism, this is Christianity; *they* died for their country, Jesus for his enemies; *they* implored the gods for themselves, Stephen for his murderers.

THE PRAYING CHRISTIAN IN THE WORLD.—THE PROMISE OF REST TO THE CHRISTIAN.

As the keeping up a due sense of religion, both in faith and practice, so materially depends on the habit of fervent and heart-felt devotion, may we be permitted, in this place, to insist on the probable effects which would follow the devout and conscientious exercise of prayer, rather than on prayer itself?

As soon as religion is really become the earnest desire of our hearts, it will inevitably become the great business of our lives; the one is the only satisfactory evidence of the other: consequently the religion of the heart and life will promote that prayer by which both have been promoted.

They, therefore, little advance the true interests of mankind, who, under the powerful plea of what great things God has done for us in our redemption by His Son, neglect to encourage our active services in His cause. Hear the words of inspiration, " Be not slothful"—" run the race"—" fight the good fight"—" strive to enter in"—" give diligence"—" work out your own salvation"—" God is not unmindful to forget your labour of love"—" but when ye have done all, say, Ye are unprofitable servants, ye have done that which was your duty to do."

But if, after we have done all, we are unprofitable servants, what shall we be if we have done nothing? Is it not obvious that the Holy Spirit, who dictated these exhortations, clearly meant that a sound faith in the word of God was meant to produce holy exertion in His cause? The activity in doing good of the Son of God was not exceeded by His devotion, and both gloriously illustrated his doctrines, and confirmed his divinity. Until we make then our religion a part of our common life, until we bring Christianity, as an illustrious genius is said to have brought philosophy, from its retreat to live in the world, and dwell among men; until we have brought it from the closet to the active scene, from the church to the world, whether that world be the court, the senate, the exchange, the public office, the private counting-house, the courts of justice, the professional departments, or the domestic drawing-room, it will not have fully accomplished what it was sent on earth to do.

We do not mean the introduction of its language, but of its spirit: the former is frequently as incompatible with public, as it is unsuitable to private business; but the latter is of universal application. We mean that the temper and dispositions which it is the object of prayer to communicate, should be kept alive in society, and brought into action in its affairs. That the integrity, the veracity, the justice, the purity, the liberality, the watchfulness over ourselves, the candour towards others, all exercised in the fear of the Lord, and strengthened by the word of God and prayer, should be brought from the retirement of devotion to the regulation of the conduct.

Though we have observed above, that it is rather the spirit than the language of religion that should be carried into business, yet we cannot forbear regretting that we seem to decline much from the sober usages of our ancestors. Formerly testamentary instruments were never made the mere conveyance of worldly possessions. They were also made the vehicle of pious sentiments, and always at least opened with a devout offering of the soul to Him who gave it. Indeed it is difficult to imagine how a man *can* write the words *my last will* without a solemn reflection on that *last* act which must inevitably follow it, and in view of which act he is making it. May not this alteration in the practice be partly ascribed to the decline of habitual prayer.*

* I beg leave to strengthen my own sentiments on this head, by quoting a passage from an eminent and truly pious barrister, with an extract from the last will of one of the greatest men of our age.

"Of late years, it has been the fashion (for there is a fashion even in the last act of a man's life) to omit these solemn preambles. I confess myself an approver of them, as believing it to be useful to the surviving relatives of the testator to draw their attention to the tremendous consequences of the separation of soul and body at a season of impressibility and reflection." By the following extract, from the will of the late Mr. Burke, it will be seen, that his sentiments, on this point, coincided with those above expressed. "First, according to the ancient good and laudable custom, of which my heart and understanding recognise the propriety, I bequeath my soul to God, hoping for His mercy through the only merits of our Lord and Saviour Jesus Christ. My body I desire, if I should die at any place very convenient for its transport thither, (but not otherwise,) to be buried at the church at Beaconsfield, near to the bodies of my dearest brother and my dearest son, in all humility praying, that, as we have lived in perfect unity together, we may together have part in the resurrection of the just." Roberts on Wills, vol. ii. p. 376.

But what fair opportunities have certain of the great officers of the law, especially in their charges, of giving to them a solemnity the most impressive, by adverting more frequently to the awful truths of Christianity! Even if such awakening appeals to the conscience should fail of their effect on the unhappy convicts to whom they are addressed, they may be of incalculable benefit to some of the numerous persons present. A counsel, a caution, a reproof, an exhortation, all on pure Christian principles, and thus coming from a profession to which it appears not immediately to belong, may, especially from not being expected, produce consequences the most salutary. The terribly affecting circumstances of the moment, the appalling scene so soon to follow, must give an unspeakable weight to the most touching admonition. He who is judging the condemned violator of divine and human laws, stands as a kind of representative of the future judge of quick and dead, and will himself soon be judged by Him, a consideration which makes his responsibility peculiarly tremendous.*

But to return.—Though we must not, in accommodation to the prevailing prejudices and unnecessary zeal against abstinence and devotion, neglect the imperative duties of retirement, prayer, and meditation; yet, perhaps, as prayer makes so indispensable an article in the Christian life, some retired, contemplative persons may apprehend that it makes the whole; whereas prayer is only the operation which sets the machine going. It is the sharpest spur to virtuous action, but not the act itself. The only infallible incentive to a useful life, but not a substitute for that usefulness. Religion keeps her children in full employ-

* The late Lord Kenyon was neither afraid nor ashamed to introduce both the doctrine and language of Christianity on these occasions; and we have lately seen other valuable instances of the adoption of this practice.

ment. It finds them work for every day in the week, as well as on Sundays.

The praying Christian, on going into the world, feels that his social and religious duties are happily comprized in one brief sentence.—"I will *think* upon thy commandments, to do them." What the Holy Spirit has so indissolubly joined, he does not separate.

He whose heart has been set in motion in the morning by prayer, who has had his spiritual pulse quickened by a serious perusal of the Holy Scriptures, will find his work growing upon him in regular proportion to his willingness to do it. He is diligently exact in the immediate duties of the passing day. Though procrastination is treated by many as a light evil, he studiously avoids it, because he has felt its mischiefs; he is active even from the love of ease, for he knows that the duties which would have cost him little, if done on the day they were due, may, by the accumulation of many neglected days, cost him much. The fear of this rouses him to immediate exertion. If the case in question be doubtful, he deliberates, he inquires, he prays; if it be clear and pressing, what his hand finds to do, he does with all his might; and in the calls of distress, he always acts on his favourite aphorism, that giving soon is giving twice.

Abroad how many duties meet him! He has on his hands the poor who want bread, the afflicted who want comfort, the distressed who want counsel, the ignorant who want teaching, the depressed who want soothing. At home he has his family to watch over. He has to give instruction to his children, and an example to his servants. But his more immediate, as well as more difficult work is with himself, and he knows that this exercise, well performed, can alone enable him wisely to perform the rest. Here he finds work for every faculty of his understanding, every conquest over his will, for every affection of his heart. Here his spirit truly labours. He has to watch, as well as to pray, that his conscience be not darkened by prejudice; that his bad qualities do not assume the shape of virtues, nor his good ones engender self-applause; that his best intentions do not mislead his judgment; that his candour do not degenerate into indifference; nor his strictness into bigotry; that his moderation do not freeze, nor his zeal burn. He has to controul his impatience at the defeat of his most wisely conceived plans. He will find, that in his best services there is something that is wrong, much that is wanting; and he feels, that whatever in them is right, is not his own, but the gift of God.

He finds that his obedience is incomplete, that his warmest affections are languid, perhaps his best intentions not realized, his best resolves not followed up. In this view, though he is abased in dust and ashes in looking up to God as the fountain of perfection, he is cheered in looking up to him also as the fountain of mercy in Christ Jesus. He prays, as well as strives, that the knowledge of his own faults may make him more humble, and his sense of the divine mercies more grateful.

He will find that his faith, even though it does not want sincerity, will too frequently want energy. He has, therefore, to watch against cold and heartless prayer, though, perhaps, the humility arising from this consciousness is a benefit in another way. He feels it difficult to bring every "thought into captivity to the obedience of Christ," yet he goes on cheerily, willing to believe that what may be difficult is not impossible.

He has to struggle against over-anxiety for temporal things. He has to preserve simplicity of intention, consistency, and perseverance. He has, in short, to watch against a long list of sins, errors, and temptations, which he will find heavier in weight, and more in number, the more closely he looks into his catalogue.

The praying Christian in the world has, above all, to watch against the rise of sin, as he may find it more easy to endure the cross than to despise the shame! Even if he have in a good degree conquered this temptation, he may still find a more dangerous enemy in the applause of the world than he found in its enmity. He has observed, that many amiable and even pious persons, who are got above the more vulgar allurements of the world, who have surmounted all the temptations of a mere sensual kind, who are no longer subdued by its softening luxuries, its seducing pleasures, its dazzling splendours, nor its captivating amusements, have not yet quite escaped this danger. The keen desire of its good opinion, the anxiety for its applause, ensnares many who are got above any thing else which the world has to offer. This is, perhaps, the last lingering sin which cleaves even to those who have made a considerable progress in religion, the still unextinguished passion of a mind great enough to have subdued many other passions.

The danger of the Christian in the world is *from* the world. He is afraid of the sleek, smooth, insinuating, and not discreditable vices; he guards against self-complacency. If his affairs prosper, and his reputation stands high, he betakes himself to his only sure refuge, the throne of God, to his only sure remedy, humble prayer. He knows it is more easy to perform a hundred right deeds, and to keep many virtues in exercise, than "to keep himself unspotted from the world," than to hold the things of the world with a loose hand.—Even his best actions, which may bring him most credit, have their dangers; they make him fear that "while he has a name to live, he is dead."

Though much above feeling any joy in vulgar acclamation, he is not insensible to the praise of those who are praised by others; but though not indifferent to the good opinion of good men, the praise even of the best, is not his object; he knows that to obtain it, is not the end for which he was sent into the world. His ambition is of a higher order; it has a loftier aim. The praise of man cannot satisfy a spirit which feels itself made for immortality.

He feels that if he had no sin but vanity, the consciousness of that alone would be sufficient to set him on his guard, to quicken him in prayer, to caution him in conduct. He does not fear vanity as he fears any other individual vice; as a single enemy, against which he is to be on the watch, but as that vice which, if indulged, would poison all his virtues.—Among the sins of the inner man, he knows that "this kind goeth not out but by prayer." When he hears it said of any popular, and especially of any religious character, "he is a good man, but he is vain," He says within himself, he is vain, and therefore I fear he is not a good man. How many right qualities does vanity rob of their value! how many right actions of their reward!

Every suspicion of the first stirring of vanity in himself, sends him with deeper prostration before his Maker. Lord what is man! shall the praise of a fellow-creature, whose breath is in his nostrils, whose ashes must soon be mingled with my own, which may even before my own be consigned to kindred dust, shall *his* praise be of sufficient potency to endanger the humility of a being, who is not only looking forward to the applause of those glorious spirits which surround the throne of God, but to the approbation of God himself?

When those with whom he occasionally mixes, see the praying Christian calm and cheerful in the world, they little suspect the frequent struggles, the secret conflicts he has within. Others see his devout and conscientious life, but he alone knows the plague of his own heart. For this plague he seeks the only remedy, to prayer, that balm of hurt minds, he constantly repairs.

The praying Christian endeavours to

make even what to some might seem casual expressions in Scripture, matter of improvement. He is not contented to devote to the distressed his mere superfluities, he makes requisitions on his frugality to add to his contributions, and he learns this lesson from the highest model.

He observes that He who could feed thousands by a word of His mouth, yet took care not to let the miracle pass without grafting on it a moral maxim for general use, a religious duty for general practice. He who could have multiplied to any extent the twelve baskets, as He had done the five loaves, condescended to say, "gather up the fragments that remain, that nothing be lost;" and that he might set an example of prayer in every possible form, He had previously *blessed* the simple but abundant meal, presenting, in this single instance, an union of three great qualities—generosity, economy, and devotion.

The practical Christian observes, with

grateful admiration, how Scripture has, as it were, let down to the plainest apprehension the habitual duty of constantly looking to God, by a familiar allusion taken from domestic life. — The fidelity, the diligent attention, the watchful observance of "the eyes of a servant looking to the hand of his master, and the eyes of a maiden to the hand of her mistress," is a simple illustration of the Christian's duty, equally intelligible to him who serves, and obligatory on him who is served.

To a worldly man, his own sin appears less than it is; to a good man, greater; not that he sees through a false medium, or aggravates the truth, or forgets the apostle's direction to think soberly; but while the nominal Christian weighs his offences in the scales of the world, the praying Christian brings his to the balance of the sanctuary. The former judges of sin only as he sees it in others; and the worst men in the rank above the vulgar, do not always appear so bad as they are. In his own heart, he sees little, because, with that heart he is not acquainted. Whereas his own bosom is the very place where the good man looks for sin, and his perceptions of what is wrong are so delicate, that he sees it in its first seed; in short, the one thinks himself worse than others, because he knows himself well; the other thinks himself better, because he knows himself not at all.

When we consider the conflicts and the trials of the conscientious, watchful, praying, Christian, we shall estimate aright the value of the consoling promise of that eternal rest from his labours, which supports him, under them. And though rest is one of the lowest descriptions of the promised bliss of heaven, yet it holds out a cheering prospect of relief and satisfaction to a feeling being, who is conscious of the fallen condition of his mortal nature in all its weakness and imperfection. *Rest*, therefore, is of itself a promise sufficiently inviting to make him, desire to depart, and to be with Christ, even independently of his higher hopes. The joy unspeakable, the crown of glory, and all those other splendid images of the blessedness of heaven, exalt and delight his mind. But it is, though with a higher, yet with a more indefinite delight. He adores, without fully comprehending the mighty blessing. But the promise of rest is more intelligible to the heavy-laden Christian; he better understands it, because it is so exactly applicable to his present wants and feelings. It offers the relief longed for by a weary, frail, and feverish being. He who best knew what man wanted, promised to His disciples *peace and rest*, and His Divine Spirit has represented the state of heaven under this image more frequently than under any other, as being in more direct contrast to his present state — a state of care, anxiety, and trouble, and a state of sin, the cause of all his other troubles. Perhaps this less elevated view of heaven may occur more rarely to persons of high-wrought feelings in religion, yet to the Christian of a contrary character, it is a never-failing consolation, a home-felt solace, the object of his fervent prayer. What a support to be persuaded that "the work of righteousness is peace, and the effect of righteousness is quietness and assurance for ever!"

THE LORD'S PRAYER, A MODEL BOTH FOR OUR DEVOTION AND OUR PRACTICE.—IT TEACHES THE DUTY OF PROMOTING SCHEMES TO ADVANCE THE GLORY OF GOD.

It is not customary for kings to draw up petitions for their subjects to present to themselves; much less do earthly monarchs consider the act of petitioning worthy of reward, nor do they number the petitions so much among the services done them, as among the burthens imposed on them. Whereas it is a singular benefit to our fallen race that the King of Kings both dictates our petitions, and has promised to recompense us for making them.

In the Lord's prayer may be found the

seminal principle of all the petitions of a Christian, both for spiritual and temporal things; and however in the fulness of his heart he will necessarily depart from his model in his choice of expressions; into whatever laminæ he may expand the pure gold of which it is composed, yet he will still find the general principle of his own more enlarged application to God, substantially contained in this brief but finished compendium.

Is it not a striking proof of the divine condescension, that knowing our propensity to err, our blessed Lord should Himself have dictated our petitions, partly perhaps as a corrective of existing superstitions, but certainly to leave behind Him a *regulator* by which all future ages should *set* their devotions; and we might perhaps establish it as a safe rule for prayer in general, that any petition which cannot in some shape be accommodated to the spirit of some part of the Lord's prayer may not be right to be adopted. Here temporal things are kept in their due subordination; they are asked for in great moderation, as an acknowledgment of our dependence on the Giver. The request for the Divine intercession we must of course offer for ourselves, as the intercessor had not yet assumed his mediatorial office.

There is in this prayer a concatenation of the several clauses, what in human composition the critics call concealed method. The petitions rise out of each other. Every part also is, as it were, fenced round, the whole meeting in a circle; for the desire that God's name may be hallowed, His will be done, and His kingdom come, is referred to, and confirmed by the ascription at the close. If the kingdom, the power, and the glory, are His, then His ability to do and to give, are declared to be infinite.

But, as we have already observed, if we do not make our prayer the ground of our practice, if we do not pray as we believe, and act as we pray, we must not wonder if our petitions are not heard, and consequently not answered.

In the tremendous scene in the Apocalyptic vision, where the dead, small and great, stand before God, and the books were opened, and another book was opened, the dead were judged out of those things, which were written in the books; were judged according—not to their prayers, but "their works." Surely then Christianity is a practical religion, and in order to use aright the prayer our Lord has given us, we must model our life by it as well as our petitions.

If we pray that the name of God may be hallowed, yet neglect to hallow it ourselves, by family as well as personal devotion, and a conscientious attendance on all the ordinances of public worship, we defeat the end of our praying, by falling short of its obligation.

The practical discrepancies between our prayers and our practice do not end here. How frequently are we solemnly imploring of God, that "His kingdom may come," while we are doing nothing to promote his kingdom of grace here, and consequently His kingdom of glory hereafter.

If we pray that God would "give His son the heathen for His inheritance," and yet make it a matter of indifference, whether a vast proportion of the globe should live heathens, or die Christians; if we pray that "the knowledge of the Lord may cover the earth, as the waters cover the sea," yet act as if we were indifferent whether Christianity ended as well as began at home. If we pray that "the sound may go out into all lands, and their words unto the ends of the world," and yet are satisfied to keep the sound within our own hearing, and the words within our own island, is not this a prayer which goeth out of feigned lips? When we pray that "His will may be done," we know that His will is, "That all should be saved, that not one should perish." When, therefore, we assist in sending the Gospel to the dark and distant corners of the earth, then, and not till then, may we consistently desire of God in our prayers, that "His saving health may be known to all nations."

For we must vindicate the veracity of our prayer by our exertions, and extend its efficiency by our influence: if we contribute not to the accomplishment of the object for which we pray, what is this but mocking Omniscience, not by unmeaning, but unmeant petitions? If we do nothing we are inconsistent; but if we do worse than nothing, if we oppose, and by our opposition hinder the good which we do not think proper to support, may we not possibly bring on ourselves the appalling charge of being "found fighting against God?"

It is indeed an easier and a cheaper way, to quiet the conscience by that common anodyne, "that the heathen are very well as they are, that the morals of the Hindoos are not inferior to those of Christians." With what sort of Christians, these asserters of the rival innocence of idolaters associate, we will not pretend to determine.

But, allowing that we do not always send abroad the very best samples of Christianity, the very best representatives of its practical effects, allowing also that too many who remain at home, and who profess and call themselves Christians, are guilty of crimes which disgrace human nature, yet Christianity renounces them. Christian governments inflict on them capital punishments. While among these poor idolaters all the social duties are trampled on, all the suggestions of natural conscience are stifled, rites the most obscene, sacrifices the most bloody are offered; and these crimes are not only committed, but sanctioned, but enjoined; they do not violate religion, they make a part of it. Surely then, politically connected with them as we are, and yet contentedly to leave them in their degraded state of morals, without any attempt for their improvement, do we not, by this neglect virtually pronounce, and awfully anticipate their dreadful sentence, "let him that is unjust be unjust still, and he that is filthy let him be filthy still."

Again, it is an easier and a cheaper way to throw the weight off our own shoulders by the cool remark, that "these things belong not to us, human efforts are superfluous; God must bring them about by a miracle."—God, it is true, introduced Christianity by miracles, but He established it by means. Miracles, indeed, are His prerogative, but man is his instrument. Had He not sent His gospel and His ministers, it is probable that the strangers scattered throughout Pontus, Galatia, Cappadocia, Bythinia, and all proconsular Asia, had never heard of Christianity to this day, which is, indeed, still the case of too many parts of that region.

But is it not equally the effect of divine grace, I had almost said, is it not equally a miracle, when, in the hottest season of the most unrelenting warfare, in the most calamitous period of unusual scarcity, when Britain had the whole civilized world in arms against her, so that she could emphatically say "There is none that fighteth for us but only Thou O God." When it might seem business enough for any but Christians to take care of themselves, even then Britain raised the banner of the cross, not in the most unprofitable crusade for the most fruitless object, but that she might carry the knowledge of Him who suffered on it, to the ends of the habitable globe. Not to redeem His sepulchre from infidels, but to communicate to them the tidings of His resurrection, and of redemption through his blood. Is it not the effect of grace, and still more nearly approaching to a miracle, when in a period immediately subsequent, while their fields were yet red with slaughter, and their rivers ran blood, their cities plundered, and their kingdoms desolated, God disposed the hearts of hostile sovereigns, ruling over opposing nations and the tenacious professors of different religions, yet as if actuated by one universal feeling, simultaneously to rise up in one common cause for the accomplishment of this mighty object—when the first use they made of the termination of war was to disseminate the gospel of peace; the first tribute they paid to the glory of God was to publish abroad that grand instrument of good will to men! Let us not then indulge groundless imaginations, as if miracles were wrought to justify indolence; as if man were to be excused the trouble of being the active agent of Divine Providence.

The miracles wrought at Ephesus seem rather to have been intended as a confirmation of the truth of St. Paul's doctrine, than as the actual instrument of conversion. Many rejected the gospel who saw the miracles. The miracles wrought did not supersede the necessity of the apostle's " speaking boldly for the space of three months, disputing and persuading the things concerning the kingdom of God. They did not supersede the necessity at another time, of his continuing to preach among them for the space of two years the two great doctrines of his mission, "Repentance towards God, and faith in our Lord Jesus Christ." Nor did they prevent his thinking it his bounden duty to send to the Ephesians his exquisite epistle, for the furtherance of their faith in the gospel. Here we behold the union of the Bible and the missionary—of the gospel sent and the gospel preached.

"Many," says the sagacious bishop Butler, "think there is but one evil, and that evil is superstition;" and we know that the epithets of superstitious and enthusiastic have been unsparingly lavished on the most sober and well-digested plans for the dispersion of the scriptures abroad. We know that every trifling errors, errors inseparable from all great undertakings, every petty indiscretion, the inevitable consequence of employing a number of inferior agents, have been

Y

carefully collected, minutely set down in the note book of observation, and triumphantly produced as unanswerable objections to the whole plan. "But," says the profound prelate above-named, in his very able defence of missions, preached before the venerable society for propagating the gospel in foreign parts*, "many well-disposed persons want much to be admonished what a dangerous thing it is to discountenance what is good, because it is not better, by raising objections to some under parts of it."

The truth is, *they* are neither enthusiasts nor superstitious, who believe that well-concerted and prudently conducted societies for the promotion of this great object, acting with a deep sense of human imperfection, and in dependance upon the favour of God, will, in due time, with His blessing, without which nothing is strong, nothing is holy, accomplish the great end of bringing all the kingdoms of the

* Preached at their anniversary meeting, February 16th, 1738—9.

world to become the kingdoms of the Redeemer. But *he* is the superstitious, he is the enthusiast, who indulges unfounded expectations, who looks for the fulfilment of declarations which have never been made, who depends upon miracles which have never been announced, who looks for consequences without their predisposing causes, who believes that the unassisted heathen, sunk in intellectual and spiritual darkness, shall call on Him of whom they have not heard, or that they shall hear without a preacher, or that the preacher will be found without being sent.

We might just as reasonably expect to see the beautiful imagery of Oriental metaphor, as displayed in the highly figurative language of the prophets, actually realized. We might as reasonably expect that the rose of Sharon shall literally blossom in the wilderness of Arabia, or the cedars of Lebanon spring up in the sandy vallies of Africa; that the thirsty desert should produce spontaneous springs of water; that the tame and savage animals should live together in friendly compact; that the material hills shall really sink and the vallies rise of themselves;—we might, I say, as rationally hope to see these lively illustrations of the fulfilment of the Divine promises literally verified, as to expect Christianity to make its own unassisted way into the distant and desolate corners of the earth. God has committed Christianity into the hands of Christians for universal diffusion.

Let it be observed, that it appears to be no real departure from the subject with which this chapter opened, that reference is not more frequently made in its progress to prayer. This seems to be the less necessary, as we are not reasoning with the irreligious man, but with the Christian, with him who professes to use the Lord's prayer as the pattern of his own devotions; and from the premises of that prayer, these observations are not forced interpretations, but natural deductions.

The Almighty is consistent in all his operations. They always exhibit simplicity and economy. He never works a superfluous miracle. There is also analogy in his works. Christ wrought miracles to relieve the bodily wants of the poor; he works miracles for them no longer, he turns them over to the rich. He wrought miracles on the first conversion of the heathen; He works miracles for them no longer, he now turns them over to Christians. He resigns to human agency, under his blessing, to provide for the spiritual wants of the ignorant, as well as for the temporal wants of the indigent. Christianity and riches are deposited in the hands of Christians, for the more general dispersion of both to the respectively destitute.

And when, if ever, through the unmerited mercy of God, that glorious and devoutly desired day shall arrive, which warms the heart even in the distant perpective of prophecy, when nation shall no more rise against nation, and they shall learn war no more; what is so likely to hasten that triumphant period, what is so likely to turn the sword into the pruning-hook, and to establish lasting peace throughout the world, as that spirit of love and concord which the universal diffusion of gospel light is calculated to impart? What is so likely to produce charity among all the children of the same common Father, as when subjects as well as sovereigns of every clime and colour, people and language, shall be brought to know God, from the greatest to the least.

Those admirable institutions, whose object it is to lead to this blessed consummation, have already enlarged the borders of Christian charity to an almost indefinite extent, by bringing into contact from every point of the compass, and from almost every city in the civilised world, Christians who had not so much as heard of each other's existence; it has already shewn them that whatever difference of education and of government, whatever modifications of opinion had hitherto divided them, the great fundamental principles of love to God, of faith in his Son, and charity to the souls of men, are at length beginning to draw them into a nearer connection. These general principles of agreement, are already bringing into one point of union, persons whom difference of sentiment had kept asunder as widely as seas had separated, and are the only means, as far as human penetration can foresee, of drawing the cords of amity into still closer bonds.

Already, even in the early stage of this vast enterprize, may we not perceive that it has had a considerable share in promoting mutual good-will, reciprocal kindness, and growing confidence, and this with foreigners, who, though they had subdued their enmity, might not so soon have conquered their jealousy? Has it not a powerful tendency to cure any remaining distrust, to confirm good faith, to promote confidence and attachment between nations, whose respect was not perhaps, altogether untinctured with suspicion? May it not break down the wall of partition, which has so long kept us asunder? May it not bring those who were aforetime separated in heart as well as country, to unite in Christian brotherhood, till we become at length of one mind in doctrine, as we already are in regard to this institution. May not the probable results of this Christian confederacy become a ratification between monarchs, firmer than any political compact, stronger than any diplomatic convention? For is it not an instrument of confederation of which the GREAT SEAL IS THE WORD OF GOD? Does it not embrace the two sublime objects of the song of the angelic hosts, by uniting, "glory to God in the highest, and on earth peace and good-will toward men?" For what means, we repeat, are so likely to bring churches, who have been hitherto kept in spiritual darkness, to a gradual and devoutly-desired reformation, as to disperse that darkness, as our being the honoured instruments of causing the full beams of divine truth to shine more directly upon them?

To descend to the very minutest wheels of this mighty engine;—with whatever derision that which has been denominated popular charity may have been treated; its inferior divisions have this advantage, that they set in motion the young and the poor. To the young female of fortune, this subordinate part of the great whole, furnishes a kind of novitiate to her future and more extended sphere of charity, for the details of which this sex has the most leisure. To the poor, like the admirable institution of the Savings Bank, though for different purposes, it gives them a little and a safe lift in the scale of society. For will they not be less likely to follow in the turbulent train of the seditious demagogue, less disposed by his pernicious but persuasive outcry, to give their stated penny for the promotion of riot and the maintenance of rioters, when that penny has been pre-engaged for the circulation of that Volume, which forbids them to speak evil of dignities, which commands to avoid those who are given to change; to work, to be quiet, to mind their own business; which imperatively says, "I exhort that prayers and intercession be made for kings and all in authority;" and above all, will not the Bible be the surest antidote against the infection of the poison contained in that profusion of books, pamphlets, and placards, which, without such a specific, threatens both our moral and political destruction.

It is the nature of man to delight in party, he delights to belong to something, to hold to his fellow-creatures, though by the least and lowest link in the chain of society; let us then take advantage of this his natural weakness. For is it not better to attach him to something that is useful to himself and to others, that he may be less likely to be drawn into such schemes as are destructive of his temporal as well as of his own highest interests, and dangerous to the security of the state, and of the country. To be connected, though by the lowest and slightest tie, with his superiors, is to the poor man at once an encouragement and a security. To belong to societies of which princes are the patrons, is at once a gratification and a guard; for will not this connection, remote as it may seem, confirm his abhorrence of those revolutionary societies whose aim is the overthrow of princes?

Let us not then grudge to the poor who have so few pleasures, that pure, and to them that hitherto untasted pleasure, that almost sacred feeling, how much more blessed is it to give than to receive. Let us not deny them the gratification of being humble contributors towards conveying that word of life to others, by which their own souls have been benefited; and to which they are indebted for the knowledge, that it is the duty of Christians to teach others what themselves have been gratuitously taught.

It is, however, most important to recommend that the petty contributions of the poor should never be extorted, nor even wrung from them by undue influence. It must be a willing offering, not pinched from their necessities, but cheerfully accepted, as the thankful tribute of successful industry. With respect to such as are in distress, and especially in debt, it would neither be honest in themselves to give, nor in the collector to receive. A very few indiscretions of this kind have given too inviting a handle, which has been unfairly laid hold of to bring the plan itself into discredit.

To venture one more passage from the prelate already quoted — and who will accuse Bishop Butler of enthusiasm? — "If the gospel had its proper influence in the Christian world in general, as this country is the centre of trade, and the seat of learning, a very few years, in all probability, would settle Christianity in every country in the world *without miraculous assistance.*"

If we, then, in this highly favoured land, are blessed with the volume of Divine Revelation, let us impart it to others with the greater alacrity, from the humiliating recollection that it was no merit of our own which brought the news of eternal life to an island of barbarians and idolaters. Freely we have received, freely let us give.

The sun of righteousnes, which first arose in the east, rejoicing as a giant to run his course, has travelled in the greatness of his strength, till, having made the circuit of the globe, having illuminated the western world, he is once again rising to shed the glories of his orient beams, where they first dawned.

" So sinks the day-star in the Ocean-bed,
 And yet again repairs his drooping head,
 And tricks his beams, and with new-spangled ore
" Flames in the forehead of his morning sky."

Let Commerce, then, wherever she spreads her sails, be assured, that whether she carries the wealth of Ormus, or of Ind, barbaric pearl and gold from the East; or from the West, the mines of Potosi or Peru, the most precious merchandize with which her vessels can be freighted, is that pearl of great price which the merchantman in the Gospel sold all that he had to purchase.

Let Discovery, wherever she pushes her bold and perilous adventure, wherever she lights on an inhabited nook of land, even should she succeed in exploring the secrets of the polar world; let her be assured that all the wonders for which gaping curiosity impatiently waits, are not to be compared with the wonders contained in that Gospel, which, it is to be hoped, she will make part of her provision for the voyage. Let her be assured, that if she carries the Bible, she will, at her return, bring back no news of equal value with that she carries out; will bring back to her native home no tidings of equal joy to the glad tidings of the Gospel she has carried abroad.

Let Conquest, though her garments have been rolled in blood, make the vanquished the only reparation in her power, not merely like the conquering Cæsar and Alexander, by carrying civilization in her train, but Christianity; by carrying them this charter of our own immortal hopes. If this mighty boon will not fully expiate the offences of the injurer, it will more than mitigate, it will even more than repay the wrongs of the injured.

CONCLUSION.

"I will be sanctified in them that draw nigh unto me," says the Almighty by his Prophet. We must, therefore, when we approach Him in our devotions, frequently endeavour to warm our hearts, raise our views, and quicken our aspirations with a recollection of His glorious attributes,—of that Omnipotence which can give to all without the least deduction from any, or from Himself; of that ubiquity which renders Him the constant witness of our actions; of that Omniscience which makes Him a discerner of our intentions, and which penetrates the most secret disguises of our inmost souls; of that perfect holiness, which should at once be the object of our adoration, and the model of our practice; of that truth, which will never forfeit any of His promises; of that faithfulness, which will never forsake any that trust in Him; of that love, which our innumerable offences cannot exhaust; of that eternity, which had place "before the mountains were brought forth, from everlasting to everlasting He is God;" of that grandeur which has set his glory above the heavens; of that long suffering of God, who is strong and patient, and who is provoked every day; of that justice which will by no means clear the guilty, yet of that mercy which forgiveth iniquity, transgression, and sin; of that compassion which waits to be gracious; of that goodness which leadeth to repentance; of that purity, which, while it hates sin, invites the sinner to return.

All these attributes are his in the abstract. He is not only strong, but our strength, not only the giver of life, but life itself, he not only bestows, but is salvation, he not only teaches truth, but *is* truth, he not only shews the way to heaven, but *is* the way, not only communicates light, but *is* light.

When we reflect that even His incommunicable attributes are employed, in never-ceasing exercise for the common benefit and happiness of mankind, adoration is melted into gratitude. When we consider, that even His justice, that flaming sword which threatened our eternal exclusion from Paradise, the attribute at which the best may tremble, for who is he that lives and sins not, is turned in our favour by the great propitiation made for sin; that heart must be hard indeed, which is not softened into love. It is because we are so little accustomed to indulge these reflections, that our natural hardness acquires additional obduracy.

Whatever good there is even in the renewed man, is but a faint adumbration of the perfections of God. The best created things, light itself, lose all their brightness, when compared with the uncreated glory from which all they have is borrowed. The heavens are not pure in His sight, behold the moon and it shineth not. He chargeth His angels with folly. The sublimest intellectual intelligencies, and the brightest visible operations of His power, are swallowed up in the contemplation of His underived original perfection. The foolishness of God is wiser than the wisdom of man, and the weakness of God is stronger than the strength of man.

Yet though the highest conceivable created excellence is thrown into utter darkness, in the comparison with this surpassing splendour, yet these remote resemblances serve to convey some idea, but Oh how weak! some reminding, but Oh how inadequate! some conception, but Oh how faint! of the Divine perfections.

Hence in the highest qualities of the best Christian we have a hint, a rudiment which serves to recal to our mind the

Divine excellence, of which they are an emanation. We use it, not as a means of overvaluing the creature, but of raising our adoration of the infinite, inexhaustible, overflowing fountain of natural, intellectual, and spiritual good. Thus, though we cannot " search out the Almighty to perfection;" yet these faint traces, are constant intimations to us to imitate, in our low measure and degree, all the imitable attributes of Almighty goodness. He would never have said, " be ye holy as I am holy," if holiness had been absolutely unattainable. There must be an aim, however low, at this conformity to our Divine pattern.

The life which the Lord of glory condescended to lead on earth, has introduced us to the nearest possible view of the Divine perfections, and exhibited a clearer prospect of the possibility of a closer imitation of them, than could have been conveyed to us by any other means. His actions are not merely objects of human admiration. They all, with the exception of his miracles, imperatively demand to be imitated, as well as admired. His meekness under reproaches the most contumelious; His patience under sufferings the most exquisite; His combination of active beneficence with unremitting devotion,—for, after days spent in successive acts of charity, He continued all night in prayer to God; His union of constant self-denial, with unwearied bounty; His enduring hunger, who could have relieved it by one of those miracles, so often performed for the relief of others; His compassion for sinners joined with His hatred of sin; His supplication for His enemies, extenuating their guilt by pleading their ignorance. "Father, forgive them, for they know not what they do!"

If this religion be not practical, if this practice be not a pattern for our's, we know not what is. While we obey him then in praying for our fellow creatures, let us remember that we must imitate his

Divine philanthropy in assisting them; while we rank ourselves among his admirers, by praising his excellencies, let us remember we shall only be known to to be his disciples when we love one another.

If good works then be indispensable, and if Faith be their great influencing principle, both must be kept alive and kept in exercise by the aliment of prayer. Prayer is the chain of communication with God himself. The readiest way to be assimilated to his likeness, the best means of promoting our conformity to His will, of advancing our love to Him and to each other. If we neglect prayer, we rob our souls of the prescribed means of our serving him here, and of the fairest foretaste of that communion with Him, which will be our highest happiness hereafter.

The obedience of the heart which grows out of a sound faith, rooted good desires, well-weighed resolutions of fidelity, formed in a higher strength than our own; a belief in the sacred Scriptures so confirmed, as not to be shaken by any objections brought against them, by any difficulties to be found in them; the comparing faithfully all we have heard urged against Religion, with all we have seen of its effects, and experienced of its benefits, all this is the solid ground on which future attainments must hereafter be built, a ground to be tried by prayer in the enquiring mind and the seeking heart.

And when our reason is become as strong on the side of Christianity as our belief—when our faith is as enlightened as it is implicit—when the growth of the one only confirms the dominion of the other, this is such an obedience of the heart as will infallibly produce obedience in the life; an obedience which will be both the cause and the consequence of effectual prayer.

The renewing of the soul after the image of God is not otherwise to be obtained than by true spiritual heart-searching prayer. There may be a form of unfelt, petitions, a ceremonious avowal of faith, a customary profession of repentance, a general acknowledgment of sin, uttered from the lips to God;—but where is His image and superscription written upon the heart? Where is the transforming power of Religion in the life? Where is the living transcript of the Divine original? Where is that holiness, to which the vision of the Lord is specifically promised? Where is the light, and life, and grace of the Redeemer exhibited in the temper and conduct? Yet we are assured, that if we are Christians, there must be an aim at this conformity.

As for the genuine Christian, however weak in faith, and defective in obedience, yet he is still seeking, though with slow and faultering steps, the things which are above; he is still striving, though with unequal progress, for the prize of his high calling;—he is still looking, though with a dim and feeble eye, for glory, honour, and immortality. He is still waiting, though not with a trust so lively as to anihilate the distance,—to see his eternal redemption drawing nigh. Though his aims will always be far greater than his attainments, yet he is not discouraged; his hope is above, his heart is above, his treasure is above; no wonder then that his prayers are directed, and a large portion of his wealth sent forward thither, where he himself hopes soon to be. It is but transmitting his riches of both kinds, not only to his future, but his eternal home.

Even if prayer were as worthless, with respect to present advantages, and religion as burthensome as some suppose, it would be a sufficient vindication of both that they lead to eternal bliss. When by a distant journey, we have been long separated from our own beloved habitation, we do not call that the most desirable road back to it which abounds with the gayest objects, but that which will bring us the most safely home. If, indeed, we can amuse ourselves with the scenery, without slackening our pace, or diverging from our path, it is well. It is no offence against the law of love, if we catch in passing, such innocent and safe delights as his bounty has scattered in our path. And if our journey have so many refreshments showered down by the hand of Divine beneficence, what shall be the delights of our home?

If the heavens grow black with clouds, and storms arise, these only serve to quicken our pace, and make us avoid digression. If sickness or accident befal us, our heart is still cheered with the thought that we are nearer home—the future supports us under the present; a little further say we—a little more fatigue, and we shall see the desire of our heart. If we are bent on security rather than amusement, the straightest and the safest way will determine our choice. Heaven is worth more sacrifices of pleasure and of profit than those to which a religious life may subject us; though, after all, it often calls for fewer and lighter than a worldly one imposes.

But if it were as rough and thorny as those who have never tried it believe, it would be a sufficient apology for voluntarily encountering its hardships, that it is the only road to heaven.

When the prosperous fool says, "soul take thine ease, thou hast much goods laid up for thee,"—the prosperous Christian says, "soul tremble at thine ease—be on thy guard. Thou hast, indeed, much goods laid up for thee, but it is in a future world. Lose not a large inheritance for a paltry possession; forfeit not an unalienable reversion for a life interest,—a life which this very night may be required of thee."

Perhaps even the worldly and thoughtless man, under an occasional fit of dejection, or an accidental disappointment, may be brought to say, "When I am in heaviness, I will think upon God."— Oh, think upon Him now, now, when you are in prosperity, now, when your fortunes are flourishing, now, when your hill is so strong that you think it shall never be moved — think upon Him when the scene is the brightest, when the world courts, flatteries mislead, and pleasures betray you; think on Him while you are able to think at all, while you possess the capacity of thinking. The time may come, when, "He may turn His face from you, and you will be troubled." Think of God when the alluring images of pleasure and of profit would seduce you from Him. Prosperity is the season of peculiar peril. "It is the bright day that brings forth the adder." Think of God when the tempting world says, "All this will I give thee." Trust not the insolvent world, it has cheated every creditor that ever trusted it. It will cheat you.

To those who are yet halting between two opinions, or rather between an opinion and an inclination, to those who approve the right, but pursue the wrong, those who are not without convictions, but which convictions pleasure stifles, or business overrules, those who are balance-ing between the world and Him who made it, who resolve to reform, but make the resolution a substitute for the performance;—and oh how large, and in many points how respectable, a class this is!—to these, to the doubting, and the dilatory, we would take the liberty to speak plainly.

It is much to be feared, that secret, unconscious infidelity lies at the bottom of the little progress you make in your spiritual attainments. If the truth, certainty, and inconceivable importance of eternal things were once rooted and grounded in the heart, it would infallibly quicken both devotion and practice. We know, but we do not act upon the knowledge, that our great business in this world is to determine our choice for eternity. This is not a bye work, which may be deferred to any time at the hazard of its not being done at all; it is the imperious business of the present hour, the next may not be granted us. It is not an affair to be kept in reserve, an affair to be postponed till other affairs are settled, for how many souls has this dilatory delusion ruined!

The resolution you may make at this moment, and the practical effect of this resolution may determine your fate for ever. The decision, if delayed, may never be made; the call, now given, may never be repeated. Think what you put to hazard by delay. There is not an hour in our lives on which eternal life, or eternal death may not depend. Shall we then, for a single moment, make it a matter of debate what our everlasting condition shall be? If it were a decision between two temporal concerns which you were called upon to make, deliberation might be wisdom, because there might be degrees of comparison between their value, and consequently a doubt as to the predominance of the object, and the prudence of your choice. But the inequalities of created things are levelled when brought into comparison with the things of eternity — the difference of more or less, richer or poorer, prosperity or privation, no longer exists; the distinction is swallowed up when contemplated in the view of endless happiness or endless misery. Here then, if you hesitate, you have already taken your part; irresolution is decision; deliberation is destruction; you have already resolved.

The hand which now holds the pen dares not denounce anathemas, but trembles as it transcribes the divinely inspired denunciation of the prophet Zephaniah. "The great day of the Lord is near, it is near, it hasteth greatly; it is the voice of the day of the Lord, when the mighty man shall cry bitterly. That day is a day of wrath; a day of trouble and distress; a day of wasteness and desolation; a day of darkness and gloominess; a day of clouds and thick darkness; a day of the trumpet and alarm."

The awful ruins of imperial Rome, the still more defaced vestiges of learned Athens, present a deeply touching spectacle of departed glory. Still more affecting is it to contemplate in the study of history on the destruction of Carthage, of Babylon, of Memphis, whose very ruins are no longer to be found! How affecting to meditate on ancient Troy, whose very scite can no longer be determined! Yet here no wonder mixes with our solemn feelings. All these noble monuments of human grandeur were made of destructible materials, they could not, from their very nature, last for ever. But, to a deeply reflecting mind, what is the ruin of temples, towers, palaces, and cities, what is the ruin of " the great globe itself" compared with the destruction of one soul meant for immortality — a soul furnished by its bountiful Creator with all the means for its instruction, sanctification, redemption, and eternal bliss? — And what presents the most mournful picture to us, and is in itself the most dreadful aggravation, is, that its consciousness cannot be extinguished, the thought of what he might have been will magnify the misery of what he is — a reflection which will accompany and torment the inextinguishable memory through a miserable eternity. Whether in the instance of the rich man, who "in hell lift up his eyes, being in torment," we might dare believe that some remains of human tenderness for his relatives might survive in a ruined soul; or, whether his anguish was made more bitter, from the reflection, that he had been their corruptor, and therefore dreaded that their punishment might hereafter aggravate his own, we pretend not to say. In any event, it offers a lesson pregnant with instruction. It admonishes every impenitent offender, of the dreadful addition that may be made to his own misery, by that corrupt example which has ruined others. And it will be the consummation of his calamity that he can see nothing but justice in his condemnation. For it is worth observing, that the man in the parable brings no accusation against the equity of his sentence. Thus shall every condemned sinner "justify God in his saying, and clear him when he is judged."

But though the anguish of an undone futurity, and the specific nature of the punishment, are exhibited with awful clearness and explicit exactness, in the gospel; how wisely has the Holy Spirit, who dictated it, avoided all particulars of that heavenly happiness which we are yet assured will be without measure and without end;—whilst the Elysian groves of the Pagan, and the paradise of the Mahometan have been graphically represented, the former by their poets, the latter in their religious code. The one describes the inhabitants reposing in gloomy bowers in cheerless indolence, with the alternative of a restless activity exercised in contemptible pursuits, and renewing on inferior objects the busy feats in which they had delighted here below! The heroes, who during life had slaughtered men, make war on beasts! The mighty warriors, who had made the earth to tremble, condescend in heaven to tame horses! The departed Mussulman receives *his* celestial rewards in scenes of revelry and banquets of voluptuousness! What gratifications for an immaterial, immortal spirit!

The whole scheme of future happiness exhibited in these two systems, is a preposterous provision for the perishable part of man, to the entire exclusion of the immortal principle; both schemes stand in direct opposition to the laws of infinite wisdom, and the express word of Scripture. Both intimate as if the body were the part of our nature which is to exist after death, while the soul is the portion which is to be extinguished. Of a spiritual heaven, neither the obsolete mythology, nor the existing Koran, affords the slightest intimation.

The Scripture views of heaven are given rather to quicken faith than to gratify curiosity. There the appropriate promises to spiritual beings are purely spiritual. It is enough for believers to know that they shall be for ever with the Lord; and though it doth not yet appear what we shall be, yet we know that when he shall appear, we shall be like Him. In the vision of the Supreme Good, there must be supreme felicity. Our capacities of knowledge and happiness shall be commensurate with our duration. On earth, part of our enjoyment — a most fallacious part — consists in framing new objects for our wishes; in heaven there shall remain in us no such disquieting desires, for all which can be found we shall find in God. We shall not know our Redeemer by the hearing of the ear, but we shall see him as he is; our knowledge, therefore, will be clear, because it will be intuitive.

It is a glorious part of the promised bliss, that the book of prophecy shall be realized; the book of providence displayed, every mysterious dispensation unfolded, not by conjecture, but by vision. In the grand general view of Revelation, minute description would be below our ideas; circumstantial details would be disparaging; they would debase what they pretended to exalt. We cannot conceive the blessings prepared for us, until he who has prepared reveal them.

If, indeed, the blessedness of the eternal world could be described, new faculties must be given us to comprehend it. If it could be conceived, its glories would be lowered, and our admiring wonder diminished. The wealth that can be counted has bounds; the blessings that can be calculated have limits. We now rejoice in the expectation of happiness inconceiveable. To have conveyed it to our full apprehension, our conceptions of it must then be taken from something with which we are already acquainted, and we should be sure to depreciate the value of things unseen, by a comparison with even the best of the things which are seen. In short, if the state of heaven were attempted to be let down to human intelligence, it would be far inferior to the glorious but indistinct glimpses which we now catch from the oracles of God, of joy unspeakable, and full of glory. What Christian does not exult in that grand outline of unknown, unimagined, yet consummate bliss — in THY presence is the fullness of joy, and at *Thy* right-hand is pleasure for evermore?

THE END.

www.ingramcontent.com/pod-product-compliance
Lightning Source LLC
Chambersburg PA
CBHW062123160426
43191CB00013B/2181